A YEAR IN MY
KITCHEN

FAVOURITE RECIPES FROM ROSE MURRAY

ROSE MURRAY

Prentice
Hall
Canada

A Pearson Company
Toronto

Canadian Cataloguing in Publication Data

Murray, Rose
   A year in my kitchen : Favourite recipes from Rose Murray

ISBN 0-13-06 2281-8

1. Cookery. I. Title.

TX714.M87 2001   641.5   C2001-901243-8

ISBN 0-13-062281-8

Editorial Director, Trade Division: Andrea Crozier
Acquisitions Editor: Nicole de Montbrun
Managing Editor: Tracy Bordian
Copy Editor: Susan Ginsberg
Proofreaders: Susan Broadhurst and Lynne Missen
Art Direction: Mary Opper
Cover and Interior Design: Carol Moskot
Cover Image: Joyce Oudkerk Pool/FoodPix
Production Manager: Kathrine Pummell
Page Layout: Arlene Edgar

1 2 3 4 5 KR 05 04 03 02 01

Printed and bound in Canada.

ATTENTION: CORPORATIONS
Books are available at quantity discounts with bulk purchase for educational, business, or sales promotional use. For information, please email or write to: Pearson PTR Canada, Special Sales, PTR Division, 26 Prince Andrew Place, Don Mills, Ontario, M3C 2T8. Email **ss.corp@pearsoned.com**. Please supply: title of book, ISBN, quantity, how the book will be used, date needed.

Visit the Pearson PTR Canada Web site! Send us your comments, browse our catalogues, and more.
www.pearsonptr.ca

A Pearson Company

FOR
ALLEN AND CHERRIE
ANNE AND ROB

CONTENTS

INTRODUCTION

In the midst of a particularly hard winter in Canada, I often wonder why our ancestors stopped here to set up house. The Caribbean is just a bit farther along. Barbados, where it's about 30°C all year round, would have been a good choice.

But then, when our fresh spring produce comes along—the first tender green shoots of asparagus or tightly curled fiddlehead fronds—I realize we would not appreciate the wonders of spring if we didn't experience winter.

Even winter has its special food. There are steaming pots of soup and warming stews that feature those hearty local vegetables like potatoes, rutabaga, carrots and onions, which, like us, can stay around and "tough out" the winter.

When winter is over, however, we are more than ready for the delights of spring. Along with those spring greens I've already mentioned will come the tart pink stalks of rhubarb and all the lovely pies, cakes and endless dishes to which this plant lends its special flavour and spring tonic. Rhubarb gets us in the mood for the parade of fruits and vegetables that come on like "gang busters" when the sun warms our once snow-covered earth.

In our age of shrinking distances and global availability, we can get fresh fruit and vegetables from any part of the world at any time of the year. I must admit, I do relish having at hand the mangos and other produce we can't grow here. But there is a difference between just "fresh" (meaning not frozen or canned) and our own "seasonal fresh." You only need to drive along a road beside a field of ripe strawberries and have their fragrance waft through your car windows to know that this is real food.

Strawberries are the true herald of summer. You can usually count on a mounded bowl for that summer-solstice party. Fast on their heels are cherries, raspberries, currants, gooseberries, blueberries, grapes, peaches, plums.... The list of fruit is endless and reaches far into the fall with melons, pears and apples.

Along with the colourful baskets of local fruit, there is a constant parade of fresh seasonal vegetables at our farmers' markets and roadside stalls. I always marvel at how early one can find large paper bags of small, tender spinach leaves, and soon after, containers of smooth baby potatoes. As all the other wonderful vegetables come on the scene, we find summer cooking easy because there is nothing much we need to do with such fresh produce, except to cook it briefly and enjoy the true taste of real food.

For that reason, you'll find my summer section a bit shorter than the others, although I could not resist adding a chapter on preserves, having learned the art from my mother as I grew up on our farm. Summer is the time to capture so many good flavours and colours for a taste of the season when winter winds blow.

Local produce is still abundant into fall with pumpkins in the fields for the Halloween crowd and Brussels sprouts resisting the first white snows. In autumn, hearty storage vegetables are harvested and put away for us to enjoy during the winter.

Fall is the time, too, for serious entertaining, so the section of the book called My Fall Kitchen is full of wonderful dishes to share with family and friends. Also, because I've written so many menus for magazines, I've included menus for entertaining family and friends at the end of the section. In fact, at the end of every section representing each of the four seasons, you will find suggested menus. Feel free to use and adapt them, and enjoy combining the individual recipes with your own menus.

Entertaining carries on into the winter, of course, with the biggest of all celebrations, Christmas. In northern countries where snow and cold winds blow, people have always feasted around the winter solstice as a kind of respite from the very climate itself. It was this thought about how important the holiday season is to Canadians that led me to write my first book. Initially called *The Christmas Cookbook* (James Lorimer & Company), it was published in 1979. Reprinted in 1990 as *Canadian Christmas Cooking* (McGraw-Hill Ryerson), it has undergone subsequent reprinting under that title and is still in print after 22 years.

After that first successful book, I wrote six others (this one will be my eighth) with substantial contributions to over 40 other cookbooks including the popular *Canadian Living* series. My own books have covered a vast number of topics—*Secrets of the Sea, Rose Murray's Vegetable Cookbook, Comfortable Kitchen Cookbook, Cellar & Silver, New Casseroles and Other One-Dish Meals* (Macmillan Canada) and *Quick Chicken* (Robert Rose).

In addition to writing cookbooks, I have been contributing to newspapers and national magazines for over 25 years. My articles have been published in Canada and Australia, and many have been translated into French. Numbering in the thousands, the recipes in those articles have covered a vast range of subjects.

When I was approached to put together a retrospective collection of my best recipes from all of these publications, I hesitated because I've always made a point of never using the same recipe in two books. My family and friends were of another mind, however, and said, "Great, now we'll have all our favourite recipes in one book." I had to go to those family members, friends and editors before I could even begin such a book. Because of the great number of recipes I've developed (not counting corporate recipes that I cannot use here), I approached other people for lists of their favourites. I refer to these lists often throughout the book.

I asked my grown children first. Both Allen and Anne are good cooks, and, along with my husband, Kent, my best critics. They are not afraid to say when a recipe needs tweaking. I have had two wonderful assistants throughout the years, Mary Lou Ruby Jonas and Sharon Boyd, who are both good cooks and know my recipes well. Editors like Julia Aitken and Elizabeth Baird gave me names of dishes they could "still taste" when they thought of the recipes. Some of the people who tested recipes at the magazines, and even producers of radio and television shows I've been on, volunteered their lists of favourites. As well, many good friends itemized recipes "they could not live without." My thanks to everyone who was so helpful.

As a result, I feel that the recipes in this book have been tested over and over again, first by me, often a number of times, then by those people who have given me their favourites and who make these recipes time after time. Some are from my own personal collection, ideas passed down by my mother and grandmother. One of the aims I've always had is to make sure my readers find my recipes doable and reliable. But more than that, I hope you find them absolutely delicious and a good salute to our wonderful seasonal food.

SPRING

MY SPRING KITCHEN

Spring usually finds everyone anxious to get out into the garden, or at least to seek out spring flowers in the market. Sometimes the season is slow in coming, but then we welcome warm days with even more exuberance. I always marvel at how the earth seems covered with snow and ice, and suddenly everything is green again.

While I'm waiting for the greening, I have to rely on finishing any bags of frozen fruits or vegetables I may have preserved at their prime last summer or those few remaining storage vegetables. Our family will enjoy the last of the good citrus fruit that comes our way from the south, and we can be happy to find in our supermarkets interesting exotic fruits like mangos that have come halfway around the world.

In spring, my meals lighten up in anticipation of warmer weather, and I'm apt to roast a chicken instead of making a hearty beef stew. Fish and pasta are big menu items to replace steaming pots of whole meal soup. I also delight in the new crop of maple syrup ... adding it to savory dishes, drizzling it over ice cream for dessert or pouring it onto pancakes for Shrove Tuesday.

When the first vegetables and fruits appear from the sun-warmed ground, I get even more excited. The curled fern fronds that show their heads along our rivers and the first tender green shoots of asparagus and pink stalks of rhubarb that poke out of the earth are harbingers, indeed, of all the wonderful produce we can enjoy throughout the coming summer.

SPRING STARTERS AND SOUPS

IN THE MENUS ...

Gravlax

MAKES 8 TO 10 SERVINGS.

This is one of my very favourite dishes for special parties because it is easy, can be made ahead, looks great, and everyone loves it. Buy the freshest fish possible for this absolutely delicious Scandinavian cured salmon. Serve it with buttered rye or pumpernickel bread. It also makes a nice addition to salads or pasta.

2	fresh centre-cut salmon fillets (1 lb/500 g each), skin on	2
1	bunch fresh dill	1
3 tbsp	EACH coarse salt and granulated sugar	45 mL
1 tbsp	white or black peppercorns, coarsely crushed	15 mL
	Lemon slices and capers	
	Mustard-Dill Sauce (recipe follows)	

1. Using a strawberry huller or tweezers, remove all bones from the salmon.
2. Place 1 fillet, skin side down, in a glass dish. Reserving a few sprigs of dill for garnish, wash dill, shake dry and cut up slightly. Place on fish. Combine salt, sugar and pepper; sprinkle over dill. Top with the other fillet, skin side up. Cover with plastic wrap. Top with a small platter and weight down with cans of food or a brick. Refrigerate for 3 days, turning every 12 hours and basting with accumulated liquid, separating halves to do so.
3. To serve, scrape all marinade and dill from salmon. Pat dry. Place on cutting board and slice salmon halves thinly on diagonal, detaching each slice from the skin. Arrange on a platter; garnish with lemon slices, capers and dill sprigs. Serve with Mustard-Dill Sauce.

Mustard-Dill Sauce

MAKES ABOUT 1-1/2 CUPS (375 ML).

This is such a delightful sauce that I've had guests go at it with a spoon!

1/2 cup	spicy brown prepared mustard	125 mL
1/3 cup	granulated sugar	75 mL
1/4 cup	white wine vinegar	50 mL
2 tsp	dry mustard	10 mL
1/2 tsp	black pepper	2 mL
1/2 cup	vegetable oil	125 mL
1/2 cup	snipped fresh dill	125 mL

1. In a medium bowl, whisk together prepared mustard, sugar, vinegar, dry mustard and pepper until sugar dissolves. Gradually whisk in oil; stir in dill. (Sauce can be prepared up to 4 days ahead, covered and refrigerated.)

Mozzarella and Prosciutto Flowers

MAKES 24 HORS D'OEUVRES.

One of my favourite quick appetizers is prosciutto wrapped around fruit—pear slices, melon balls or fresh fig wedges. This pretty variation is a taste-tempter using Italian soft cheese. You can buy fresh mozzarella, called ciliegine or bocconcini, in Italian grocery stores. If unavailable, cut regular mozzarella into 1/2-inch (1 cm) cubes.

1	tangerine or orange	1
1/4 cup	olive oil	50 mL
1	clove garlic, minced	1
2 tbsp	EACH chopped black olives and fresh parsley	25 mL
1/4 tsp	hot pepper flakes	1 mL
24	ciliegine (or 6 bocconcini, quartered)	24
8	thin slices prosciutto	8

1. With a zester,* remove the zest (outer rind) from the tangerine and place it in a medium bowl. Squeeze the juice from the tangerine into the bowl; stir in oil, garlic, olives, parsley and hot pepper flakes. Add cheese balls. Cover and marinate overnight in the refrigerator, stirring occasionally.

2. Cut the prosciutto slices lengthwise into 3 strips each. Wrap a strip around each cheese ball and secure with a toothpick if necessary.

A zester is a small tool with a stainless steel end in which there are five small holes whose sharp cutting edges remove tiny strips of only the coloured, outer layer of citrus fruit. The cutting action releases the citrus oil, so work over the bowl to capture the flavour. If you don't have a zester, cut off only the coloured layer of rind with a sharp knife, then shred into little strips.

Spiced Almonds

MAKES 1-1/2 CUPS (375 ML).

Sharon Boyd, a friend who often helps me with my testing, frequently makes this delicious snack for her own parties or for the parties she caters. It is high on her list of favourites among my recipes.

2 tbsp	unsalted butter	25 mL
1 tbsp	Worcestershire sauce	15 mL
1/2 tsp	ground cumin	2 mL
Dash	hot pepper sauce	Dash
1-1/2 cups	unblanched almonds	375 mL
1 tbsp	coarse pickling salt	15 mL

1. In a small saucepan, melt butter over low heat. Stir in Worcestershire sauce, cumin and hot pepper sauce; simmer gently for 5 minutes. Stir in almonds to coat well.
2. Spread nuts on baking sheet; bake in 325°F (160°C) oven, stirring occasionally, for 15 to 20 minutes or until toasted. Sprinkle with salt. Serve warm.

TIP

Nuts can be toasted ahead of time and reheated.

Cream of Fiddlehead Soup

MAKES 6 SERVINGS.

My husband, Kent, goes out picking fiddleheads every spring. When he brings them home, we clean them, and after enjoying many fresh ferns, we freeze the rest for colder months. If you pick fiddleheads, remember that the only one you should eat is the tightly curled head of the ostrich fern, and always leave a couple of fronds on each plant. To clean them, pull out each stalk and head carefully, shake to remove any brown scales and wash in several changes of lukewarm water. Fresh fiddleheads are best enhanced with only butter, salt and pepper and a sprinkling of fresh lemon juice. Or, enjoy their delicate flavour in this classic soup.

1/4 cup	butter	50 mL
1 cup	sliced leeks or onion	250 mL
2 tbsp	all-purpose flour	25 mL
2-1/2 cups	chicken stock	625 mL
4 cups	cooked fresh fiddleheads	1 L
2 cups	light cream	500 mL
1 tbsp	fresh lemon juice	15 mL
1/4 tsp	black pepper	1 mL
Pinch	cayenne pepper	Pinch
	Salt	
1/4 cup	sour cream	50 mL

1. In a large saucepan, melt butter over low heat. Cook leeks, covered, stirring often, for 10 to 15 minutes or until softened but not browned. Sprinkle with flour; cook, stirring, for 2 minutes. Gradually stir in stock; bring to a boil over medium-high heat, stirring constantly.

2. Add fiddleheads and return to a boil; reduce heat to medium, cover and simmer for 5 to 6 minutes or until fiddleheads are tender.

3. Remove 6 fiddleheads and set aside for garnish. In a blender or food processor (a blender makes a smoother soup), purée soup until smooth, in batches if necessary and holding down the blender lid.

4. Return soup to the saucepan. Stir in cream; heat through over medium heat, stirring often and being careful not to boil. Stir in lemon juice, pepper, cayenne and salt to taste. Serve garnished with sour cream and reserved fiddleheads.

TIP

If using frozen fiddleheads, thaw and drain before adding to soup.

SPRING MAIN DISHES

IN THE MENUS ...

Wild Mushroom, Leek and
Prosciutto Strata   45
Baked Glazed Ham   49

Crisp-Skinned Salmon on Spicy Lentils

MAKES 6 SERVINGS.

The skin becomes wonderfully crisp and the fish remains moist and flavourful with a spicy rub
before it goes into a hot oven.

1 tbsp	EACH ground cumin and ground coriander 15 mL
2 tsp	fennel seeds, slightly crushed 10 mL
1 tsp	salt 5 mL
1/2 tsp	ground cardamom 2 mL
3 tbsp	olive oil 45 mL
6	thick centre-cut salmon fillets with skin 6
	Pepper
	Spicy Lentils (recipe follows)

1. In a small bowl, stir together cumin, coriander, fennel seeds, salt and cardamom. Stir in 1 tbsp (15 mL) oil. (Mixture can be made several hours ahead.)
2. Place 2 ovenproof skillets over high heat. Add 1 tbsp (15 mL) oil to each skillet. Sprinkle salmon with pepper and coat on both sides with spice mixture. When oil is very hot, add 3 fillets to each pan, skin side down. Cook for 3 minutes; then without turning the fillets over, transfer the skillets to 400°F (200°C) oven. Roast for 8 to 9 minutes or until skin is very crisp and fish is just cooked through.
3. Spoon warm lentils onto 6 warm dinner plates and set salmon fillets on top, skin side up. Serve immediately.

Spicy Lentils

MAKES 6 SERVINGS.

Lentils take on the flavours of whatever they are cooked with; for example, in the Crisp-Skinned
Salmon recipe above, they are enlivened with the spices that make up the salmon coating to
become a perfect accompaniment for the fish.

1-1/2 cups	green or brown lentils 375 mL
2 tbsp	olive oil 25 mL
1 tsp	cumin seeds 5 mL
1	onion, sliced 1
2	cloves garlic, minced 2
1-1/2 tsp	ground cumin 7 mL
1 tsp	ground coriander 5 mL
1/4 tsp	cayenne 1 mL
Pinch	turmeric Pinch
	Salt and pepper
1/2 cup	chopped fresh coriander 125 mL

1. Pick over and rinse lentils. Place in a medium saucepan; cover with 4 cups (1 L) water. Bring to a boil, reduce heat, cover and simmer, stirring occasionally, for about 25 minutes or until soft but not mushy. Reserving cooking water, drain lentils.
2. Meanwhile, heat oil in heavy skillet over medium heat. Add cumin seeds; fry for 1 minute. Add onion and garlic; cook, stirring often, for 5 minutes. Stir in ground cumin, ground coriander, cayenne, turmeric and cooked lentils. Season with salt and pepper to taste. Cook over low heat for 5 minutes, adding a bit of cooking water if dry. (Lentils can be prepared, cooled, covered and refrigerated for up to 6 hours. Refrigerate cooking water as well. Bring out lentils to room temperature and reheat slowly, adding more cooking water if necessary.)
3. Stir fresh coriander into lentils and serve hot.

New-Style Tuna Casserole

MAKES 4 SERVINGS.

The tuna noodle casserole of the 1950s goes formal with bow ties, wild mushrooms and fresh rosemary. Quick and easy to make, it would be just right to serve with a green salad to unexpected company. You can, of course, use ordinary white mushrooms if wild mushrooms are not available. This is one of my friend Sharon Boyd's favourite recipes from my *New Casseroles and Other One-Dish Meals*.

3 cups	bow-tie pasta (farfalle) 750 mL
3 tbsp	butter 45 mL
4 oz	wild mushrooms (crimini, portobello or shiitake), coarsely chopped 125 g
3	cloves garlic, minced 3
1 tbsp	chopped fresh rosemary (or 1 tsp/5 mL crumbled dried rosemary) 15 mL
1-1/2 cups	milk 375 mL
4 oz	unripened (fresh) goat cheese or cream cheese, in bits 125 g
1/2 cup	sour cream 125 mL
1	can (6 oz/170 g) tuna, drained 1
1 cup	fresh bread crumbs 250 mL
2 tbsp	chopped fresh parsley 25 mL
1 tsp	grated lemon zest (outer rind) 5 mL

1. Cook pasta in a large pot of boiling salted water for 8 to 10 minutes or until tender but firm; drain well and return to the pot.

2. Meanwhile, melt the butter in a large skillet and transfer 1 tbsp (15 mL) to a medium bowl; set aside.

3. To the remaining butter, add mushrooms and two-thirds of the garlic; cook over medium-high heat for 7 minutes. Stir in the rosemary. Reduce heat to low; stir in the milk, then add the cheese and stir to melt. Stir in the sour cream. Combine with pasta and gently stir in tuna. Transfer to a greased 6-cup (1.5 L) casserole.

4. To the reserved butter, add bread crumbs, parsley, lemon zest and remaining garlic. Spread evenly over top of the pasta mixture and bake in a 350°F (180°C) oven for 20 to 30 minutes or until the top is golden brown and the casserole is bubbly.

Tuna Florentine

MAKES 4 TO 6 SERVINGS.

Spinach adds a Florentine touch and is a natural with pasta. This is a great dish to "pull out of your cupboard" on a busy weeknight. To make it even easier, replace the fresh spinach with a package of frozen.

2 tbsp	butter 25 mL	
1	onion, sliced 1	
1	clove garlic, minced 1	
1	can (19 oz/540 mL) tomatoes, undrained 1	
1	can (7-1/2 oz/213 mL) tomato sauce 1	
1/2 tsp	EACH dried basil, granulated sugar and salt 2 mL	
1/4 tsp	pepper 1 mL	
4 oz	medium egg noodles 125 g	
1	pkg (10 oz/284 g) fresh spinach 1	
1	can (6-1/2 oz/184 g) tuna, drained 1	
1/4 cup	freshly grated Parmesan cheese 50 mL	

1. In a large skillet, melt butter over medium heat; cook onion and garlic for about 3 minutes or until softened. Stir in tomatoes, tomato sauce, basil, sugar, salt and pepper; simmer for about 20 minutes or until thickened.

2. Meanwhile, in a large pot of boiling salted water, cook noodles for 8 to 10 minutes or until tender but firm; drain well and set aside.

3. Rinse spinach; shake off excess water. In a covered saucepan, cook spinach (with only the water clinging to the leaves) over medium-high heat for about 5 minutes or just until wilted. Drain well and squeeze dry; chop coarsely and set aside.

4. Break tuna into chunks and stir into tomato mixture along with cooked noodles. Transfer to a 6-cup (1.5 L) casserole. Spoon chopped spinach around the edge. Sprinkle Parmesan cheese over top. Bake, uncovered, in a 375°F (190°C) oven for about 25 minutes or until bubbling.

Baked Shells with Spinach and Prosciutto

MAKES 6 TO 8 SERVINGS.

I always marvel at how early in the spring lovely local spinach appears at our farmers' market. This simple make-ahead casserole from my *New Casseroles* cookbook is an excellent choice for a potluck contribution or just good family fare. Use a homemade (or good-quality commercial) meatless spaghetti sauce. Accompany with lots of crusty bread and a crisp green salad.

8 oz	jumbo pasta shells (about 32) 250 g
1	pkg (10 oz/284 g) fresh spinach, trimmed 1
1 tbsp	olive oil 15 mL
1	onion, chopped 1
4 oz	prosciutto, diced 125 g
1-1/2 cups	shredded Fontina cheese (6 oz/175 g) 375 mL
1 cup	ricotta cheese 250 mL
1	egg, beaten 1
1 tbsp	chopped fresh basil (or 1 tsp/5 mL dried) 15 mL
1/4 tsp	EACH grated nutmeg and black pepper 1 mL
3-1/2 cups	meatless spaghetti sauce 875 mL
1/2 cup	freshly grated Parmesan cheese 125 mL

1. In a large pot of boiling salted water, cook pasta for 7 to 8 minutes or until tender but firm (al dente). Lift out with a slotted spoon, then rinse in a colander under cold water and set aside.

2. In the same pot of boiling water, cook spinach for about 2 minutes or until tender.

3. Drain well and let cool. Squeeze out any liquid and chop.

4. Meanwhile, in a large deep skillet, heat oil over medium heat; cook onion for 5 minutes. Remove from the heat. Stir in spinach, prosciutto, half the Fontina cheese, the ricotta cheese, egg, basil, nutmeg and pepper.

5. Spread 1 cup (250 mL) of the sauce in a greased 13 x 9-inch (3 L) glass baking dish. Fill each pasta shell with about 1 rounded tablespoon (15 mL) of the spinach mixture; arrange shells in a single layer in the dish.

6. Spoon remaining sauce over top. Sprinkle with remaining Fontina cheese and the Parmesan cheese. (Recipe can be prepared to this point, covered and refrigerated for up to 1 day. Remove from the refrigerator 30 minutes before baking or bake a little longer.)

7. Bake, covered with foil, in a 350°F (180°C) oven for about 30 minutes or until bubbly.

Old-Fashioned Baked Macaroni and Cheese with Tomatoes

MAKES 6 TO 8 SERVINGS.

My son and his girlfriend often treat me to my own recipe for macaroni and cheese when I go for dinner, but Allen has tweaked it by doubling the cheese and adding some Tabasco sauce. I must admit, I like this new version. If you wish, you can divide the casserole between two 6-cup (1.5 L) dishes and reduce the baking time to 35 minutes. Freeze one dish to have on hand when the craving for macaroni and cheese—like your mother (or your son) used to make—strikes again.

1/2 lb	elbow macaroni (2 cups/500 mL) 250 g
1 lb	Cheddar cheese, preferably old 500 g
1	can (28 oz/796 mL) tomatoes 1
1 tsp	EACH granulated sugar and Worcestershire sauce 5 mL
1/2 tsp	EACH dried summer savory or thyme, salt and Tabasco 2 mL
1/4 tsp	pepper 1 mL
2	eggs, beaten 2
1 cup	milk 250 mL

1. In a large pot of boiling salted water, cook macaroni until just tender, about 8 minutes; do not overcook. Drain well and transfer to a well-buttered 12-cup (3 L) casserole. Meanwhile, shred half of the cheese; set aside. Thinly slice remainder; set aside.

2. Drain 3/4 cup (175 mL) of the juice from the tomatoes and reserve for another use. Pour tomatoes and remaining juice into a bowl; chop tomatoes. Stir in shredded cheese, sugar, Worcestershire sauce, savory, salt, Tabasco and pepper; pour over the macaroni and mix well. Top with cheese slices.

3. In a small bowl, blend eggs with milk; pour over cheese-covered macaroni but do not stir. Bake, uncovered, in a 350°F (180°C) oven for 40 to 50 minutes or until the top is golden brown.

Texas Brisket with Spicy Barbecue Sauce

MAKES 8 SERVINGS.

When I wrote a Tex-Mex Barbecue menu for *Homemaker's,* Julia Aitken was the food editor; she lists this beef dish among her favourites. Beef brisket epitomizes the Texan barbecue. Traditionally cooked for hours in a backyard barbecue pit, this indoor version of beef brisket would impress any Southerner and will give you a spring taste of barbecues to come. Start preparing the recipe at least one day ahead.

1 cup	EACH red wine and beef broth 250 mL
1/3 cup	fresh lime juice 75 mL
1/4 cup	EACH Worcestershire sauce and packed brown sugar 50 mL
1/4 cup	**Spicy Barbecue Sauce** (recipe follows) 50 mL
2 tbsp	chopped fresh parsley 25 mL
4	cloves garlic, minced 4
2	jalapeño peppers, seeded and minced 2
1 tsp	EACH salt, pepper and paprika 5 mL
1	beef brisket, rolled and tied (about 5 lb/2.2 kg) 1
1 tbsp	vegetable oil 15 mL

1. In a medium bowl, stir together red wine, beef broth, lime juice, Worcestershire sauce, brown sugar, Spicy Barbecue Sauce, parsley, garlic and peppers; set aside.

2. In a small bowl, combine salt, pepper and paprika. Rub salt mixture all over brisket; place in a sturdy plastic bag set in a large bowl. Pour wine mixture into the bag; seal well. Refrigerate at least 24 hours or up to 3 days, turning brisket occasionally.

3. Reserving 3/4 cup (175 mL) marinade, remove brisket from marinade; dry well. Rub brisket with oil. Sear brisket on a hot barbecue or in a large skillet over medium-high heat, turning often until browned all over.

4. Transfer brisket, fat side up, to a large sheet of heavy-duty foil; place in a shallow roasting pan. Pour reserved marinade over brisket; wrap securely in foil. Roast in a 250°F (120°C) oven for 8 hours, until tender. Slice thinly across the grain; serve with heated Spicy Barbecue Sauce.

Hint

When seeding and mincing jalapeño peppers, wear rubber gloves.

Spicy Barbecue Sauce

MAKES ABOUT 2-1/2 CUPS (625 ML).

Sauces are of primary importance to a Texan barbecue, but they should never hide the meat's flavour. This easy sauce is also a great addition to any barbecue chef's repertoire throughout the summer and can be brushed onto grilled ribs, beef or sausage.

2 tbsp	vegetable oil	25 mL
4	cloves garlic, minced	4
1	onion, chopped	1
1 tbsp	EACH drained horseradish and dry mustard	15 mL
1 tsp	dried oregano	5 mL
1/3 cup	red wine vinegar	75 mL
1/2 tsp	salt	2 mL
1-1/2 cups	ketchup	375 mL
1/3 cup	liquid honey	75 mL
3 tbsp	packed brown sugar	45 mL
2 tbsp	Worcestershire sauce	25 mL
1 tbsp	sambal oelek* (approx.)	15 mL

1. In a medium saucepan, heat oil over medium heat; cook garlic and onion 3 minutes or until softened.
2. Add horseradish, mustard, oregano, vinegar and salt. Simmer for 3 minutes. Stir in ketchup, honey, brown sugar, Worcestershire sauce and sambal oelek. Simmer, uncovered, for 30 minutes, stirring occasionally. Taste and add more sambal oelek if necessary. (Sauce can be made up to 1 week ahead; refrigerate covered. Reheat gently to serve.)

* Sambal oelek is a spicy Indonesian sauce available in the international section of most large supermarkets. If unavailable, use a hot red pepper paste to taste or chopped canned jalapeño peppers.

Maple Apricot Pork Chops

MAKES 4 SERVINGS.

This is my easy, everyday way of cooking pork chops and one of my daughter, Anne's, favourites. They're delicious with a wild and white rice mixture and steamed spinach.

12	dried apricots	12
4	pork chops, loin or butt	4
1/2 tsp	dried thyme	2 mL
	Salt and pepper	
1/3 cup	maple syrup	75 mL

1. Soak apricots in 1/2 cup (125 mL) warm water for 20 minutes. Meanwhile, remove any fat from the chops and render it in a large ovenproof skillet over medium-high heat just to coat the pan. Discard the solid fat. Brown chops on both sides.

2. Sprinkle the chops with the thyme and salt and pepper to taste. Reserving the soaking liquid, place the apricots on top of the chops. Stir maple syrup into the reserved liquid; pour around the chops in the skillet. Cover and bake in a 350°F (180°C) oven for 30 minutes. Uncover and bake for about 10 minutes longer or until tender. The time will depend on the thickness of the chops.

Roast Chicken

MAKES 6 SERVINGS.

There's something very satisfying and homey about putting a whole chicken in the oven to roast for a Sunday dinner, hearing it spattering and sending out irresistible aromas. Since leftovers make such good weekday fare, you might like to roast a bigger bird. Just adjust the time, allowing about 20 minutes per pound (500 g).

1	roasting chicken or capon (about 5 lb/2.2 kg)	1
Half	lemon	Half
	Salt and pepper	
1	onion, quartered	1
1 tbsp	butter, softened	15 mL
1 tbsp	Dijon mustard	15 mL
1/2 tsp	dried thyme	2 mL
1/2 tsp	crumbled dried sage	2 mL

1. Remove neck and any giblets from the chicken. Rinse and pat chicken dry inside and out. Rub inside and out with the lemon half, squeezing out the juice as you work. Sprinkle inside and out with salt and pepper. Place the onion in the cavity. With your fingers, loosen the skin as far back as possible on the breast; be careful not to break the skin.

2. Combine the butter, mustard, thyme and sage. Rub some of the mixture under the breast skin and the remainder on top of the breast and legs. Tie legs together with string; tuck wings under the back or tie to the body with string. Place breast side up on a rack in a shallow roasting pan.

3. Roast in a 325°F (160°C) oven for about 2 hours or until juices run clear when chicken is pierced and a meat thermometer inserted in the thigh registers 185°F (85°C); baste occasionally with pan drippings.

4. Transfer chicken to a warm platter and tent with foil; let stand for about 15 minutes before carving so juices can settle into the meat.

Goat Cheese and Sun-Dried Tomato Cheesecake

MAKES ABOUT 8 SERVINGS.

Serve thin wedges of this easy-to-make savory cheesecake warm or at room temperature over a bed of dressed greens for a delicious brunch dish. It's high on Sharon Boyd's list of favourites and one of the dishes she served at a lovely shower she gave my daughter.

3/4 cup	all-purpose flour 175 mL
1/4 cup	butter, softened 50 mL
1/4 cup	toasted chopped walnuts 50 mL
1	egg yolk 1
1/4 tsp	salt 1 mL
1/2 lb	mild goat cheese 250 g
1/4 lb	cream cheese 125 g
3	eggs 3
1 tbsp	chopped fresh basil (or 1 tsp/5 mL dried basil) 15 mL
1/4 tsp	hot pepper sauce 1 mL
	Salt and white pepper
1/4 cup	finely chopped, oil-packed sun-dried tomatoes, drained 50 mL

1. In an 8-inch (2 L) springform pan, gently combine flour, butter, walnuts, egg yolk and salt with your hands; pat evenly over the bottom of the pan. Bake in a 350°F (180°C) oven for 10 minutes.

2. In a food processor or bowl, beat together goat cheese, cream cheese, eggs, basil, hot pepper sauce, and salt and pepper to taste only until smooth and blended. Stir in tomatoes. Pour into the crust; bake in a 350°F (180°C) oven for 20 to 25 minutes or until almost set and starting to crack around the outside, yet still wobbly in the centre.

3. Remove from the oven. Immediately run a sharp knife around the inside of the pan to prevent cheesecake from cracking when cooling. Cool slightly to serve. (Cheesecake can be cooled completely, covered and refrigerated for up to 2 days. Let stand at room temperature for about 1 hour before serving.)

TIP

Sun-dried tomatoes are usually found dry in bags in the produce department and are less expensive than those packed in oil. Rehydrate them in warm water for 30 minutes, drain and pack in olive oil, and refrigerate for a day or two. Or, just pack in oil for several days until they are rehydrated.

Spring Risotto with Escarole, Morels and Prosciutto

MAKES 3 MAIN-COURSE SERVINGS OR 6 TO 8 FIRST-COURSE SERVINGS.

Escarole adds character and crunch to this comforting dish. Because the prosciutto and Parmesan are both salty, you may prefer using a low-sodium chicken stock to balance the flavouring.

4 cups	chicken stock	1 L
1 oz	dried morels or other dried wild mushrooms	30 g
1	small head escarole (about 6 cups/1.5 L, chopped)	1
2 tbsp	butter	25 mL
1 tbsp	olive oil	15 mL
1	onion, chopped	1
2 tsp	finely chopped fresh thyme (or 1/2 tsp/2 mL dried thyme)	10 mL
1 cup	arborio rice	250 mL
2 oz	thinly sliced prosciutto, coarsely chopped	60 g
2 tbsp	snipped chives or green onion tops, chopped	25 mL
1/2 cup	freshly grated Parmesan cheese, plus more for serving	125 mL
	Black pepper	

1. In a medium saucepan, bring stock to a boil. Add dried mushrooms, remove from the heat, cover and let stand for 30 minutes. Meanwhile, wash and chop 6 cups (1.5 L) outer leaves of escarole; set aside.

2. Remove soaked mushrooms with a slotted spoon. When cool enough to handle, coarsely chop. Strain stock through cheesecloth or a paper towel; return to the pan and place over low heat.

3. In a large saucepan or deep skillet over medium heat, melt 1 tbsp (15 mL) butter with olive oil. Add onion and thyme; cook for 5 minutes, stirring often. Add reconstituted mushrooms; stir for 2 minutes. Add rice and stir for 1 minute.

4. Pour in hot stock, 1/2 cup (125 mL) at a time, stirring constantly and waiting several minutes until stock is mostly absorbed before adding more; keep rice at a brisk simmer. The risotto should always be moist. After 12 minutes, stir in escarole. After 5 more minutes, taste rice; it should be al dente (tender but firm to the bite). Some Italian cooks like the middle of the rice grain to be chalky; if you do not like this texture, add more stock and cook for 5 more minutes, stirring constantly. Never cook grains until soft in the centre because they will continue to cook after they are removed from the heat.

5. Stir in prosciutto, chives, cheese, remaining 1 tbsp (15 mL) butter and pepper to taste. Serve immediately in warm shallow bowls, with cheese for garnish.

Light Eggs Benedict

MAKES 4 SERVINGS.

Prosciutto and a butterless Hollandaise sauce make a lighter version of this classic dish.

Light Hollandaise Sauce

4	English muffins (or 8 slices of French bread)	4
2 tbsp	unsalted butter	25 mL
1/4 lb	prosciutto, slivered or sliced	125 g
8	poached eggs	8

PERFECTLY POACHED EGGS

3	eggs	3
3 tbsp	fresh lemon juice	45 mL
1/4 cup	hot water	50 mL
1/4 tsp	white pepper	1 mL
Dash	hot pepper sauce	Dash

Variation

Substitute smoked salmon or shaved ham for the prosciutto. Substitute fried polenta for the muffins and a tomato bruschetta topping for the Hollandaise sauce.

1. To prepare the Hollandaise sauce, whisk together eggs, lemon juice and hot water in a large heatproof bowl. Place over a pan of hot, not boiling, water and whisk until fluffy and thickened, 3 to 4 minutes. Whisk in pepper and hot pepper sauce; cover and keep warm over hot water for up to 30 minutes.
2. Meanwhile, split muffins; toast and place on hot plates. Keep warm. In a small skillet, melt butter; sauté prosciutto just until heated through. Place prosciutto on top of muffins; top each with a poached egg and spoon sauce over.

1. Use the freshest eggs possible; the fresher the eggs the less the whites will stray from the yolks. In a deep skillet or saucepan, bring 2 to 3 inches (5 to 8 cm) of water to a boil. For each egg, stir water to create a whirlpool effect and carefully slip the egg into the centre of the whirlpool. Do not crowd the pan with eggs. Reduce the heat, cover and simmer for about 4 minutes or until the eggs are soft cooked. Lift out with a slotted spoon and drain on a paper towel. Use immediately or transfer to a bowl of ice water. Poached eggs can be covered and refrigerated for up to 2 days. To reheat, slip poached eggs into a saucepan of barely simmering water; cook for 1 to 2 minutes or until heated through. If your eggs are less than fresh, adding white vinegar at the rate of 2 tbsp (25 mL) to 4 cups (1 L) water will help keep the egg whites together.
2. To determine whether an egg is fresh, place it in a container of water. A newly laid egg will sink and lie flat on the bottom. As the egg ages, the air pocket continues to expand until the egg becomes buoyant enough to stand upright in the water (about 3 weeks old or so).

Buttermilk Pancakes

MAKES ABOUT 12 PANCAKES.

When I made these easy pancakes for Shrove Tuesday on my regular spot on the news at Kitchener, Ontario's CKCO-TV, the switchboard was inundated with calls for days. Top with a bit of butter, if desired, and maple syrup or a fruit sauce.

2 cups	all-purpose flour*	500 mL
2 tbsp	granulated sugar	25 mL
1-1/2 tsp	baking powder	7 mL
1 tsp	baking soda	5 mL
1/2 tsp	salt	2 mL
2	eggs	2
2 cups	buttermilk	500 mL
2 tbsp	vegetable oil or melted butter	25 mL

1. In a large bowl, sift or stir together flour, sugar, baking powder, baking soda and salt.
2. In a small bowl, stir together the eggs, buttermilk and oil. Pour into dry ingredients and stir just enough to combine, ignoring lumps. Let rest for 5 minutes.
3. Heat a nonstick griddle or skillet until drops of water dance and sputter; grease lightly. Drop batter in 1/4-cup (50 mL) amounts onto the hot pan. Cook for 2 to 3 minutes or until top is covered with fine bubbles. Do not flatten with a spatula. Turn pancake over and cook until bubbly side is well browned. Serve immediately.

Or use 1 cup (250 mL) EACH of all-purpose and whole-wheat flour.

SPRING SIDES AND SALADS

Oven-Roasted Asparagus

MAKES 4 SERVINGS.

One year, when I was doing a lot of work with asparagus, I discovered that oven-roasting it at a high temperature was not only fast, but also easy and provided a new dimension to the vegetable. It becomes nuttier and has a more substantial texture. I do it often for guests, and it never fails to impress them. The recipe can be doubled easily and is also great with a drizzle of balsamic vinegar after roasting.

1 lb	fat asparagus spears, trimmed 500 g
1 tbsp	vegetable or olive oil 15 mL
	Salt and pepper

1. Spread asparagus out in a single layer in a large, shallow baking pan or sheet. Drizzle with oil; sprinkle with salt and pepper to taste.
2. Roast, uncovered, in a 500°F (260°C) oven for about 8 minutes, stirring once, until asparagus is tender but still slightly firm.

Oven-Roasted Asparagus with Hazelnut Vinaigrette

MAKES 2 TO 4 SERVINGS.

Here is a delicious variation. I've done many articles on asparagus over the years, and this simple recipe is from a recent article in *Elm Street*. My editor wrote, "It's so delicious two people could happily share a portion this size."

2 tbsp	minced shallots 25 mL
2 tbsp	finely chopped toasted hazelnuts 25 mL
1 tbsp	hazelnut or olive oil 15 mL
1 tbsp	red wine vinegar 15 mL
1/2 tsp	Dijon mustard 2 mL
1 lb	asparagus, roasted as above 500 g

1. Whisk together shallots, hazelnuts, hazelnut oil, vinegar and mustard. Transfer hot asparagus to a warm platter and spoon dressing over the top. Toss gently to coat asparagus with dressing and serve at once.

Special-Occasion Carrots Glazed with Honey and Mint

MAKES ABOUT 4 SERVINGS.

I sometimes cook mini-carrots in a skillet with a bit of water, then finish them off with herbs and honey or maple syrup. Although this is a little extra fuss, it is easily doubled and is a delicious side dish with lamb. For a wonderful accompaniment to roast chicken, substitute sage for the mint, cutting the amount in half.

15	thin carrots (about 1-1/4 lb/ 625 g) 15 (or 1 lb/500 g peeled mini-carrots)
2 tbsp	butter 25 mL
1/2 tsp	granulated sugar 2 mL
1/4 tsp	EACH salt and pepper 1 mL
1/3 cup	water 75 mL
2 tbsp	liquid honey 25 mL
1/4 cup	whipping cream 50 mL
2 tbsp	finely chopped fresh mint 25 mL

1. Trim carrots and cut into 1-inch (2.5 cm) pieces; set aside. (Leave mini-carrots as they come.)

2. In a large skillet, melt butter over medium heat; cook carrots, sugar, salt and pepper for 3 minutes, stirring occasionally. Add water, bring to a boil and reduce heat; cover and simmer for 5 minutes or just until tender-crisp.

3. Uncover and increase the heat to medium-high; cook for 2 to 4 minutes or until the liquid has evaporated. Add honey and stir for 1 minute to coat carrots. Pour in cream; boil until thick enough to coat a spoon, about 2 minutes. Taste and adjust seasoning if necessary. Sprinkle with mint.

Rosemary Breaded Parsnips

MAKES 6 TO 8 SERVINGS.

I always think of parsnips as spring vegetables because on our farm we would leave them in the garden all winter and dig them up in the spring before they started to sprout; this ensured that they would taste particularly sweet. Parsnips done this way in a crunchy herb coating will be well received by all as a side dish to roast poultry or meat.

2 lb	parsnips (about 6)	1 kg
1/4 cup	EACH all-purpose flour and dry bread crumbs	50 mL
2 tsp	crumbled dried rosemary	10 mL
1/2 tsp	EACH salt and pepper	2 mL
1/4 cup	butter (approx.)	50 mL

1. Peel parsnips and cut into pieces about 2 inches (5 cm) long and 1 inch (2.5 cm) wide. Cook, covered, in boiling salted water for about 5 minutes or until almost tender. Drain well.

2. In a shallow bowl, combine flour, bread crumbs, rosemary, salt and pepper. Using tongs, roll hot parsnips in crumb mixture to coat well, setting each on a tray lined with waxed paper. (Recipe can be prepared to this point, cooled, covered and left at room temperature for 2 hours, or refrigerated for up to 24 hours.)

3. In a large skillet or 2 small skillets, melt butter over medium heat. Cook parsnips, turning, for about 10 minutes until golden brown on all sides.

Dandelion Salad with Warm Mustard Dressing and Croutons

MAKES 4 MAIN-COURSE SERVINGS OR 6 OR MORE SIDE-SALAD SERVINGS.

When we first moved to Cambridge, Ontario, I remember our dear friend Edna Staebler arriving at our house one spring with two huge shopping bags full of dandelions. She proceeded to show my son, Allen, how to make her delicious dandelion salad that appears in her best-selling cookbook, *Food That Really Schmecks*. "In Waterloo County," she explained, "we say that dandelion greens purify the blood, grown sluggish and thick through the winter." This recipe is not quite the same as Edna's, but you might add her touch of 2 sliced, hard-cooked eggs with the croutons and bacon.

If you use dandelions from your lawn, be sure they haven't been sprayed. Otherwise, look for those grown under sawdust or straw specifically for supermarkets. Failing that, substitute curly endive.

3	slices whole-grain or whole-wheat bread 3
8 oz	dandelion greens or curly endive 250 g
4	slices side bacon 4
1/4 cup	thinly sliced shallots 50 mL
1 cup	sour cream 250 mL
1 tbsp	white wine vinegar 15 mL
1 tbsp	coarse-grained mustard (like moutarde de Meaux) 15 mL
2 tsp	granulated sugar 10 mL
2 tsp	all-purpose flour 10 mL
	Salt and pepper

1. Remove crusts from bread and cut into 1/2-inch (1 cm) cubes. Spread out in a single layer on a baking sheet. Bake in a 350°F (180°C) oven for about 15 minutes, or until golden.

2. Meanwhile, wash and dry dandelion greens well. Trim off any tough stems, break up if necessary and arrange in a large salad bowl.

3. In a medium skillet over medium heat, cook bacon until crisp. Drain on paper towels and crumble; set aside. Pour off all but 2 tbsp (25 mL) of the drippings. Over medium heat, cook shallots in drippings for about 3 minutes or until soft but not brown. Reduce heat to low.

4. In a small bowl, stir together until smooth the sour cream, vinegar, mustard, sugar, flour, and salt and pepper to taste. Add to shallots and heat, stirring until slightly thickened. Do not boil. Pour over dandelion greens and toss to coat well. Sprinkle warm croutons and bacon over top. Serve immediately.

Watercress and Orange Salad

MAKES 8 TO 10 SERVINGS.

When I first started writing for *Recipes Only Magazine* (now part of *Homemaker's Magazine*), Carroll Allen was the editor, and she put together a lovely hard-cover *Recipes Only Cookbook* in 1989. In an article launching that book in September 1989, Carroll is quoted as saying, "This is one of the best salad recipes ever to appear in *Recipes Only.*"

Watercress is a true herald of spring. For this easy and colourful salad, you also might like to try tender, young spinach leaves that appear in the spring markets.

3	bunches watercress	3
4	seedless oranges	4
1 tbsp	granulated sugar	15 mL
1/2 cup	toasted slivered almonds	125 mL
1/4 cup	fresh lemon juice	50 mL
1/4 cup	minced shallots or onion	50 mL
1/2 tsp	curry powder or to taste	2 mL
	Salt and pepper	
1/2 cup	olive oil	125 mL

1. Remove stems from watercress; wash and dry well. Wrap in paper towels and place in a plastic bag in the refrigerator if preparing ahead of time. Or, arrange on a large platter.

2. Peel oranges and remove all white pith. Cut in thin, crosswise slices and arrange in an overlapping pattern on top of the watercress. Sprinkle with sugar and almonds.

3. Stir together lemon juice, shallots, curry powder, and salt and pepper to taste in a small bowl. Slowly whisk in the oil. (Dressing can be prepared ahead, covered and left at room temperature for up to 2 hours. Whisk just before using to recombine.) Pour dressing all over the salad and serve immediately.

Spinach and Mushroom Salad with Creamy Buttermilk Dressing

MAKES 6 TO 8 SERVINGS.

Look for tender local spinach for this crunchy salad, a favourite with Elizabeth Hay, the producer of CBC's *Ontario Today*. Elizabeth especially likes the dressing. This was evident in a note she sent me telling me how much she uses my *Comfortable Kitchen Cookbook*: "I use the buttermilk dressing from the spinach salad on a weekly basis, on everything from potato salad to poached eggs ... of course on your spinach salad as well."

1 cup	buttermilk	250 mL
1/2 cup	light mayonnaise	125 mL
2	cloves garlic, crushed	2
2 tsp	Dijon mustard	10 mL
	Salt and pepper	
10 oz	spinach	284 g
1/2 lb	mushrooms, sliced	250 g
1/4 lb	bean sprouts (about 2 cups/500 mL)	125 g
5	slices crisply cooked side bacon, crumbled	5

1. In a small bowl, whisk together buttermilk, mayonnaise, garlic, mustard, and salt and pepper to taste until frothy. (Dressing can be covered and refrigerated for up to 8 hours.)
2. Wash and dry spinach well; remove any thick stems and tear into bite-sized pieces. Toss in a large salad bowl with mushrooms and bean sprouts. (Salad can be covered and refrigerated without the dressing for up to 3 hours.)
3. Just before serving, toss the spinach mixture gently with the dressing to coat. Sprinkle with bacon.

TIP
Always shake the container of buttermilk well before using it.

Hot and Spicy Rhubarb Chutney

MAKES ABOUT 4 CUPS (1 L).

Carol Ferguson was the food editor for *Canadian Living* when I started writing for the magazine—my first article, in fact. She was also food editor for *Homemaker's Magazine* when I did this chutney recipe for that magazine. I was very happy when she asked if she could use it in her wonderful book, *The New Canadian Basics Cookbook*. In her lead she says, "This excellent, inexpensive chutney rivals the most costly store-bought." Serve it with meats or cheese.

2 cups	packed brown sugar	500 mL
1-1/2 cups	cider vinegar	375 mL
1 tbsp	ground ginger	15 mL
1 tsp	EACH salt, ground allspice and cinnamon	5 mL
1/2 tsp	EACH ground cloves, black pepper and cayenne	2 mL
6 cups	rhubarb, cut in 1-inch (2.5 cm) pieces	1.5 L
2 to 3	fresh small chilies such as jalapeño, minced	2 to 3
2 tbsp	EACH minced fresh ginger and garlic	25 mL
1 cup	chopped onions	250 mL
1 cup	golden raisins	250 mL

1. In a large, heavy saucepan, combine sugar, vinegar, ground ginger, salt, allspice, cinnamon, cloves, pepper and cayenne. Bring to a boil, stirring to dissolve the sugar. Add the rhubarb, chilies, fresh ginger, garlic, onions and raisins; return to a boil. Reduce heat and simmer uncovered, stirring often, for about 1 hour or until thick.

2. Immediately pour into 1-cup (250 mL) warm, clean canning jars, leaving 1/2-inch (1 cm) headspace. Seal. Process in a boiling water bath for 10 minutes. Let cool on a rack.

SPRING DESSERTS

IN THE MENUS ...

Maple Crème Brûlée

MAKES 6 SERVINGS.

Easy elegance personified, this creamy dessert gains a whole new dimension of flavour when finely grated maple sugar is caramelized on top. If you can't find maple sugar, grate or finely chop the maple leaf moulds found in farmers' markets. The broiler works well for caramelizing the sugar, but you could also use a small kitchen blowtorch.

1-1/2 cups	whipping cream	375 mL
1/4 cup	maple syrup	50 mL
4	egg yolks	4
1/3 cup	finely grated maple sugar	75 mL

1. In a small, heavy saucepan, heat cream and maple syrup together until bubbles just start to form around the outside. Remove from the heat. In a bowl, whisk egg yolks slightly without allowing them to foam. Very gradually pour hot cream into yolks, stirring constantly.

2. Strain custard through a fine sieve into a pitcher or measuring cup. Pour into six 1/2-cup (125 mL) heatproof ramekins.* Place in a baking pan just big enough to hold them; pour hot water into the pan to come two-thirds up the sides of the ramekins.

3. Cover with foil; bake in a 325°F (160°C) oven for about 25 minutes or until custards are just set but still slightly jiggly in centres. Remove ramekins to cool on rack; refrigerate until very cold. (Custards can be prepared a day ahead.)

4. Just before serving, sprinkle custards with maple sugar; broil on rack nearest heat for about 3-1/2 minutes, watching carefully, or until sugar caramelizes to golden brown. Serve immediately.

*Small, usually round dishes for baking and serving an individual portion.

Candied Lemon Tart

MAKES 8 SERVINGS.

This is the simple, elegant tart you see in smart pastry-shop windows. Although there are various steps, they can be done in stages for a completely make-ahead company dessert. Add a tablespoon (15 mL) of sugar to your favourite regular pastry recipe or use a sweet short-crust pastry. According to my co-author for *Cellar & Silver,* Tony Aspler, a Late Harvest Riesling or an Austrian Beerenauslese would be a good accompanying wine.

2	large lemons 2
	Pastry for 9-inch (23 cm) single-crust pie (see **Pie Pastry,** page 33)
1/4 cup	unsalted butter 50 mL
1-1/3 cups	granulated sugar 325 mL
1	egg 1
1 tbsp	finely grated lemon zest 15 mL
1/4 tsp	almond extract 1 mL
1/2 cup	ground blanched almonds 125 mL
1 tbsp	all-purpose flour 15 mL
1/4 tsp	vanilla 1 mL

1. With a sharp knife, slice lemons as thinly as possible, still keeping slices whole. Place in a heatproof bowl and cover with boiling water; let stand, covered, for 6 hours.

2. Drain slices and place in a saucepan; cover with fresh, cold water and bring to a boil. Once again, drain and cover with fresh, cold water; bring to a boil. Reduce heat, cover and simmer for 30 minutes or until rinds are soft and pulp has partly disintegrated. Let cool in liquid.

3. On a lightly floured surface, roll out the pastry. Line a tart tin (preferably with a removable bottom). Prick the bottom of the pastry all over with a fork and line it with parchment paper or foil. Fill with dried beans or rice as weights and bake in a 400°F (200°C) oven for 5 minutes. Remove paper and weights; set aside.

4. In a bowl, beat butter with 1/3 cup (75 mL) of the sugar until light and fluffy. Beat egg lightly; stir in lemon zest and almond extract. Gradually blend into butter mixture. Stir together almonds and flour; blend into butter mixture. Spread evenly over partially baked pastry. Bake in 375°F (190°C) oven for 25 to 30 minutes or until puffed, golden brown and firm to the touch. Cool.

5. Meanwhile, reserving 1 cup (250 mL) of the liquid, drain lemon slices in a sieve. In a saucepan, combine reserved liquid, remaining 1 cup (250 mL) of sugar and vanilla; stir and cook over low heat until sugar is dissolved. Add lemon slices and simmer, uncovered, for 5 minutes. Transfer lemon slices to a plate and boil syrup for 18 to 20 minutes, or until a small amount on a cold saucer crinkles when pushed with a finger. Arrange lemon slices attractively (overlapping somewhat) over tart; spoon hot syrup on top. Let cool to room temperature to serve.

Pie Pastry

MAKES ENOUGH PASTRY FOR TWO 9-INCH (23 CM) PIE CRUSTS.

When making pastry, be sure all the ingredients are cold and work quickly for best results. Although flaky, the pastry is sturdy enough for a tart shell. The recipe is enough for two 9-inch (23 cm) crusts; if you need only one, wrap the other half well and freeze for up to 2 months.

3 cups	all-purpose flour 750 mL
1 tsp	salt 5 mL
1/4 tsp	baking powder 1 mL
3/4 cup	chilled lard or shortening, cubed 175 mL
1/4 cup	chilled butter, cubed 50 mL
1	egg 1
2 tsp	white vinegar 10 mL
	Cold water

1. Stir together flour, salt and baking powder in a large bowl. Cut in lard and butter with a pastry blender or 2 knives, until mixture resembles coarse crumbs. In a glass measure, whisk together egg, vinegar and enough cold water to measure 2/3 cup (150 mL). Stir egg mixture into flour mixture until dough begins to clump together; then gather dough into a ball. Divide into 2 even pieces and form each into a disc. Wrap in plastic wrap and refrigerate for 30 minutes before rolling out.

Lemon Mousse Cheesecake with Raspberry Sauce

MAKES 12 SERVINGS.

A fluffy cheesecake is a suitable ending for any celebration, and this one can be made weeks in advance. Freezing it ensures perfect wedges for serving. Instead of using fresh raspberries as a garnish, you might like to place each wedge of cheesecake on Raspberry Sauce. The recipe follows.

CRUST

1 cup	all-purpose flour	250 mL
1/4 cup	EACH finely chopped almonds and granulated sugar	50 mL
1 tsp	grated lemon zest	5 mL
1/3 cup	butter, softened	75 mL
1	egg yolk	1
1/2 tsp	vanilla	2 mL

FILLING

1-1/2 lb	cream cheese, at room temperature	750 g
1-1/4 cups	granulated sugar	300 mL
5	eggs, separated	5
1/4 cup	all-purpose flour	50 mL
4 tsp	grated lemon zest	20 mL
1 tsp	vanilla	5 mL
2/3 cup	fresh lemon juice	150 mL
	Icing sugar	
	Fresh raspberries and sprigs of mint, or **Raspberry Sauce** (recipe follows)	

1. In a bowl, stir together flour, almonds, sugar and lemon zest; make a well in the centre. Place butter, egg yolk and vanilla in the well. Blend with a fork, then mix with your fingers just until dough holds together, yet is still fairly crumbly. Press onto bottom of lightly greased 10-inch (3 L) springform pan; bake in a 325°F (160°C) oven for 15 to 20 minutes or until crust is lightly browned around the edges. Cool on rack; then wrap bottom of the pan with foil.

1. In a large bowl with electric mixer, break up cream cheese. Gradually beat in 1 cup (250 mL) of the sugar. Beat in egg yolks one at a time, then flour, lemon zest and vanilla until well blended. Slowly blend in lemon juice.

2. In a clean bowl with clean beaters, beat egg whites slightly; gradually beat in remaining sugar until stiff (but not dry) peaks form. Fold into cream cheese mixture. Pour over crust and place pan in a bigger, shallow pan (broiler pan or big foil roaster). Pour 1 inch (2.5 cm) of hot water into outer pan. Bake for 55 to 65 minutes until puffed and golden but still wobbly in the middle. Remove to a rack and immediately run a sharp knife around the inside edge of the pan. Let cool to room temperature. (Cake will sink as it cools. Don't worry if a crack appears; using a water bath will help prevent it.) Cover and freeze for at least 24 hours or up to 2 months.

3. While frozen, cut into serving wedges with a sharp knife. Dip knife into hot water and wipe clean in between each cut. With the aid of a metal spatula, remove serving pieces to individual dessert plates and cover each with plastic wrap. Refrigerate for at least 4 hours or up to 1 day before serving.

4. To serve, sieve icing sugar over each piece and garnish with a couple of fresh raspberries and a sprig of mint, or place each piece on Raspberry Sauce.

Raspberry Sauce

MAKES ABOUT 1 CUP (250 ML).

A drizzle of this easy sauce is delicious with Lemon Mousse Cheesecake, chocolate cake or just plain vanilla ice cream.

1	pkg (300 g) frozen, unsweetened raspberries, partially thawed 1	1. Purée raspberries in a food processor until smooth. Rub purée through a fine sieve into a bowl, discarding the seeds. Whisk icing sugar and lemon juice into the purée until smooth.
1/3 cup	icing sugar 75 mL	
2 tbsp	fresh lemon juice 25 mL	

Tangerine Chiffon Cake with Fresh Lemon Glaze

MAKES 10 TO 12 SERVINGS.

This light, easy-to-make cake not only has a delicious hit of citrus, but also has the added appeal of staying moist for 2 or 3 days if kept in an airtight container.

2 cups	sifted cake and pastry flour 500 mL
1-1/3 cups	granulated sugar 325 mL
1 tbsp	baking powder 15 mL
1/2 tsp	salt 2 mL
1/3 cup	vegetable oil 75 mL
5	eggs, separated 5
2 tbsp	minced tangerine or orange zest (outer rind) 25 mL
1 cup	strained fresh tangerine or orange juice 250 mL
2	egg whites 2
1/2 tsp	cream of tartar 2 mL

1. In a large bowl, sift together flour, 1 cup (250 mL) of the sugar, baking powder and salt. Make a well in the centre and add the oil, egg yolks, tangerine zest and juice. With a wooden spoon, beat wet ingredients into dry mixture until smooth.
2. In a separate, clean, large bowl, beat the 7 egg whites and cream of tartar together until they hold soft peaks. Gradually add the remaining sugar, beating constantly until whites are shiny and stiff.
3. Pour flour mixture over egg whites; fold in just until combined. Pour cold water into a 10-inch (4 L) tube pan with removable base; tip water out and shake pan well to drain. Spoon batter into damp pan; bake for 50 minutes in a 325°F (160°C) oven. Increase the oven temperature to 350°F (180°C); bake for 5 to 15 minutes longer or until a toothpick inserted into the cake comes out clean.
4. Invert the pan on a wire rack. Let the cake cool completely upside down in the pan before removing. Place the cake on a serving plate.

FRESH LEMON GLAZE

2-1/2 cups	icing sugar 625 mL
2 tbsp	grated lemon zest (outer rind) 25 mL
1/4 cup	fresh lemon juice 50 mL
	Icing sugar

1. In a small bowl, stir together the sugar, lemon zest and juice until smooth. Pour the glaze over top of the cake, letting it run down the sides. Let the glaze set before slicing the cake. Just before serving, sift icing sugar on top of the cake.

TIP

When grating the zest from citrus fruit, always avoid the bitter white pith underneath the rind, using only the coloured part of the rind.

Rhubarb Custard Pie

MAKES 6 SERVINGS.

If my family thought they could have only one pie all year, this is the one they would choose ...
reason enough for nicknaming rhubarb the "pie plant." This was my mother's recipe—the very
first recipe I ever demonstrated on television almost 30 years ago. And it's on almost everyone's list
of favourites. Wait for fresh, local rhubarb since the forced rhubarb tends to be too juicy and may
make the filling runny.

3 cups	rhubarb, coarsely chopped (1-inch/2.5-cm pieces) 750 mL
1 cup	granulated sugar 250 mL
3 tbsp	all-purpose flour 45 mL
2 tbsp	butter, cubed 25 mL
2	egg yolks, beaten 2
1	unbaked 9-inch (23 cm) pie shell (see **Pie Pastry, page 33)** 1

1. In a large bowl, stir together rhubarb, sugar, flour and butter; stir in egg yolks. Spoon into pie shell. Bake in a 425°F (220°C) oven for 10 minutes. Reduce heat to 350°F (180°C) and bake another 30 minutes or until filling is bubbling and rhubarb is tender. Remove pie from oven. Place on a wire rack and let cool to lukewarm.

MERINGUE

2	egg whites 2
1/4 tsp	cream of tartar 1 mL
1/4 cup	granulated sugar 50 mL
2 tbsp	water 25 mL
1/2 tsp	vanilla 2 mL
1/4 tsp	salt 1 mL

1. In a large bowl and using an electric mixer, beat egg whites with cream of tartar for 3 to 5 minutes until stiff, and moist peaks form. Very gradually beat in sugar. Add water, vanilla and salt; beat until very stiff, shiny peaks form. Spread meringue over lukewarm pie, making sure meringue touches pastry edges all the way around. Swirl meringue decoratively with a knife. Bake in a 375°F (190°C) oven for about 12 minutes or until tips of meringue are golden brown. Let pie cool slowly.

Rhubarb Cream Cheese Coffee Cake

MAKES 8 TO 10 SERVINGS.

This was a dessert I included in a "Spring Fling Brunch" I wrote for *Homemaker's Magazine*. Julia Aitken, the food editor at the time, included this cake in her list of favourites and referred to it as "fabulous" in her addition to my lead. It's best served warm, straight from the oven, but you can prepare the rhubarb and the cream cheese mixtures and even combine the dry ingredients the day before, and then put it together quickly the morning of the brunch.

1-1/4 cups	finely diced rhubarb (about 3 stalks) 300 mL
1-1/2 cups	granulated sugar 375 mL
1	lemon 1
2-1/4 cups	all-purpose flour 550 mL
3/4 cup	butter 175 mL
1/2 cup	chopped walnuts 125 mL
1/2 tsp	cinnamon 2 mL
1/2 tsp	EACH baking powder and baking soda 2 mL
1/4 tsp	salt 1 mL
8 oz	cream cheese, softened 250 g
2	eggs 2
3/4 cup	sour cream 175 mL
1 tsp	vanilla 5 mL

1. In a small, heavy saucepan, combine rhubarb, 1/2 cup (125 mL) of the sugar and 1 slice cut from the lemon. Bring to a boil over high heat, stirring until sugar melts. Reduce heat to medium; simmer for 12 to 13 minutes or until thickened and reduced to about 1/2 cup (125 mL). Let cool.

2. In a large bowl, combine flour and 3/4 cup (175 mL) of the sugar. Cut in the butter until the mixture resembles coarse crumbs. Measure 1 cup (250 mL) of the flour mixture into a small bowl. Stir walnuts and cinnamon into this portion of flour mixture; set aside. Add baking powder, baking soda and salt to the remaining flour mixture; set aside. Grate 1 tsp (5 mL) of rind from the rest of the lemon. In a small bowl, combine lemon rind, cream cheese, 1/4 cup (50 mL) of the sugar and 1 egg. Set aside.

3. In a small bowl, stir together sour cream, vanilla and remaining egg. Stir sour cream mixture into flour/baking powder mixture until just blended; do not overmix. With floured fingers, press sour cream mixture evenly over the bottom and 2 inches (5 cm) up the sides of a greased 10-inch (3 L) springform cake pan. Spread cream cheese mixture over sour cream mixture; top with rhubarb mixture. Sprinkle walnut mixture evenly over top. Bake in a 350°F (180°C) oven for 1 hour or until a knife inserted in the centre of the cake comes out clean of batter (it will be moist from the cream cheese and rhubarb). Place pan on wire rack; let cake cool in pan for 15 minutes. Remove from pan. Serve warm, cut into wedges. Refrigerate any leftovers.

Mango Sorbet

Nice ripe mangos are becoming more available in our stores, and I enjoy them just as they are, or in this silky smooth sorbet—a true taste of the tropics. Let the sorbet stand for a few minutes at room temperature to soften slightly before serving. If you wish, arrange a few extra slices of the fresh fruit around the side of each bowl.

1 cup	water	250 mL
1/2 cup	granulated sugar	125 mL
2 cups	cubed, peeled ripe mangos	500 mL
3/4 cup	fresh orange juice	175 mL
1/4 cup	fresh lime juice	50 mL

1. In a saucepan, bring water and sugar to boil over high heat; boil rapidly, uncovered, for about 5 minutes or until reduced to 2/3 cup (150 mL). Let cool and chill.

2. In a food processor or blender, purée mangos, orange juice, lime juice and chilled syrup. Transfer to an ice-cream maker and freeze according to manufacturer's directions. Or, pour into a shallow cake pan; freeze until firm, about 4 hours. Purée in a food processor until smooth and creamy; pack into an airtight container and refreeze for 4 hours or until firm.

Pecan Lace Cookies

MAKES 5 DOZEN.

These crisp, lacy cookies were on several lists of favourites, perhaps because they are elegant and extremely quick to make, and they go wonderfully well with sorbets or ice cream.

1/2 cup	EACH unsalted butter, packed brown sugar and corn syrup 125 mL
1 cup	all-purpose flour 250 mL
1/2 tsp	vanilla 2 mL
3/4 cup	finely chopped pecans 175 mL

1. In a heavy saucepan, combine butter, brown sugar and corn syrup; bring to a boil over medium heat, stirring just until the sugar is dissolved. Remove from the heat; stir in flour, vanilla and nuts.
2. Drop scant teaspoonfuls (5 mL) of mixture 4 inches (10 cm) apart onto greased baking sheets. Bake in a 325°F (160°C) oven for 8 to 10 minutes or until set and lightly browned.
3. Remove from the oven and let cool on pans for 2 minutes. Remove to let cool perfectly flat on finely meshed racks or waxed paper. Store in an airtight container with waxed paper between the layers.

Variation

To make **Maple Lace Cookies**, substitute maple syrup for the corn syrup and chopped maple sugar, if available, for the brown sugar.

SPRING

SPRING MENUS

In this country, where winter always outlasts its welcome, I like to greet spring with a special celebration. One of my favourite ways to do this is to invite good friends over for brunch and while away a warm, sunny Sunday with relaxed conversation and good food.

I enjoy serving simple, straightforward food that makes use of fresh ingredients that are seasonal and available. I also like to make as much as possible the day before so I don't have to get up at the crack of dawn. And when guests arrive, I can visit with everyone.

We greet guests with chilled flutes of raspberry champagne ... champagne with raspberry liqueur or raspberry-flavoured brandy.

Throughout the book, you'll find any number of main courses that would work well with this menu—Light Eggs Benedict (page 20) or even Gravlax (page 4) set out with cream cheese and lovely rye bread.

Welcome Spring Brunch

RASPBERRY CHAMPAGNE

FRESH FRUIT SALAD WITH LIME CREAM

POPPY SEED MUFFINS

WILD MUSHROOM, LEEK AND PROSCIUTTO STRATA

SALAD OF MIXED GREENS

RHUBARB CUSTARD TORTE

COFFEE

Fresh Fruit Salad with Lime Cream

MAKES 8 SERVINGS.

A dollop of lime-flavoured cream and a bit of liqueur turn a simple fruit salad into company fare.
Serve it at room temperature for best flavour.

2 cups	seedless green grapes, halved	500 mL
2 cups	orange segments (about 4 oranges)*	500 mL
2 cups	sliced peeled kiwifruit (about 7)	500 mL
2 cups	red grapefruit segments (about 2 grapefruits)*	500 mL
1/4 cup	granulated sugar	50 mL
1/4 cup	orange juice	50 mL
1/4 cup	orange liqueur or more orange juice	50 mL

1. In an 8-cup (2 L) glass bowl, layer grapes, oranges, kiwifruit and grapefruit. Sprinkle with sugar; pour in orange juice and liqueur, but do not stir. Cover and refrigerate for at least 1 hour or up to 12 hours.

LIME CREAM

2/3 cup	whipping cream	150 mL
2 tsp	icing sugar	10 mL
2 tsp	grated lime zest (outer rind)	10 mL
2 tbsp	sour cream	25 mL

1. Up to 1 hour before serving, whip cream with icing sugar and lime zest for 1 minute. Add sour cream and beat for 3 minutes. Spoon fruit into individual bowls; top with dollops of cream.

Using a sharp knife, peel fruit, removing the outside membrane. Cut out sections from the inner membranes, holding the fruit over a container to catch any juice.

Poppy Seed Muffins

MAKES 12 MUFFINS.

Simple and crunchy, these easy muffins are just right with a fruit salad or your favourite jam and Cheddar cheese.

1/2 cup	butter, softened 125 mL
3/4 cup	granulated sugar 175 mL
2	eggs 2
1 tsp	vanilla 5 mL
1 tbsp	grated lemon zest (outer rind) 15 mL
2 cups	all-purpose flour 500 mL
1/3 cup	poppy seeds 75 mL
1 tsp	baking powder 5 mL
1/2 tsp	EACH baking soda and salt 2 mL
3/4 cup	sour cream 175 mL

1. In a large bowl, cream together butter and sugar until fluffy. Beat in eggs, one at a time, blending in well. Mix in vanilla and lemon zest.
2. In a separate bowl, stir together flour, poppy seeds, baking powder, baking soda and salt; stir into butter mixture alternately with sour cream, making 3 additions of dry ingredients and 2 of sour cream, stirring just enough to combine.
3. Spoon into 12 greased muffin cups and bake in a 400°F (200°C) oven for 15 to 20 minutes or until a tester inserted in the middle of a muffin comes out clean.

Wild Mushroom, Leek and Prosciutto Strata

MAKES 8 SERVINGS.

I love having a do-ahead casserole for brunches because you just pop the dish in the oven on the morning of the party, then delight in its aroma while it cooks. So-called wild or exotic mushrooms are readily available now in every supermarket. If you are lucky enough to find the truly wild morel, it would be exquisite in this dish.

12	slices homemade-style dry bread (Italian loaf) 12
4 cups	light cream (or 2 cups/ 500 mL EACH light cream and milk) 1 L
1/4 cup	butter 50 mL
4	leeks (white and 1 inch/2.5 cm of pale green), thinly sliced 4

1. Spread dry bread out in a large, shallow dish; pour cream over top. Set aside to let soak.
2. In a large, deep skillet, melt three-quarters of the butter over medium heat; cook leeks until softened, about 8 minutes. Add mushrooms; cook for 5 minutes. Add prosciutto; cook for 2 or 3 minutes. Reserving 1 tbsp (15 mL) of the parsley, stir fresh herbs into the leek mixture; set aside.
3. Gently squeeze moisture from the bread, reserving cream in a bowl. (Don't worry if the bread breaks up.)

continued

1/2 lb	shiitake or portobello mushrooms, stemmed and cut into 1/4-inch (5 mm) wide strips 250 g
1/2 lb	thinly sliced prosciutto, cut into 1/4-inch (5 mm) strips 250 g
1/4 cup	chopped fresh parsley 50 mL
2 tbsp	chopped fresh thyme or marjoram (or a combination) 25 mL
2 cups	shredded Gruyère cheese (about 8 oz/250 g) 500 mL
6	eggs 6
2 tsp	dry mustard 10 mL
	Pepper

4. In a greased, shallow 12 x 8-inch (3 L) baking dish, arrange one-third of the bread, top with half of the leek mixture, then one-third of the cheese. Repeat layers once. Arrange remaining bread on top. (Don't worry if the bread doesn't cover each layer.)

5. To the cream in the bowl, add eggs, mustard and pepper to taste; whisk until well combined. Pour over bread layer. Sprinkle with remaining cheese; dot with remaining butter. Sprinkle with remaining parsley. Cover well and refrigerate overnight.

6. Bake, uncovered, in a 325°F (160°C) oven for 35 to 45 minutes or until the top is golden brown and a knife inserted in the centre comes out clean.

Rhubarb Custard Torte

MAKES 8 TO 10 SERVINGS.

This elegant torte with its tender shortbread crust is one of my friend Sharon Boyd's favourite ways of enjoying spring's first fruit.

CRUST

3/4 cup	butter 175 mL
1/3 cup	granulated sugar 75 mL
2	egg yolks 2
2 cups	all-purpose flour 500 mL
1 tsp	baking powder 5 mL
1/2 tsp	salt 2 mL

1. In a large bowl and using an electric mixer, cream together the butter and granulated sugar; add egg yolks and beat until light and fluffy. Sift or stir together the flour, baking powder and salt; add to egg mixture, mixing with your hands, until crumbly. Press two-thirds of the mixture onto the bottom of a 10-inch (3 L) springform pan. Bake in a 400°F (200°C) oven for 10 minutes or until crust is light golden but not browned. Let cool. Press remaining mixture up the sides of the pan.

FILLING

6 cups	chopped rhubarb, cut into 1-inch (2.5 cm) pieces (about 1-1/2 lb/750 g) 1.5 L
1/2 cup	granulated sugar 125 mL
1/4 cup	quick-cooking tapioca 50 mL
1/2 tsp	cinnamon 2 mL

1. In a heavy, stainless steel saucepan, stir together the rhubarb, granulated sugar, tapioca and cinnamon; let stand for 15 minutes. Stir in water and bring to a boil; reduce heat to medium-low and cook covered, stirring often, for about 10 minutes, just until the rhubarb is tender but not mushy. (Mixture should be quite thick.) Let cool slightly; pour into crust.

1/4 cup	water 50 mL
6	eggs 6
2 cups	sour cream 500 mL
1/2 cup	packed brown sugar 125 mL
2 tsp	finely grated lemon zest 10 mL
1 tsp	vanilla 5 mL
	Icing sugar
	Grated lemon zest

2. In a large bowl, beat eggs until light in colour; stir in sour cream, brown sugar, 2 tsp (10 mL) lemon zest and vanilla. Pour over rhubarb and bake in a 350°F (180°C) oven for about 1 hour or until the top is golden and the custard is set. Let cool and refrigerate, covered, for at least 3 hours or overnight. Run a sharp knife around the outside of the torte and inside the edge of the pan; remove the edge of the pan.

3. To serve, sprinkle icing sugar over torte. Sprinkle a little lemon zest in the centre.

TIP

If you use frozen rhubarb, place it in a large sieve and pour hot water over it for a few seconds before proceeding; increase the tapioca to 1/3 cup (75 mL).

Easter or the start of spring is always a lovely time to fill your house with bright spring flowers and gather family or friends around for a celebration. Nothing much has started in our gardens yet, but we can make marvelous dishes with the last of the storage vegetables and some imported exotic fruit. If fiddleheads have not started to show their heads, I steam a bag left from those I froze the year before.

Easter Dinner

SMOKED TROUT MOUSSE WITH SLICES OF BAGUETTE

BAKED GLAZED HAM

OLD-FASHIONED SCALLOPED POTATOES (SEE PAGE 208)

STEAMED FIDDLEHEADS WITH LEMON

GINGERED SWEET POTATOES

MAPLE-GLAZED ONIONS

PAVLOVA WITH KIWI AND PASSION FRUIT

Smoked Trout Mousse

MAKES 10 TO 12 SERVINGS.

Smooth, light and slightly smoky, this easy mousse is perfect to serve in Belgian endive leaves, which have an edge of bitterness. Or, spread the mousse onto Melba toast, baguette slices or crackers. Two trout, a bit over a pound (500 g) in total, should give you the right amount. If you wish, use the same amount of any other smoked fish.

3/4 lb	boned, skinned smoked trout 375 g	
1/4 cup	fresh lemon juice 50 mL	
3 tbsp	EACH mayonnaise and whipping cream 45 mL	
Pinch	EACH salt, black pepper and cayenne Pinch	

1. Cut fish into small pieces and purée in a food processor or blender. Add lemon juice, mayonnaise, whipping cream, salt, pepper and cayenne; process for about 30 seconds or until smooth but not watery. Transfer to a bowl; cover and refrigerate for up to 1 day. Remove from refrigerator for 30 minutes before serving.

Baked Glazed Ham

MAKES ABOUT 10 SERVINGS.

"Fully cooked" smoked hams are greatly improved by a short cooking time to finish them off; a spicy fruit-honey mixture applied for the last few minutes gives a seductive and delicious glaze. Such a ham would make the perfect focus of any festive dinner table.

1	fully cooked bone-in smoked ham (about 7-1/2 lb/3.3 kg) 1 Whole cloves	
1/2 cup	peach or apricot jam 125 mL	
1/4 cup	liquid honey 50 mL	
2 tbsp	fresh lemon juice 25 mL	
1 tbsp	cornstarch 15 mL	
1/4 tsp	ground cloves 1 mL	
Pinch	cinnamon Pinch	

1. With a sharp knife, remove any rind and excess fat (leaving a thin layer) from the ham. Place, fat side up, on a rack in a shallow pan.
2. With a sharp knife, score the outside layer of fat diagonally in both directions to make 2-inch (5 cm) diamonds. Do not cut too deeply. Insert whole cloves at the corners or in the centre of the diamonds. Bake in a 325°F (160°C) oven for 2 to 2-1/2 hours or until a meat thermometer registers 130°F (55°C).
3. Meanwhile, in a small saucepan, stir together the jam, honey, lemon juice, cornstarch, cloves and cinnamon; bring to a boil over medium heat, stirring. During the last 30 minutes of cooking time, spoon some of the glaze onto the ham 2 or 3 times until all the glaze is used, basting with pan juices, too.

Gingered Sweet Potatoes

MAKES 8 TO 10 SERVINGS.

Roasting the potatoes for this brightly coloured side dish gives them an extra dimension of flavour, but you could, of course, steam or boil them.

6	medium sweet potatoes 6
2 tbsp	butter 25 mL
2 tbsp	sour cream 25 mL
3/4 tsp	ground ginger (or more to taste) 4 mL
	Salt and pepper

1. Scrub the potatoes, but do not peel. Pierce them in several places and arrange on a baking sheet. Roast in a 400°F (200°C) oven for about 1 hour or until tender.
2. While still hot, peel into a large bowl. With an electric mixer, beat the potatoes until smooth, adding the butter, sour cream, ginger, and salt and pepper to taste.
3. Transfer to a greased 6-cup (1.5 L) baking dish. (Potatoes can be cooled, covered and refrigerated for up to 1 day. Bring to room temperature before reheating.)
4. Reheat, covered, in a 350°F (180°C) oven for about 30 minutes or until hot throughout.

Maple-Glazed Onions

MAKES 6 TO 8 SERVINGS.

Maple syrup adds a wonderful depth of flavour to little pearl onions in a simple side dish that is delicious served with roast pork or chicken.

2	pkg (each 10 oz/283 g) pearl onions 2
1/3 cup	maple syrup 75 mL
1/4 cup	butter 50 mL
	Salt and pepper

1. In a small saucepan of boiling water, blanch onions for 3 minutes; drain and refresh under cold running water. Drain well and peel; cut an "X" in the bottom of each. Place in a greased, shallow baking dish just big enough to hold the onions in a single layer.
2. In a small saucepan, boil maple syrup until reduced by one-quarter; stir in butter until melted. Pour over onions; sprinkle with salt and pepper to taste and stir to coat. Bake uncovered, basting occasionally, in a 350°F (180°C) oven for about 45 minutes or until tender and browned.

Pavlova with Kiwi and Passion Fruit

MAKES 8 TO 12 SERVINGS.

Since this meringue dessert, named after a famous ballerina, hails from a part of the world where exotic fruit grows in abundance, it's usually garnished with passion fruit. Add some slices of kiwi and you will have a pretty spring dessert, just right for a special holiday dinner like Easter. If passion fruit is unavailable, try peeled, sliced mango. Use any other fresh fruit as it comes into season—strawberries, raspberries, peaches—for this easy but elegant dessert ... one of my favourites.

You can bake the meringue on a parchment-lined baking sheet and remove to a plate, but it's easier to bake it, and then serve it, in a ceramic dish.

8	egg whites 8
1-1/2 cups	granulated sugar 375 mL
4 tsp	EACH vinegar, cornstarch and vanilla 20 mL
1 cup	whipping cream, whipped 250 mL
2	kiwifruits, peeled and sliced 2
1 or 2	passion fruit (depending on size) 1 or 2

1. In a large bowl, beat egg whites until stiff. Gradually beat in the sugar until stiff and glossy. In a small bowl, stir together vinegar, cornstarch and vanilla. Fold into egg whites and transfer to a greased 11-inch (28 cm) shallow, round dish about 2 inches (5 cm) deep. With a spatula, make an indentation in the middle and swirl the mixture up around the sides of the dish. Bake in a 300°F (150°C) oven for 1/2 hour. Reduce the temperature to 200°F (93°C) and bake another 1-1/2 hours. Let cool slowly in the turned-off oven with the door ajar, if possible. (Meringue can be made a day or two ahead.)

2. Just before serving, pile whipped cream in the indentation and arrange kiwi slices on top. Cut passion fruit in two and spoon out flesh; arrange around kiwi slices.

SUMMER

MY SUMMER KITCHEN

Summer is that lovely time of the year when everyone wants to be outside, the barbecues are lit and the living is easy ... as the song goes.

Everyday meals are based on quick grills and garden-fresh produce that need no special work to be sensational. Entertaining, too, can take the form of alfresco meals on the patio or even a picnic in the park.

Although I miss the big vegetable garden I used to have, I delight in going to our local farmers' market twice a week. I've grown to know the vendors there, and when Shirley tells me the corn was picked late the night before, I know it will be fresher than any I can get in a supermarket. Peter's tiny cucumbers that are just hours old will be perfect for the cornichons I make every year. Dave's lovely purple garlic will hang in a rope in my kitchen far into the colder months. Peaches are picked when they're ripe for this market, and there is nothing like a lovely, ripe, local peach that you have to eat leaning over the kitchen sink with the juice running down your arms. In fact, I usually plan a party in peach season, just so that I can make Peaches Catherine (page 90).

The season is short, and everything comes tumbling along. Strawberries are not finished by the time cherries are ready; then raspberries, currants, gooseberries, blueberries, grapes, peaches, plums and melons are mounded on vendors' stalls. Spinach, tiny smooth potatoes, tender green peas, beans, carrots, corn, beets, summer squash and tomatoes are there in a myriad of colour. There's such a bounty in the summer months that "What will I have for dinner?" is no longer a question.

All I can do is enjoy everything while it comes and preserve some of the season's abundance for the winter months when I can only dream of freshly picked peaches.

SUMMER STARTERS AND SOUPS

Caponata Cups

MAKES ABOUT 2 DOZEN APPETIZERS.

These little mouthfuls of crisp toast and tangy, soft vegetable mixture will disappear from your appetizer tray in no time, as they have from mine over the years. You can even serve the caponata mixture on crackers or in little, crisp tart shells that you can purchase.

TOAST CUPS

8	thin slices white bread (approx.) 8
	Olive oil

1. Cut crusts from bread. With a rolling pin, roll out bread until flat; cut into quarters. Press into greased miniature muffin cups. (Or, roll out enough bread to cut into rounds with a cookie cutter to fit muffin or tart cups.) Brush lightly with oil. Bake in a 350°F (180°C) oven for 5 to 7 minutes or until crisp and golden. Let cool. (Cups can be stored for days in an airtight tin.)

CAPONATA

1 cup	diced, peeled eggplant 250 mL
1/2 tsp	salt 2 mL
2 tbsp	olive oil (approx.) 25 mL
1	onion, chopped 1
2	cloves garlic, minced 2
1/3 cup	chopped celery 75 mL
1 cup	drained canned tomatoes, chopped 250 mL
1/2 cup	chopped sweet red pepper 125 mL
1 tsp	granulated sugar 5 mL
1/4 tsp	EACH pepper, dried oregano and basil 1 mL
1 tbsp	chopped fresh parsley 15 mL
1/4 cup	chopped, pitted black olives 50 mL
2 tbsp	drained capers 25 mL
2 tbsp	red wine vinegar 25 mL

1. In a colander, sprinkle eggplant with salt; let drain for 30 minutes. In a skillet, heat half the oil over medium-high heat; sauté onion and garlic for 5 minutes. Add celery and tomatoes; cook for 5 minutes. Remove from the heat.

2. Rinse eggplant and pat dry. In a separate skillet, fry eggplant in remaining oil until golden. With a slotted spoon, remove and drain on paper towels. Add red pepper to the skillet; fry until wilted, adding a teaspoon (5 mL) more oil if necessary.

3. Add eggplant, tomato mixture, sugar, pepper, oregano, basil, parsley, olives, capers and vinegar; cook for 15 minutes over low heat, stirring occasionally. (Caponata can be cooled and refrigerated in a covered container for up to 3 days. Serve at room temperature.) Spoon into toast cups.

Mexican Spirals

MAKES ABOUT 5 DOZEN.

When I developed this recipe for *Homemaker's Magazine,* Julia Aitken was my editor, and she still lists this easy appetizer recipe as one of her favourites.

Rolling tortillas around a spicy chicken filling is a quick way of creating a good number of delicious appetizers in short order.

8 oz	cream cheese, softened 250 g
1 cup	diced cooked chicken 250 mL
1/4 lb	Monterey Jack cheese, shredded 125 g
1/4 cup	chopped fresh coriander 50 mL
2 tbsp	diced fresh or canned jalapeño peppers 25 mL
2 tsp	ground cumin 10 mL
	Salt
4	(10-inch/25 cm) flour tortillas 4
	Vegetable oil
	Salsa and sour cream to serve

1. In a large bowl, combine cream cheese, chicken, Monterey Jack, coriander, jalapeño peppers, cumin and salt to taste.

2. Spread mixture evenly over tortillas. Roll up each tortilla tightly around chicken mixture. Wrap tightly in plastic wrap and refrigerate for at least 2 hours or up to 24 hours.

3. Just before serving, cut each tortilla roll into 1/2-inch (1 cm) slices. Arrange on greased baking sheet; brush with oil. Bake in a 350°F (180°C) oven for 12 to 15 minutes or until lightly browned. Serve hot with salsa and sour cream for dipping.

Grilled Eggplant Dip with Grilled Pita Toasts

I wrote an article for *Homemaker's Magazine* on snacks and appetizers cooked on the grill. This is one of my favourites—a soft, smoky dip just right with garlicky, crisp pita triangles.

6	small eggplants (Oriental or baby Italian) 6 (2 lb/1 kg total)
6	cloves garlic, thinly sliced 6
2	plum tomatoes 2
1/3 cup	chopped fresh coriander or parsley 75 mL
2 tbsp	EACH olive oil and fresh lemon juice 25 mL
1 tsp	EACH ground cumin and salt 5 mL
1/3 cup	chopped toasted walnuts, optional 75 mL
	Grilled Pita Toasts (recipe follows)

1. Cut deep slits in the eggplants and insert garlic slices. Place on a greased grill over medium-high heat. Cook, turning occasionally, for 20 to 30 minutes or until eggplants are charred and beginning to collapse. Grill tomatoes, turning occasionally, for 5 minutes or until they begin to char.
2. Strip off and discard eggplant skins; finely chop eggplant with garlic; place in a bowl.
3. Peel, seed and chop tomatoes; add to eggplant. Stir in coriander, oil, lemon juice, cumin and salt. Taste and adjust seasoning. (Can be covered and refrigerated for up to 8 hours.) Just before serving, stir in walnuts, if using. Serve with Grilled Pita Toasts.

Grilled Pita Toasts

I often make pita toasts in the oven as well. In that case, I follow the recipe below as far as brushing each round with the oil mixture. Then I cut each round into 8 wedges with scissors and place the wedges on baking sheets. I toast them in a 350°F (180°C) oven for 7 to 9 minutes or until golden brown and crisp.

4	pita breads (7 inch/18 cm) 4
1/4 cup	olive oil 50 mL
2	cloves garlic, minced 2
1 tsp	paprika 5 mL

1. Split each pita horizontally into 2 rounds. In a small saucepan at the edge of the grill, heat oil with garlic and paprika. Brush lightly onto both sides of each pita round. Grill over medium heat for 1 minute on each side or until grill-marked and crisp. Cut or break each into 4 wedges.

Chilled Cucumber Soup with Walnuts

MAKES 6 SERVINGS.

This easy-to-make soup is a refreshing start to a summer meal. Borage blossoms (the purple-blue star-shaped flowers of the herb) are perfect as a garnish since they have a slight cucumber flavour.

3	medium field cucumbers (about 1-1/2 lb/750 g total) 3
	Salt
2 cups	buttermilk 500 mL
2	cloves garlic 2
1	small onion, chopped 1
1/4 cup	chopped fresh parsley 50 mL
1 tbsp	snipped fresh chives 15 mL
1 cup	EACH plain yogurt and light sour cream 250 mL
1 tbsp	fresh lemon juice 15 mL
1 tbsp	granulated sugar 15 mL
	White pepper
Pinch	cayenne pepper Pinch
1/2 cup	finely chopped walnuts, toasted 125 mL
	Borage blossoms, snipped chives or parsley sprigs

1. Peel cucumbers and slice in half lengthwise. With a teaspoon, scoop out the seeds and discard. Chop the cucumbers coarsely; transfer them to a sieve. Sprinkle lightly with salt and let stand for 30 minutes.
2. Drain cucumbers and pat dry. Place in a blender along with the buttermilk, garlic, onion, parsley and chives; purée until smooth.
3. Transfer to a large bowl; stir in the yogurt, sour cream, lemon juice, sugar, salt and white pepper to taste, and the cayenne. Stir in walnuts. Cover and chill for at least 1 hour or for up to 2 days.
4. Serve in chilled bowls, garnished with borage blossoms.

TIP

To toast walnuts, spread them out on a baking sheet and bake in a 350°F (180°C) oven for about 5 minutes, watching carefully. In the summer, I use my toaster oven to avoid heating up the kitchen.

Spinach Vichyssoise

MAKES 8 TO 10 SERVINGS.

My daughter, Anne Loxton, told me she had a delicious soup at an Easter dinner party in Bermuda this year. When she said her hostess told her it was from the *Recipes Only Cookbook* (1989), I realized it was mine and felt happy people are still enjoying my fresh-tasting twist on a classic.

1/4 cup	butter 50 mL
2 cups	sliced leeks (white part of 3 large) 500 mL
1/4 cup	finely chopped celery and leaves 50 mL
2	cloves garlic, minced 2
4 cups	sliced, peeled potatoes (4 medium) 1 L
5 cups	chicken broth 1.25 L
2 tbsp	fresh lemon juice 25 mL
1 tsp	salt 5 mL
1/4 tsp	white pepper 1 mL
1 lb	fresh spinach 500 g
2 cups	light cream 500 mL
	Thin lemon slices for garnish

1. In a large saucepan over medium heat, melt butter. Add leeks, celery and garlic; cook over low heat for about 20 minutes, stirring often. Do not brown. Stir in potatoes, broth, lemon juice, salt and pepper. Bring to a boil, reduce heat and simmer mixture, covered, for about 10 minutes, or until potatoes can be pierced easily with a fork.

2. Stir in spinach; bring back to a boil and simmer for 5 minutes. Purée soup in a blender or food mill, or push through a sieve into a large bowl. (A food processor will spoil the soup's texture.) Cool. Stir in cream and taste for seasoning. Add more salt, white pepper and lemon juice if necessary. Cover and refrigerate for several hours or overnight.

3. After chilling, adjust seasoning if necessary and, if too thick, stir in more cream. Serve in chilled bowls or glasses and float thin slices of lemon on each serving.

Oven-Roasted
Tomato Soup with Avocado Purée

MAKES 6 SERVINGS.

This vibrant soup can be served hot or chilled. Ladle it into shallow bowls so that the green avocado purée can be seen.

SOUP

3 lb	ripe plum tomatoes (16 to 20) 1.5 kg
2	cloves garlic, minced 2
1 tbsp	chopped fresh parsley 15 mL
2 tsp	dried basil 10 mL
	Salt and pepper
1/4 cup	olive oil 50 mL
5 cups	chicken stock 1.25 L
1 tsp	EACH ground coriander and cumin 5 mL
Pinch	cayenne Pinch

1. Wash tomatoes and with a small sharp knife, cut out cores at stem end. Cut tomatoes in half lengthwise. Arrange halves, cut sides up, on a large baking sheet. Sprinkle evenly with garlic, parsley, basil, and salt and pepper to taste; drizzle with oil. Bake in a 250°F (120°C) oven for about 2 hours or until tomatoes have shrunk slightly.

2. In batches, transfer tomatoes and any juice on the baking sheet to a blender or food processor; blend until smooth. Transfer tomato mixture to a large saucepan. Stir in chicken stock, ground coriander, ground cumin, cayenne, and salt and pepper to taste. Bring to a boil over high heat. Reduce heat to medium-low; simmer, covered, for 20 minutes. Rub through a fine sieve into a large bowl to remove tomato skins.

3. To serve cold, refrigerate, covered, until thoroughly chilled. Taste and adjust seasoning before serving.

4. To serve hot, heat through gently until hot; taste and adjust seasoning before serving.

AVOCADO PURÉE

1	large ripe avocado 1
1 tsp	fresh lime juice 5 mL
2 tsp	chopped fresh coriander 10 mL
Pinch	salt Pinch
	Fresh coriander sprigs

1. Just before serving, cut avocado in half; remove the pit. Scoop out the flesh into a small bowl; mash with a fork until smooth. Stir in lime juice, coriander and a pinch of salt. Ladle soup into shallow bowls and place a spoonful of avocado purée in the centre of each; garnish with coriander sprigs.

Hint

To check if an avocado is ripe, cradle it in your hand; it should yield to gentle pressure.

SUMMER MAIN DISHES

IN THE MENUS ...

Grilled Lamb Shanks

MAKES 4 SERVINGS.

My friends Diane and Gary Slimmon say they "cannot live without" the recipe for these scrumptious lamb shanks that are braised to a melting tenderness, cooled in their liquid, then grilled over a hot fire. The braising juice makes a delicious sauce for pasta or mashed potatoes to go alongside. A crisp green salad completes the menu. It was Neil Baxter, chef of Rundles Restaurant in Stratford, Ontario, who first showed me how good lamb shanks taste prepared this way.

2 tbsp	olive oil	25 mL
4	lamb shanks	
	(about 1-3/4 lb/875 g total)	4
1	carrot, diced	1
1	onion, chopped	1
12	cloves garlic	12
2 cups	beef stock	500 mL
1/4 cup	chopped fresh parsley	50 mL
1/2 tsp	dried thyme	2 mL
1	bay leaf	1
	Salt and pepper	

1. In a large Dutch oven, heat oil over medium-high heat; brown shanks on all sides, 8 to 10 minutes. Remove lamb from the pan and set aside.

2. Reduce heat to medium; cook carrot, onion and garlic for 5 minutes, stirring often. Stir in stock, parsley, thyme, bay leaf, and salt and pepper to taste; bring to a boil.

3. Return lamb to the pan; cover and cook in a 325°F (160°C) oven for 2-1/2 hours, turning meat occasionally. Let cool until steaming stops; cover and refrigerate overnight.

4. Remove lamb from braising mixture. Lift off and discard any fat from braising mixture and reserve. Place lamb on a greased grill over high heat; grill for 10 to 15 minutes without turning. Turn lamb and grill until browned crust forms on the other side and shanks are warmed through.

5. Meanwhile, heat braising liquid and vegetables; push through a sieve and boil for 5 minutes or until reduced and thickened. Serve with lamb.

Flank Steak Southwestern Style

MAKES 4 TO 6 SERVINGS.

This is a great recipe to have in your repertoire for times when you've marinated steak in anticipation of barbecuing, and the rain starts to come down. You can cook the steak inside or out. I originally developed the recipe in a braising article I wrote for *Elm Street* called "Humble Cuts." Later, I tested the recipe on the barbecue grill. Flank steak is one of those humble cuts that people pass by, but if it's marinated, there is nothing nicer than this lean meat.

1	flank steak (about 1-1/2 lb/750 g) 1
1/2 cup	bottled salsa 125 mL
2 tbsp	EACH vegetable oil and fresh lime juice 25 mL
2	cloves garlic, minced 2
2	canned chipotle chilies,* drained and minced 2
1 tbsp	packed brown sugar 15 mL
2 tsp	ground cumin 10 mL
1 tsp	EACH chili powder and dried oregano 5 mL
	Salt and pepper
	Fresh coriander sprigs

1. With a sharp knife, remove any membrane from the surface of the steak; then score the steak by making very shallow cuts at 2-inch (5 cm) intervals on both sides. In a shallow glass dish just big enough to hold the steak, stir together the salsa, half the oil, the lime juice, garlic, chilies, brown sugar, cumin, chili powder and oregano. Add steak to the marinade, spooning marinade over meat to coat both sides completely. Refrigerate, covered, for at least 3 hours or overnight.

2. Reserving marinade, remove steak from the marinade and sprinkle with salt and pepper. Place marinade in a small saucepan, bring to a boil and simmer for 5 minutes. Keep warm on the side of the grill. Brush steak and grill with remaining oil; place steak 4 inches (10 cm) from medium-hot coals or on medium-high setting. Grill, brushing often with marinade, for 4 to 6 minutes per side or until rare. Do not overcook.

3. Transfer to a cutting board. Let stand for 5 minutes; then thinly slice on the diagonal across the grain. Arrange on a warm platter. Spoon on any remaining marinade, then garnish with coriander.

4. Alternatively, heat the remaining oil in a large, heavy skillet over medium-high heat. Add the steak and marinade. Cook for about 10 minutes for rare, turning often. Let rest, carve and serve as above.

Chipotle chilies are smoked jalapeños, usually canned in adobo sauce and available at specialty food stores. Any leftover chilies with sauce can be refrigerated in a covered container for up to 2 weeks. Or, pour them and the sauce into a freezer bag, gently pressing out the air. Manipulate the bag to separate the peppers so that it will be easy to break off a section of pepper and sauce without thawing the whole package.

Asian Grilled Salmon

Cooking a large salmon fillet on the grill is easy. Try to buy a fillet of even thickness. Use the removable bottom of a tart pan to transfer the salmon from the grill to a serving platter.

2 lb	salmon fillet, with skin 1 kg
2 tbsp	EACH vegetable oil, fresh lemon juice and soy sauce 25 mL
1 tbsp	EACH brown sugar and minced fresh ginger 15 mL
2	cloves garlic, minced 2
Pinch	EACH black pepper and cayenne pepper Pinch

1. Make several shallow diagonal slashes in skinless side of salmon. Place fish, skin side up, in a shallow glass dish. Whisk together oil, lemon juice, soy sauce, sugar, ginger, garlic, pepper and cayenne; pour over salmon and marinate for 30 minutes.

2. Discarding marinade, place fillet, skin side down, on greased grill over low heat; close lid and cook for about 30 minutes or until fish is opaque and flakes easily when tested with a fork.

Rosemary Grilled Veal Chops

MAKES 4 SERVINGS.

Marinating and grilling need not be complicated. The simplest recipes are sometimes the best, and when I want to serve something that's fast and easy but a bit on the elegant side for company, I do these chops.

4	thick veal loin chops	4
1/3 cup	dry white wine	75 mL
1/4 cup	olive oil	50 mL
1 tbsp	chopped fresh rosemary (or 1 tsp/5 mL crumbled dried)	15 mL
1/2 tsp	grated lemon zest (outer coloured rind)	2 mL
	Salt and pepper	

1. Place chops in a glass dish just big enough to hold them in a single layer. Whisk together wine, oil, rosemary and lemon zest; pour over chops. Cover and marinate at room temperature for 30 minutes or up to 4 hours in the refrigerator. Remove from refrigerator 30 minutes before grilling.

2. Sprinkle with salt and pepper. Place on greased grill over medium-high heat; grill for 5 to 10 minutes per side, depending on thickness, or until desired doneness. (Do not overcook.)

TIP

A lemon zester is a good investment because it makes fast work of taking off just the outer bit of rind from citrus fruit.

Ginger Grilled Pork Loin

MAKES ABOUT 8 SERVINGS.

Pork loin is often sold as a double roast, that is, two loins tied together. For this recipe, buy a long, single loin; or in some areas, you can purchase a sirloin of pork. You could also use 2 large or 3 smaller pork tenderloins, but grill them only for about 25 minutes.

3 tbsp	finely chopped fresh thyme (or 1 tbsp/15 mL crumbled dried thyme) 45 mL
1 tbsp	dry mustard 15 mL
1	single boneless centre-cut pork loin (about 4 lb/2 kg) 1
1/2 cup	EACH green ginger wine* and low-salt soy sauce 125 mL
1/4 cup	vegetable oil 50 mL
3	large cloves garlic, crushed 3

1. In a small bowl or mortar, crush together thyme and mustard with the tip of a spoon or pestle to form a paste; rub all over the pork.
2. Place pork in a sturdy plastic bag set in a shallow dish. Stir together wine, soy sauce, oil and garlic; pour over pork. Seal the bag and turn to coat meat well; refrigerate several hours or overnight, turning occasionally. Remove from refrigerator 30 minutes before cooking.
3. Reserving marinade, remove pork and pat dry with paper towels. Sear pork on greased grill over high heat, turning often, for 10 minutes.
4. Raise grill or reduce setting to low. Cover with barbecue lid or tent pork with foil. Grill, turning often and basting occasionally with reserved marinade, for about 30 to 45 minutes or until meat thermometer inserted in the thickest part registers 160°F (70°C). The time will vary with thickness of meat, type of barbecue and wind conditions. (If cooking on a rotisserie, omit searing and baste often.) Pork is best not overcooked. Bring to a boil any marinade that's left and simmer for 5 minutes.
5. Transfer roast to a carving board; cover loosely with foil and let stand for 10 minutes before slicing thinly. Drizzle with any marinade.

Green ginger wine is available from a liquor store.

Hoisin-Glazed Ribs

MAKES 8 SERVINGS.

Everyone will love these Oriental-flavoured, finger-licking-good ribs I developed for a "Summer Celebration" for *Family Magazine.* Look for hoisin sauce, sesame oil and chili paste in the Asian section of your supermarket, adding more chili paste if you like spicier ribs.

6 to 8 lb	meaty pork back ribs 2.7 to 3.5 kg
1 cup	hoisin sauce 250 mL
3/4 cup	ketchup 175 mL
1/3 cup	liquid honey 75 mL
1/4 cup	fresh lemon or lime juice 50 mL
1/4 cup	rice vinegar 50 mL
3	cloves garlic, minced 3
1 tbsp	chopped fresh ginger 15 mL
1 tbsp	sesame oil 15 mL
1 tsp	Oriental chili paste (or 1/2 tsp/2 mL hot pepper flakes) 5 mL

1. Cut ribs into serving-size pieces and put in a large pot (or 2). Add enough cold water to cover the ribs; bring to a boil over high heat. Reduce the heat to medium-low; simmer, covered, for 40 to 45 minutes or until the meat is tender. Drain well.

2. In a medium bowl, whisk together the hoisin sauce, ketchup, honey, lemon juice, vinegar, garlic, ginger, sesame oil and chili paste. Brush ribs on both sides with some of the hoisin mixture. Put ribs in a large bowl; pour any remaining hoisin mixture over ribs. Let cool; cover and refrigerate for at least 4 hours or up to 24 hours.

3. About 30 minutes before cooking, remove ribs from the refrigerator. Preheat the barbecue to medium. Remove ribs from the bowl, shaking off and reserving marinade. Pour marinade into a small saucepan. Put ribs, meaty side down (in batches if necessary), on a greased grill. Cook, covered, for about 10 minutes, moving ribs occasionally so that they don't get too brown in one spot. Turn and baste with some of the reserved marinade halfway through cooking, until crisp and glazed. If cooking ribs in batches, keep the first batch warm while grilling the rest.

4. Heat the remaining marinade over medium heat until piping hot; serve as a sauce with the ribs. (Since the ribs are cooked before being marinated, there will be no uncooked meat juices in the marinade.)

Bistro Burgers

MAKES 4 BURGERS.

A green salad of curly endive with crisp bacon and walnuts, along with a fresh fruit tart as a finale, would complete this menu perfectly. If you can find a French loaf about 4 inches (10 cm) wide, cut burger-width rounds from it. Slice each round from the side, nearly through to open up like a book, and enclose a burger. Otherwise, use 2 thin slices of wider bread to hold each burger. Creamy goat cheese makes a nice foil for peppery arugula with this juicy burger.

3 tbsp	Pesto	45 mL
2 tbsp	dry bread crumbs	25 mL
1/4 tsp	pepper	1 mL
1 lb	ground beef	500 g
2 oz	fresh, mild goat cheese, formed into 4 rounds	50 g
4	pieces French bread (see above)	4
	Olive oil	
	Dijon mustard	
	Arugula leaves	
4	thin slices red onion	4

1. In a bowl, combine pesto, crumbs and pepper. Gently mix in beef and lightly shape into 4 round patties 3/4-inch (2 cm) thick.

2. Place on greased grill over medium heat; cook, turning once, for 10 to 12 minutes or until meat is no longer pink inside. About 1 minute before removing burgers from the grill, top each with a round of cheese, pressing it down onto the burger with a spatula.

3. Meanwhile, brush cut side of bread with oil and toast on the side of the grill. Spread cut sides liberally with Dijon mustard, top with several leaves of arugula, an onion slice and a burger.

Veal Burgers with Roasted Peppers on Panini

MAKES 4 BURGERS.

If panini (Italian rolls) are not available, use crusty Kaisers (and form round patties) for this full-flavoured burger with its juicy, sweet-pepper strips. Begin supper with a cold tomato soup before the burgers and finish with a selection of gelati or spumoni.

2	green onions, finely chopped	2
2	cloves garlic, minced	2
2 tbsp	tomato paste	25 mL
1 tbsp	water	15 mL
1 tsp	Italian herb seasoning	5 mL
	Salt and pepper	
1 lb	ground veal	500 g
3	sweet peppers, preferably 2 red and 1 yellow	3
3 tbsp	olive oil	45 mL
1 tbsp	wine vinegar	15 mL
1/4 tsp	hot pepper flakes	1 mL
4	Italian panini	4

1. In a bowl, combine onions, 1 clove garlic, tomato paste, water, seasoning, 1/4 tsp (1 mL) EACH salt and pepper. Working quickly, add ground veal and gently mix until blended. Lightly form into 4 oval patties about 3/4-inch (2 cm) thick. (Cover and refrigerate if making ahead.)

2. Roast peppers over high heat on barbecue grill, turning often, until the skin is black all over. Remove to an overturned bowl for 10 minutes. Peel, seed and slice into 1/2-inch (1 cm) strips. Toss with oil, vinegar, 1/4 tsp (1 mL) EACH salt and pepper, hot pepper flakes and remaining garlic.

3. Place burgers on greased grill over medium heat; cook, turning once, for about 12 minutes, or until meat is well browned on the outside and no longer pink but still juicy inside.

4. Meanwhile, split open buns and toast on cut sides on the grill until warm and lightly browned. Place cooked burgers on rolls and top with roasted pepper mixture.

Greek-Style Chicken Burgers

MAKES 4 SERVINGS.

The whole family will love this light, Mediterranean version of the classic hamburger. Add a salad for a nice, light lunch.

1	egg	1
1/3 cup	fine dry bread crumbs	75 mL
2 tbsp	milk	25 mL
2 tbsp	fresh lemon juice	25 mL
1/2 tsp	EACH dried mint and oregano	2 mL
1/4 tsp	EACH salt and pepper	1 mL
1 lb	ground chicken	500 g
1 tbsp	vegetable oil	15 mL
2	7-inch (18 cm) pitas	2
1/4 cup	light mayonnaise	50 mL
	Thinly sliced red onion, tomato and cucumber	

1. In a medium bowl, beat egg; then stir in bread crumbs, milk, 1 tbsp (15 mL) lemon juice, mint, oregano, salt and pepper. Gently mix in chicken until well combined. (Mixing too vigorously will result in tough burgers.) Shape into 4 patties, each about 3/4-inch (2 cm) thick.

2. In a large nonstick skillet, heat oil over medium-high heat. Cook patties about 8 minutes, turning once, until golden brown and no longer pink inside. Alternatively, brush with oil and place on greased barbecue grill over medium-high heat; cook, turning once, for 12 to 14 minutes or until patties are no longer pink inside.

3. Meanwhile, cut pitas in half crosswise to make 4 pockets. Warm in a 300°F (150°C) oven for 5 minutes or in a microwave on High for 1 minute, or place on the side of the grill for 5 minutes.

4. In a small bowl, combine mayonnaise and remaining lemon juice; spread mixture inside pita halves. Place cooked patty in each pita half; tuck in slices of red onion, tomato and cucumber.

Jerk Chicken

MAKES 4 TO 6 SERVINGS.

Authentic Jamaican jerk chicken, with its smack of hot peppers and island spices, is marinated for a couple of days, then smoked over wood and charcoal for 2 to 3 hours. This version—which you can grill or broil—replicates the flavour without the fuss. Serve with rice and peas, coleslaw and ice-cold beer.

4	chicken leg quarters 4
6	green onions, coarsely chopped 6
2 or 3	Scotch bonnet peppers, halved and seeded* 2 or 3
2	cloves garlic, coarsely chopped 2
2 tbsp	EACH olive oil and white wine vinegar 25 mL
1 tbsp	ground allspice 15 mL
1 tsp	ground cinnamon 5 mL
1/2 tsp	EACH grated nutmeg, dried thyme, salt and black pepper 2 mL

1. Cut each of the chicken quarters into 2 pieces through the joint; trim away any excess fat. Wipe chicken pieces with a damp paper towel; place in a glass dish just large enough to hold them in a single layer.

2. In a blender or food processor, combine green onions, peppers, garlic, olive oil, white wine vinegar, allspice, cinnamon, nutmeg, thyme, salt and pepper; then blend until a smooth paste forms. Spread paste on chicken. Cover and refrigerate for 24 hours, turning chicken occasionally.

3. Place chicken on a greased grill over medium heat or on a greased broiler rack about 4 inches (10 cm) from the preheated element. Cook for 35 to 45 minutes, turning often, until the juices run clear when the thickest part of the chicken is pierced with a skewer.

Scotch bonnet peppers are small, hot chili peppers that look like squashed hats. If unavailable, substitute any small hot peppers and use 3 if you prefer a nice biting heat. Wear rubber or plastic gloves when preparing hot peppers, avoid touching your face, and wash your knife and cutting board in hot, soapy water immediately afterward.

Variation

To prepare **Jerk Pork**, substitute 1-inch (2.5 cm) thick, boneless pork chops for the chicken. Grill over medium-high heat, or broil 3 inches (8 cm) from the element, for about 15 minutes, turning once, until the juices run clear when chops are pierced with a skewer; the pork should still be tinged pink inside.

Hoisin-Orange Chicken Legs

MAKES 4 SERVINGS.

The combination of hoisin and orange gives a dark mahogany appearance and loads of flavour to grilled chicken. Accompany with plain or fried rice and a stir-fried green vegetable like sugar snap peas.

4	chicken legs 4
1/4 cup	hoisin sauce 50 mL
1 tsp	grated orange zest (outer orange rind) 5 mL
1/4 cup	fresh orange juice 50 mL
2	cloves garlic, minced 2
1 tbsp	EACH minced fresh ginger and vegetable oil 15 mL
1 tbsp	bitter orange marmalade 15 mL

1. Wipe chicken dry; place in a shallow glass dish or sturdy plastic bag.
2. In a small bowl, stir together the hoisin sauce, orange zest, orange juice, garlic, ginger and oil; pour over the chicken. Cover and refrigerate for at least 3 hours or up to 8 hours, turning occasionally. Remove from the refrigerator 30 minutes before cooking.
3. Remove chicken from marinade, reserving marinade in a small saucepan. Bring marinade to a boil and simmer for 5 minutes. Stir in marmalade; set aside on the edge of the grill.
4. Meanwhile, place chicken legs on a greased grill on medium-high setting for gas barbecue or 6 inches (15 cm) from medium-hot coals; cook for 15 minutes, turning often. Brush marinade liberally over chicken and cook on the grill, turning often and brushing with marinade, for 10 to 20 minutes longer or until juices run clear when chicken is pierced with a fork.

Greek-Style Baked Chicken

MAKES 4 SERVINGS.

My son Allen and his girlfriend Cherrie often make this colourful and delicious dish from *Quick Chicken* (Robert Rose). You can garnish it with some black olives if you wish and serve it with rice and green beans for a fast and easy supper.

4	small, skinless boneless chicken breast halves 4
	Black pepper
2	small tomatoes (preferably plum), diced 2
2 tbsp	diced sweet red or yellow pepper 25 mL
2 tbsp	chopped fresh parsley 25 mL
1/2 tsp	dried oregano 2 mL
2	cloves garlic, minced 2
1 cup	crumbled feta cheese 250 mL
1 tbsp	olive oil 15 mL

1. Arrange chicken breasts in a greased baking dish just big enough to hold them in a single layer. Sprinkle with pepper and set aside.
2. In a bowl, toss together tomatoes, sweet pepper, parsley, oregano, garlic and feta cheese. Spoon over chicken, drizzle with olive oil and bake, uncovered, in a 400°F (200°C) oven for 25 to 30 minutes or until chicken is no longer pink inside.

Short-Cut Rotini with Broccoli and Clams

MAKES 2 SERVINGS.

This is a regular with my son, Allen. He and Cherrie frequently take the ingredients to the cottage or when they go camping.

1/4 lb	rotini or other pasta (1-1/3 cups/325 mL) 125 g
2 cups	small broccoli florets (1/4 lb/125 g) 500 mL
1 tbsp	butter 15 mL
1 tbsp	olive oil 15 mL
2	cloves garlic, minced 2
Pinch	hot pepper flakes Pinch
1	can (5 oz/142 g) clams 1
	Pepper
	Freshly grated Parmesan cheese

1. In a large pot of boiling salted water, cook rotini for 4 minutes. Add broccoli and cook for 2 minutes or until rotini is tender but firm.
2. Meanwhile, in a large skillet, melt butter with oil over low heat; cook garlic and hot pepper flakes for 3 minutes. Reserving liquid, add clams to the skillet and heat through; stir in liquid.
3. Drain broccoli and pasta well; stir into the skillet. Increase heat to high; cook until pasta has absorbed most of the liquid, stirring often, about 4 minutes. Sprinkle generously with pepper. Serve on warmed plates. Sprinkle with lots of cheese and serve immediately.

Scotch Eggs

MAKES 4 SERVINGS.

Also a good picnic treat, these cold, make-ahead eggs are delicious with cheese, scones and fruit for a summer breakfast.

1/2 lb	pork sausage meat	250 g
1/4 tsp	dried thyme	1 mL
Pinch	dried sage	Pinch
4	hard-cooked eggs, peeled	4
	All-purpose flour	
1	egg, beaten	1
1/2 cup	dry bread crumbs	125 mL
2 tbsp	vegetable oil or butter (approx.)	25 mL

1. In a bowl, mash sausage meat with thyme and sage; divide into 4 portions. Dust hard-cooked eggs with flour.
2. Wrap each portion of meat mixture evenly around an egg, sealing well. Dip into beaten egg; roll in bread crumbs.
3. In a medium skillet, heat oil over medium-low heat; fry coated eggs, turning frequently and adding more oil if necessary, until sausage meat is cooked and browned on all sides, about 10 minutes.

TIP

Moisten hands before forming meat for easier handling.

Prosciutto & Cheese Toasts

MAKES 4 SERVINGS.

Since fresh basil is the intensely flavoured ingredient in this new take on a grilled cheese sandwich, make these toasts for lunch when your basil is at its best in the garden. This is one of the recipes my friends the Slimmons "can't live without." They like to serve the sandwiches with sliced, fresh ripe tomatoes, drizzled with balsamic vinegar.

8	1/2-inch (1 cm) slices Italian bread 8
8 oz	thinly sliced Fontina or mozzarella cheese 250 g
4	slices prosciutto or cooked ham 4
1/4 tsp	black pepper 1 mL
32	fresh basil leaves 32
1/3 cup	olive oil, plus a little more if necessary 75 mL
1	large clove garlic, peeled and crushed with flat blade of a large knife 1

1. Cover half the bread slices with half the cheese. Top each with a prosciutto slice, folding to fit if necessary; sprinkle with pepper. Arrange an overlapping layer of basil leaves over prosciutto, dividing evenly; cover with remaining cheese. Top each with a second slice of bread.

2. In a large skillet, heat 2 tbsp (25 mL) oil with garlic over medium-low heat. Pushing garlic to the side of the skillet so that it doesn't get too brown, cook sandwiches in batches, for about 6 minutes, adding more oil as necessary, until bottoms of sandwiches are golden. Turn over with a spatula and cook for 5 minutes, until other side is golden and cheese is melted and runny. Remove sandwiches from skillet; cut each in half diagonally. Serve at once.

Goat Cheese & Vegetable Focaccia

MAKES 4 SERVINGS.

I was testing this recipe for *Owl Canadian Family Magazine* when I was also entertaining some visitors for lunch. When my friend Bernie Yew heard that it was a vegetable sandwich, he was not excited, but he ended up having two helpings and is still talking about how good it was.

Focaccia is an Italian-style flatbread, sometimes garnished with herbs. Look for it in the bread or deli section of your supermarket. Roasted peppers are available in jars in the pickles section if you do not have your own.

1	small eggplant (about 1 lb/500 g)	1
2	zucchini (12 oz/375 g total)	2
1/4 cup	olive oil	50 mL
1/4 tsp	salt	1 mL
1	focaccia (7 to 8 inches/ 18 to 20 cm across)	1
2/3 cup	soft goat cheese or cream cheese (about 4 oz/125 g)	150 mL
1/2 tsp	minced fresh rosemary (or a pinch crumbled dried rosemary)	2 mL
1/2 tsp	black pepper	2 mL
2/3 cup	bottled roasted red peppers, drained	150 mL

1. Preheat broiler to high. Trim stem ends from eggplant and zucchini; slice eggplant and zucchini lengthwise into 1/4-inch (5 mm) slices. Reserving 1 tbsp (15 mL) oil, brush vegetable slices on both sides with remaining oil; sprinkle with salt. Put vegetable slices in a single layer on a broiler pan or in a shallow baking pan; broil 4 inches (10 cm) from the element for 8 to 12 minutes, turning once, until tender and golden brown. Remove from broiler pan; set aside (you may need to do this in 2 batches). Don't switch broiler off.

2. Cut focaccia in half horizontally. Lightly brush cut sides with reserved oil; broil for 2 to 4 minutes, until lightly toasted. Keep warm.

3. In a small bowl, stir together cheese, rosemary and pepper until smooth. Spread cheese mixture on toasted sides of focaccia. Arrange eggplant, zucchini and red pepper on bottom half of focaccia; top with remaining half of focaccia. With a large serrated knife, cut focaccia into quarters; serve at once.

SUMMER SIDES AND SALADS

IN THE MENUS ...

New Potatoes Roasted with Olive Oil and Garlic

MAKES ABOUT 4 SERVINGS.

When I can buy waxy, little new potatoes at my local farmers' market, I love to toss them with olive oil, garlic and herbs and roast them until they're tender but crusty on the outside.

12	small new potatoes (about 2 lb/1 kg), unpeeled 12
4	cloves garlic, crushed 4
2 tbsp	olive oil 25 mL
2 tsp	finely chopped fresh rosemary or thyme (or 1/2 tsp/2 mL dried) 10 mL
1 tsp	paprika 5 mL
	Salt and pepper

1. Scrub potatoes and dry them. In a small roasting pan, toss together the potatoes, garlic, oil, rosemary and paprika.

2. Cover and roast in a 375°F (190°C) oven until potatoes are tender, 30 to 40 minutes, stirring occasionally. Season with salt and pepper to taste.

Down-Home Potato Salad

I could sit down to a big plate of this delicious salad and ask for nothing more. It does, however, go awfully well with ribs or chicken.

5	potatoes 5
2 tbsp	white wine vinegar 25 mL
1 tsp	granulated sugar 5 mL
4	hard-cooked eggs, finely chopped 4
1/4 cup	EACH diced red onion, celery and sweet green pepper 50 mL
2	cornichons (or 1 small dill pickle), minced 2
1 cup	light mayonnaise 250 mL
1 tbsp	Dijon mustard 15 mL
Pinch	cayenne pepper Pinch
	Salt and pepper

1. Peel and quarter potatoes. Cook in boiling, salted water for about 20 minutes or until tender; drain well and coarsely chop. Place in a bowl and combine with vinegar and sugar while still hot.
2. Add eggs, onion, celery, green pepper and pickles; toss gently.
3. Stir together the mayonnaise, mustard, cayenne, and salt and pepper to taste; stir into potato mixture. Serve warm or cover and refrigerate for up to 8 hours; bring to room temperature to serve.

Mussel and New Potato Salad

MAKES 10 FIRST-COURSE SERVINGS OR 6 TO 8 LUNCHEON MAIN-COURSE SERVINGS.

I can still taste this lovely salad with its homemade mayonnaise, which Elizabeth Baird and I did for a *Canadian Living* story on Prince Edward Island many years ago. This recipe celebrates two of the province's best products.

4 lb	mussels, steamed and shucked (see Marinated Mussels, Summer Menus, page 108) 2 kg
1/4 cup	fresh lemon juice 50 mL
2 tbsp	finely chopped shallots 25 mL
1/4 cup	chopped fresh parsley 50 mL
1-1/2 lb	new potatoes 750 g
2 tbsp	dry white wine 25 mL
2 tbsp	olive oil 25 mL
	Salt and pepper
1	egg 1
1-1/2 tsp	Dijon mustard 7 mL
1/2 tsp	dry mustard 2 mL
1 tbsp	white wine vinegar 15 mL
1-1/2 tsp	finely chopped fresh oregano (or 1/2 tsp/2 mL dried oregano) 7 mL
1/2 cup	olive or vegetable oil 125 mL
	Oak or other leaf lettuce
2	hard-cooked eggs, cut into wedges 2
	Fresh parsley sprigs

1. In a large bowl, combine mussels, lemon juice, shallots and half the chopped parsley. Cover and refrigerate for 1 hour.

2. Scrub potatoes. Boil in salted water to cover until tender but firm; drain and peel. If large, cut into quarters; if tiny, leave whole.

3. In a medium bowl, combine warm potatoes with wine, 2 tbsp (25 mL) oil, remaining chopped parsley, and salt and pepper to taste. Set aside and let marinate at room temperature for 30 to 60 minutes.

4. In a blender or food processor, combine egg, Dijon and dry mustards, vinegar, oregano, and salt and pepper to taste. With the machine running, slowly add the oil, a drop at a time at first, then in a thin stream as the dressing thickens.

5. Combine mussel mixture, potato mixture and dressing; stir gently. Cover and refrigerate for at least 2 hours. To serve, line individual plates with lettuce and mound salad on top. Garnish with egg wedges and parsley sprigs.

Sage Green Beans with Parmesan Slivers

MAKES 8 SERVINGS.

In the summer, when green or yellow beans are so abundant in gardens and markets, they need little embellishment, but this do-ahead treatment will make them even more special for company fare. To make Parmesan slivers, run a vegetable parer across a short piece of Parmesan cheese.

2 lb	green beans, trimmed	1 kg
3 tbsp	olive oil	45 mL
2	cloves garlic, each halved	2
1 tbsp	chopped fresh sage (or 1 tsp/5 mL dried crumbled sage)	15 mL
	Salt and pepper	
2 tsp	fresh lemon juice	10 mL
1/2 cup	slivered Parmesan cheese	125 mL

1. In a big saucepan, bring a large quantity of salted water to boil; add beans and cook over medium-high heat, uncovered, for 3 to 5 minutes or until just tender but still firm. Drain and refresh under cold running water. (Beans can be prepared to this point, wrapped in a clean tea towel and refrigerated for up to 8 hours.)

2. In a large skillet, heat oil over medium heat and cook garlic until golden brown. Remove and discard garlic. Add beans to the skillet and shake the pan to coat them. Season with sage, and salt and pepper to taste. Cover and cook over low heat for about 2 minutes or until heated through. Toss with lemon juice and arrange in a warm, shallow serving dish. Sprinkle with Parmesan slivers.

Spinach-Strawberry Salad with Honey-Pecan Dressing

MAKES ABOUT 4 SERVINGS.

Strawberries not only add colour, but texture and loads of flavour to this delicious salad with its creamy nut dressing.

10 oz	fresh spinach	284 g
2 cups	strawberries	500 mL
1	sweet yellow pepper, in strips	1
1/3 cup	pecan halves, toasted	75 mL

HONEY-PECAN DRESSING

1/3 cup	olive or vegetable oil	75 mL
3 tbsp	chopped pecans, toasted	45 mL
2 tbsp	white wine vinegar	25 mL
2 tbsp	liquid honey	25 mL
	Salt and pepper	

1. Wash and dry spinach well. Remove big stems and tear leaves into bite-sized pieces; place in a large salad bowl. Wash, dry, hull and halve strawberries; add to the bowl with yellow pepper and pecans.

1. In a blender, combine the oil, chopped pecans, vinegar, honey and a generous amount of salt and pepper to taste. Blend until smooth. Dressing will be quite thick. Thin to pouring consistency with about 2 tbsp (25 mL) water. (Dressing can be made up to 4 hours ahead, covered and refrigerated.)
2. Pour dressing onto spinach salad and toss well to coat.

Fresh Peach and Roquefort Salad with Walnut Dressing

MAKES 4 SERVINGS.

An assertive blue cheese, tangy greens and a nut dressing are happy companions to juicy, fresh peach slices in this quick summer salad.

1/3 cup	fresh lime juice 75 mL
1/4 cup	walnut or olive oil or a combination 50 mL
2 tsp	white wine vinegar 10 mL
1/2 tsp	Dijon mustard 2 mL
	Salt and pepper
3	peaches 3
1	bunch watercress or arugula 1
3 oz	Roquefort cheese (or other blue cheese) 75 g
1/4 cup	toasted, coarsely chopped walnuts 50 mL

1. In a medium bowl, whisk together lime juice, oil, vinegar, mustard, and salt and pepper to taste. Peel, pit and slice peaches 1/4-inch (5 mm) thick; add to the dressing and toss to coat. Let stand to marinate for 30 minutes.

2. Arrange watercress on a large platter or individual plates. Arrange peach slices on top, drizzling with dressing. Crumble cheese over peaches; sprinkle with walnuts. Serve immediately.

Greek Pasta Salad

MAKES ABOUT 10 SERVINGS.

High on Allen and Cherrie's list of favourites, this delicious salad is one they often make to take to the cottage where even the least adventurous eaters love it. It would be perfect, too, for a family pic-nic or backyard barbecue. Bow-tie pasta or farfalle is an excellent choice for salads because it's firm enough to withstand cooking, tossing and a day in the refrigerator without getting mushy.

8 cups	farfalle (1 lb/500 g)	2 L
1/2 cup	extra virgin olive oil	125 mL
1/3 cup	fresh lemon juice	75 mL
1 tbsp	anchovy paste	15 mL
2	cloves garlic, minced	2
1 tsp	dried oregano	5 mL
Pinch	EACH salt and pepper	Pinch
1	small cucumber	1
2 cups	small cherry tomatoes	500 mL
1 cup	small black olives	250 mL
1 cup	chopped red onion	250 mL
1/2 cup	chopped fresh parsley	125 mL
1 cup	finely diced feta cheese (about 4 oz/125 g)	250 mL

1. In a large pot of boiling salted water, cook farfalle for 8 to 10 minutes or until tender but firm; drain well.

2. Meanwhile, whisk together oil, lemon juice, anchovy paste, garlic, oregano, salt and pepper; toss half with the pasta. Let cool to room temperature, stirring occasionally.

3. Cut cucumber in half, lengthwise. Scoop out seeds and thinly slice crosswise.

4. Add to the pasta along with the tomatoes, olives, onion, parsley and remaining dressing; toss to coat well. Gently stir in feta cheese. (Salad can be covered and refrigerated for up to 1 day.)

SUMMER DESSERTS

Strawberries with Almond Cream Sauce

MAKES 6 SERVINGS.

As I was growing up on our farm, we always had fruit to pick from the first pink stalks of rhubarb in the spring to the last crisp apple in late fall. But there was something special about getting out in the warm June sun to find perfectly ripe, red strawberries hidden under their protective green leaves.

When I have flavourful, freshly picked berries, I like to present them simply—mounded in a dish to enjoy with cream and sugar or to eat out-of-hand, perhaps with some sour cream or crème fraîche and a bit of brown sugar for dipping.

The following recipe is one of my favourites. It's very simple, celebrating the rich flavour of ripe fruit. Yet there's a touch of elegance that lends itself well to the finale of a dinner party.

5 cups	ripe strawberries 1.25 L
1/4 cup	instant dissolving or fruit sugar 50 mL
1 cup	light sour cream 250 mL
2 tbsp	Amaretto 25 mL

1. Rinse berries, dry and hull. If large, slice; if small, leave whole. Place in a sieve set over a large bowl. Sprinkle with sugar and refrigerate, covered, for 1 hour.
2. To serve, divide berries among 6 serving dishes. Whisk sour cream and liqueur into the juice that has collected in the bowl until smooth. Pour over the berries and serve immediately.

Old-Fashioned Strawberry Shortcake

MAKES 6 SERVINGS.

Throughout the decades, strawberry shortcake has been the focus of many festivals and summer suppers—a dessert everyone craves at least once when local strawberries are in season. This sweet biscuit base my mother always made is excellent for other fruit throughout the summer—peaches, blueberries or raspberries.

2 cups	all-purpose flour	500 mL
3 tbsp	granulated sugar	45 mL
1 tbsp	baking powder	15 mL
1/2 tsp	salt	2 mL
1/2 cup	butter	125 mL
2/3 cup	light cream	150 mL
1	egg	1
1 cup	whipping cream	250 mL
4 cups	strawberries, hulled	1 L
1/3 cup	icing sugar	75 mL
1 tsp	vanilla	5 mL
	Butter, softened	

1. In a large bowl, sift or stir together flour, 2 tbsp (25 mL) of the granulated sugar, baking powder and salt; cut in butter until mixture resembles fine crumbs. In a measuring cup, beat together light cream and the egg; quickly stir all at once into the dry ingredients to moisten.

2. Form dough into a ball; pat into an ungreased 8-inch (2 L) square cake pan. Brush with 2 tsp (10 mL) of the whipping cream; sprinkle with remaining granulated sugar. Bake in a 450°F (230°C) oven for 12 to 15 minutes or until golden brown on top. Place on a rack and let cool for about 30 minutes.

3. Meanwhile, set aside 6 whole strawberries for garnish. Slice or chop the remaining berries and place in a bowl; sprinkle them with all but 1 tbsp (15 mL) of the icing sugar. Set aside for at least 30 minutes.

4. In a chilled bowl, beat remaining whipping cream with the remaining icing sugar and vanilla. Cut warm shortcake into 6 pieces; slice each horizontally in half. Set bottom halves on individual serving plates, cut side up. Butter both cut sides. Spoon on sliced berries and their juices; top with remaining shortcake. Spread whipped cream on top; garnish each with a whole berry.

TIP

Just before using, wash berries briefly under cold running water and then remove hulls. If you remove hulls before washing the berries, water will soak into the holes left from the green tops.

Peaches Catherine

MAKES 12 SERVINGS.

Many of my friends and family list this easy recipe as one of their all-time favourites. Everyone just calls it Peaches Catherine despite never having met my friend Catherine Betts who gave me the recipe. It is one of those wonderful desserts that takes very little time to prepare and is loved by all. Make it only in peach season when juicy local peaches are the best in the world!

15	ripe peaches	15
2 tbsp	fresh lemon juice	25 mL
2 cups	whipping cream	500 mL
3/4 cup	packed brown sugar	175 mL

1. Peel, slice and arrange peaches in a 12-cup (3 L) shallow gratin dish or other attractive baking dish, sprinkling slices with the lemon juice as you work.
2. Whip the cream and spread it all over the peaches. Sprinkle with brown sugar by putting the sugar through a fine sieve. Cover with plastic wrap and refrigerate overnight. (This is a necessary step.)
3. Just before serving, broil peaches about 4 inches (10 cm) from the heat for about 2 minutes or until crispy golden on top.

Summer Fruit Cobbler

MAKES 8 SERVINGS.

There are so many wonderful desserts you can make when our local fresh fruit abounds. This
easy and versatile cobbler, one of my favourites, can take you right through the summer season:
thinly sliced rhubarb; hulled, sliced strawberries (or a combination of the two); whole raspberries,
blackberries or blueberries (or a combination of the three); pitted cherries; sliced pitted peaches—
alone or in any combination; and, finally, sliced pitted plums. Adjust the sugar to the sweetness of
the fruit, and for best flavour, serve the cobbler warm with ice cream or lightly whipped cream.
My husband also loves his with a bit of nice old Cheddar.

COBBLER TOPPING

2 cups	sifted cake and pastry flour	500 mL
4 tsp	EACH granulated sugar and baking powder	20 mL
Pinch	salt	Pinch
1/2 cup	cold butter	125 mL
1 cup	whipping cream	250 mL
1/4 cup	milk	50 mL

1. In a large bowl, stir together the flour, sugar, baking powder and salt.
   With a pastry blender or 2 knives, cut in butter until mixture resembles coarse meal. (Topping mixture can be prepared up to this point
   and refrigerated in a sealed plastic bag for up to 5 days.)
2. Just before placing the topping mixture on the fruit, add whipping
   cream and milk to the mixture; stir gently until ingredients are
   combined, dry ingredients are moistened and a soft, slightly sticky
   dough forms.

FRUIT LAYER

8 cups	fresh fruit (see above)	2 L
3/4 cup	granulated sugar (or more depending on sweetness of fruit)	175 mL
2 tbsp	all-purpose flour	25 mL
	Additional granulated sugar	

1. In a 9-inch (2.5 L) square, shallow baking dish or gratin dish of the
   same volume, toss fruit with sugar and flour. Spoon topping over fruit in
   8 rough rounds or patties no more than 1/2-inch (1 cm) thick; sprinkle
   with additional sugar. Bake in a 375°F (190°C) oven for 40 to 45 minutes
   or until the topping is golden brown and fruit juices are bubbly.
2. Serve warm with vanilla ice cream or dollops of softly whipped cream.

Plum Clafouti with Cognac Cream

MAKES 4 SERVINGS.

When I want something elegant but quick, I enjoy serving a fruit dessert like this one. A kind of custard or thick fruit pancake from Limousin, France, clafouti (also spelled "clafoutis") was originally made with black cherries. I love the look of it with purple plums, but use whatever fruit is in season, varying the liqueur to complement the fruit and adjusting the sugar to the fruit's sweetness.

2 cups	halved, pitted, purple prune plums (about 10) 500 mL
1/2 cup	granulated sugar 125 mL
1 tbsp	kirsch or brandy 15 mL
1-1/4 cups	light cream 300 mL
2	eggs 2
2 tbsp	all-purpose flour 25 mL
Pinch	salt Pinch
1/2 tsp	vanilla 2 mL
	Icing sugar

1. Toss plums with 2 tbsp (25 mL) of the sugar and kirsch. Set aside.
2. Butter a 6-cup (1.5 L) shallow, pretty baking dish; sprinkle with 1 tbsp (15 mL) of the sugar.
3. In a blender, blend light cream, eggs, flour and salt for 1 minute. Add remaining sugar and vanilla; blend a few seconds longer.
4. Arrange plums, cut side down, and their juice in prepared dish; pour egg mixture over top. Bake in a 375°F (190°C) oven for about 45 minutes or until well puffed and golden. Let cool until barely warm. Sprinkle with icing sugar to serve.

COGNAC CREAM

1/2 cup	whipping cream 125 mL
1 tbsp	EACH cognac or brandy and icing sugar 15 mL

1. Whip cream, cognac and icing sugar together to form soft peaks. Serve with clafouti.

Layered Almond-Plum Trifle

MAKES 6 SERVINGS.

When plums are in season, I love using them in all kinds of desserts and sauces. Easier to make than a traditional trifle with a cooked custard, this pretty little dessert seems just as decadent. This recipe uses amaretti—almond-flavoured Italian cookies available in Italian grocery stores, gourmet shops and some large supermarkets.

1 lb	large red or purple plums (about 7)	500 g
1/2 cup	granulated sugar	125 mL
1/4 cup	water	50 mL
1-1/2 cups	coarsely chopped amaretti cookies (about 26 cookies)	375 mL
1/4 cup	brandy	50 mL
8 oz	light cream cheese	250 g
2 tbsp	light sour cream	25 mL
1 cup	whipping cream	250 mL
2 tbsp	icing sugar	25 mL
1/3 cup	toasted sliced almonds	75 mL

1. Pit and slice plums; combine in a large skillet with sugar and water. Cook over medium-low heat, stirring occasionally, until sugar dissolves. Bring to a boil, reduce heat to low, cover and simmer for 8 to 12 minutes or until plums are soft.

2. With a slotted spoon, transfer plums to a bowl, draining well. Boil cooking syrup for about 5 minutes or until reduced to 1/4 cup (50 mL). Refrigerate plums and syrup separately for at least 1 hour or up to 3 days, covering them after they cool.

3. Moisten cookie crumbs with 3 tbsp (45 mL) of the brandy and set aside.

4. Using a food processor or an electric mixer, blend cream cheese, reserved plum syrup and sour cream until smooth.

5. In a separate bowl, whip cream with icing sugar until soft peaks form; blend in remaining 1 tbsp (15 mL) brandy.

6. Sprinkle half the amaretti mixture in the bottom of a 4-cup (1 L) straight-sided glass bowl. Spread with half the cream cheese mixture, half the plums and then half the whipped cream. Repeat layers, cover with plastic wrap and refrigerate for at least 3 hours and up to 6 hours before serving. Sprinkle almonds over top just before serving.

Hint

To toast almonds, spread them out in a small, heavy skillet; cook over medium heat, stirring occasionally and watching carefully, for 3 to 5 minutes until golden and fragrant.

Zucchini Almond Cake

MAKES 12 SERVINGS.

This recipe has been a long-time favourite with all my friends who have kids, because it makes a big cake that children (and adults) love. I developed it when I had lots of zucchini in my huge vegetable garden at Keith and Jean Medley's farm near Owen Sound, Ontario. As a result, their "grown" boys still ask for this cake when they go home for a visit.

3 cups	all-purpose flour	750 mL
2 tsp	baking powder	10 mL
1 tsp	baking soda	5 mL
1 tsp	salt	5 mL
4	eggs	4
3 cups	granulated sugar	750 mL
1-1/4 cups	vegetable oil	300 mL
1 tsp	almond extract	5 mL
3 cups	finely grated, peeled zucchini	750 mL
1 cup	ground almonds	250 mL

1. Sift or stir together flour, baking powder, soda and salt.
2. In a large bowl, with an electric mixer, beat eggs until thick and light-coloured. Gradually add sugar, 1/4 cup (50 mL) at a time, beating well after each addition. Stir in oil and almond extract. Blend in dry ingredients, mixing until smooth.
3. Stir in zucchini and ground almonds. Pour into a well-greased and floured 10-inch (4 L) tube pan. Bake in a 350°F (180°C) oven for 1 hour and 15 minutes, or until a tester inserted in the centre of the cake comes out clean.
4. Cool in the pan on a rack for 15 minutes. Remove from the pan and cool completely on a rack.

ALMOND GLAZE

1-1/2 cups	icing sugar	375 mL
2 tbsp	milk	25 mL
1/4 tsp	almond extract	1 mL
1/4 cup	toasted sliced almonds	50 mL

1. Meanwhile, in a small bowl, stir together the icing sugar, milk and almond extract until smooth; spread over the top of the cake. Let icing run down the sides and sprinkle the top with sliced almonds.

SUMMER PRESERVES

Small-Batch Strawberry Preserves

MAKES ABOUT 1-3/4 CUPS (425 ML).

Because you want the fruit to stay whole, choose small, firm strawberries for these decadent preserves. Made in the microwave oven, they are so easy that you could even serve them warm with scones or tea biscuits for a company breakfast.

4 cups	strawberries (about 1 lb/500 g) 1 L	
1-1/4 cups	granulated sugar 300 mL	
1	orange 1	
1 tbsp	Cointreau or other orange liqueur (optional) 15 mL	

1. Wash, dry and hull the berries. In an 8-cup (2 L) glass measure, combine berries and sugar. Let stand for 5 minutes.
2. Remove 1 tsp (5 mL) zest from the orange and set aside. Cut the orange in two and squeeze out juice to make 1/4 cup (50 mL). Stir zest and juice into berries. Microwave, covered with plastic wrap, on High for 5 to 6 minutes or until boiling; stir well. Microwave, uncovered, on High for 15 to 17 minutes or until thickened, stirring often and watching that mixture doesn't bubble over. Stir in liqueur if using. Pour into a clean jar and, if storing, cover when cool and refrigerate.

Note
Recipe was tested in a 700-watt oven.

Small-Batch Peach-Rum Jam

MAKES ABOUT 1-1/4 CUPS (300 ML).

The microwave makes short work of small batches of jam like this one. Be sure to use the size of container called for and don't be tempted to double the recipe. The flavour is intensely peachy, so serve it spooned over ice cream or slathered on hot toast.

2 cups	very finely chopped peeled, pitted peaches 500 mL
3/4 cup	packed brown sugar 175 mL
1/2 cup	granulated sugar 125 mL
3 tbsp	dark rum 45 mL
2 tbsp	fresh lemon juice 25 mL

1. In an 8-cup (2 L) glass measure, combine the peaches, brown sugar, granulated sugar, 2 tbsp (25 mL) of the rum and the lemon juice. Microwave, covered with waxed paper, on High for 5 to 6 minutes or until boiling. Stir well. Microwave, uncovered, on High for 15 to 17 minutes or until thickened and set, stirring each time the mixture bubbles up to the top. Watch carefully. Stir in remaining tablespoon (15 mL) of rum. Pour jam into hot, sterilized jars, leaving 1/2-inch (1 cm) headspace. Seal tightly and leave at room temperature overnight. Refrigerate for up to 1 month or freeze for up to 1 year.

Note
Recipe was tested in a 700-watt oven.

Old-Fashioned Chili Sauce

MAKES ABOUT 10 (2-CUP/500 ML) JARS.

This was my mother's recipe for chili sauce—that old-fashioned Canadian relish that is like no other. My husband waits in great anticipation each year to come home to the heady aroma of a great pot of sauce bubbling away on the stove. It's his very favourite condiment, and he is sad indeed if we run out before the next tomato harvest. In Ontario, we still find tomatoes in baskets (quarts and litres), but in some areas tomatoes are weighed.

6 quarts	very ripe tomatoes (about 10 lb/ 4.5 kg)	6 L
8	onions, chopped	8
5	sweet red peppers, chopped	5
3 cups	chopped celery	750 mL
1/4 cup	finely chopped hot red peppers	50 mL
1 cup	cider vinegar	250 mL
2 tbsp	coarse pickling salt	25 mL
1 tsp	EACH black pepper, ground cloves, ground allspice, ground ginger, cinnamon, freshly grated nutmeg and celery seed	5 mL
2 cups	packed brown sugar	500 mL

1. Dip tomatoes into boiling water for 15 to 30 seconds, then into cold water; slip off skins. Cut out cores and chop coarsely. Place in a large, heavy non-aluminum saucepan. Add onions, peppers, celery, hot peppers, vinegar, salt, pepper, cloves, allspice, ginger, cinnamon, nutmeg and celery seed. Stir to mix well. Bring to a boil, reduce heat and simmer, uncovered, for about 2-1/2 hours or until sauce is dark red and thickened; stir often.

2. Add sugar and continue to simmer for another 30 minutes, stirring more often.

3. Ladle hot sauce into clean sealers, leaving 1/2-inch (1.25 cm) headspace. Process in boiling water bath for 10 minutes.

Cornichons

MAKES 16 CUPS (4 L).

If I don't take time to make any other pickles during the summer, I still make a batch of these little sour gherkins so that I have a supply to serve with pâté and other spreads during the winter. Seek out the smallest and freshest pickling cucumbers you can find.

16 cups	small pickling cucumbers (gherkin size) 4 L
1-3/4 cups	pickling salt 425 mL
2 tbsp	white vinegar 25 mL
3/4 lb	small pickling onions 375 g
16	cloves garlic 16
8	sprigs EACH fresh thyme and tarragon 8
8	bay leaves 8
4 tsp	black and white peppercorns (mixed or all black) 20 mL
4 tsp	whole cloves 20 mL
8	dried hot chili peppers 8
6 cups	white wine vinegar 1.5 L

1. Wash cucumbers well; rub with a towel to remove spikes. Place in a stainless steel or glass bowl; sprinkle with salt and let stand overnight.
2. Rinse eight 2-cup (500 mL) preserving jars with boiling water; turn upside down to drain.
3. Drain cucumbers; cover with cold water and add the white vinegar. Drain again and pat dry. Evenly divide cucumbers among the jars along with onions, garlic, thyme, tarragon, bay leaves, peppercorns, cloves and chili peppers. Cover with vinegar. Seal jars and refrigerate for 5 weeks before using. Cornichons can be refrigerated for up to 1 year.

Peach and Red Pepper Relish

MAKES ABOUT 14 CUPS (3.5 L).

This colourful and delicious relish recipe was inspired by my friend's mother, Alma MacLennan. I try to make it every peach season because it remains one of my favourite relishes to serve with roast pork or poultry.

12	large peaches	12
12	large sweet red peppers	12
1-1/4 cups	white vinegar	300 mL
2 tsp	pickling salt	10 mL
2	lemons, halved crosswise	2
6 cups	granulated sugar	1.5 L

1. Peel, pit and finely dice peaches. Chop peppers in a food processor. Combine peaches, peppers, vinegar and salt in a large kettle; bring to a boil. Reduce heat and simmer, uncovered, for 15 minutes, stirring often.

2. Squeeze juice from the lemons and cut rinds into quarters; add juice and lemon quarters with sugar to the peach mixture. Bring back to a boil, stirring gently to dissolve sugar; reduce heat and simmer for 20 minutes, stirring often.

3. Remove lemon-rind quarters and cook relish for 45 to 55 minutes or until thickened, stirring often.

4. Ladle into hot, clean preserving jars, leaving 1/2-inch (1 cm) headspace. Top with disk and apply screw band until fingertip tight.

5. Process for 10 minutes in a boiling water bath with water 2 inches (5 cm) above jar tops. Remove jars and (without tightening screw bands) place them upright on folded dry cloth or rack to cool. Label and store in a cool, dark and dry place.

TIP

After the jars have cooled, check for a seal. If the disk has snapped down, i.e., is curving downward, a seal has occurred. If you wish, you can remove the screw band to use again. Any unsealed jars can be refrigerated for immediate use.

SUMMER

SUMMER MENUS

To hold a wedding in your home is to make a personal gesture more elegant and satisfying than is possible anywhere else. This is the menu from the wedding for our daughter, Anne, and her husband, Rob Loxton.

The wedding was on the first day of summer after an unusually cold spring. As a result, we were pleased to have some local asparagus (really a spring treat), but I had to drop fresh strawberries (which usually start in this area by now) from the menu. My friends did, however, find a flat of local strawberries at the farmers' market that day, so we served them for the brunch we had for guests the next morning.

When I wrote the story for the June 1998 issue of *Canadian Living*, I received more comments from readers than I gleaned from any other story. People love weddings, but these recipes would be lovely to serve at any kind of party. The Cheddar Chutney Tarts will become a winning appetizer throughout the year, and the Fruited Wild Rice Salad a potluck favourite.

A Summer Garden Wedding

FOIE GRAS ON MELBA TOAST

RADICCHIO AND CORN CHIVE MUFFINS WITH CRÈME FRAÎCHE AND CAVIAR

CHEDDAR CHUTNEY TARTS*

ENDIVE WITH SMOKED TROUT MOUSSE (SEE PAGE 49)

MIXED GREENS WITH PROSCIUTTO PASTA PINWHEELS*

TURKEY BALLOTINE WITH CRANBERRY CREAM

ROASTED BEEF TENDERLOIN WITH HORSERADISH SAUCE*

FRUITED WILD RICE SALAD*

OVEN-ROASTED ASPARAGUS (SEE PAGE 23)

TRIPLE CHOCOLATE WEDDING CAKE ON RASPBERRY COULIS

*Recipe included. Although the entire wedding menu is shown above, only those recipes I developed myself especially for the wedding appear in this collection.

Cheddar Chutney Tarts

MAKES 6 DOZEN TARTS.

Bake these easy, make-ahead appetizers right from the freezer and serve hot for rave reviews.

8 oz	cream cheese, softened 250 g
1 cup	old Cheddar cheese (4 oz/ 125 g), shredded 250 mL
1	clove garlic, minced 1
1 tsp	curry powder 5 mL
1/3 cup	Major Grey mango chutney 75 mL
4	green onions, finely chopped 4
2 tsp	dry sherry or apple juice 10 mL
Pinch	cayenne pepper Pinch
Dash	Worcestershire sauce Dash
1	pkg (about 14 oz/397 or 411 g) frozen puff pastry, thawed 1

1. In a bowl, mash cream cheese with wooden spoon. Add Cheddar cheese, garlic and curry powder; mix well. Chop large pieces of mango in the chutney; add to cheese mixture along with remaining chutney, onions, sherry, cayenne and Worcestershire sauce; mix well. (Filling can be made several days ahead, covered and refrigerated.)
2. Working with half of the pastry at a time, roll out the pastry on a lightly floured surface into a 12-inch (30 cm) square. Cut into 2-inch (5 cm) squares. Press each square into 1/2-inch (1 cm) deep mini-tart cups and prick with a fork in 2 or 3 places. Spoon 1 tsp (5 mL) filling into each. (Can be frozen in airtight container for up to 1 week.)
3. Bake in the centre of a 400°F (200°C) oven for about 15 minutes or until pastry is golden. Serve hot.

Mixed Greens with Prosciutto Pasta Pinwheels

MAKES 20 SERVINGS.

15	lasagna noodles 15
30	large fresh spinach leaves 30
8 oz	spreadable herbed cream cheese 250 g
8 oz	prosciutto or smoked ham, thinly sliced 250 g
10 cups	mesclun mix 2.5 L

CHUNKY TOMATO VINAIGRETTE

1/4 cup	olive oil 50 mL
16	plum tomatoes, diced 16
4	green onions, diced 4
3	cloves garlic, minced 3
1/4 cup	red wine vinegar 50 mL

1. In a large pot of boiling salted water, cook noodles, in batches, for about 10 minutes or until tender but firm. (If you do use fresh noodles, reduce this time considerably.) Chill under cold, running water and pat dry.
2. Meanwhile, trim, wash and dry spinach.
3. Spread cream cheese evenly over noodles. Arrange 2 spinach leaves over each noodle. Cut prosciutto into strips to fit noodles; divide evenly over spinach. Roll up each noodle tightly from 1 short end. Wrap well in plastic wrap and refrigerate for at least 1 hour or for up to 2 days.

1. In a large skillet, heat oil over high heat; cook tomatoes, onions and garlic for 1 to 2 minutes or just until tomatoes start to soften. Remove from the heat; stir in vinegar, basil, salt, pepper and sugar. (Vinaigrette can be cooled, covered and refrigerated for up to 1 day; bring to room temperature to serve.)

1/4 cup	chopped fresh basil 50 mL
3/4 tsp	salt 4 mL
1/4 tsp	EACH pepper and granulated sugar 1 mL

2. Thirty minutes before serving, cut each roll into 4 slices. Let stand at room temperature. To serve, divide mesclun mix among salad plates; spoon dressing over each and place 3 pinwheels on top.

Mesclun is a mixture of colourful baby greens; it comes ready to use so you don't need to wash or dry it.

TIP

If you make your own mesclun mixture, use Boston lettuce, endive, radicchio, baby spinach, watercress and leaf lettuce. Wash it the day before and dry it thoroughly; refrigerate in plastic bags with paper towels interspersed throughout to absorb the moisture.

Roasted Beef Tenderloin with Horseradish Sauce

MAKES ABOUT 16 SERVINGS.

This easy, do-ahead recipe makes beef tenderloin even more special. Multiply it by 6 for 100 people. You can marinate the beef a day in advance, then cook and refrigerate it up to 2 days ahead. Remove from the refrigerator and cut into 1/4-inch (5 mm) thick slices when cold. Arrange the slices on platters, cover tightly and let them come to room temperature to serve, accompanied by the Horseradish Cream sauce (recipe follows).

1/2 cup	Worcestershire sauce 125 mL
2 tbsp	Scotch whisky 25 mL
2 tbsp	packed brown sugar 25 mL
1 tsp	pepper 5 mL
2	cloves garlic, minced 2
1	piece (1 inch/2.5 cm) fresh ginger, thinly sliced 1
1	whole beef tenderloin (4 lb/2 kg) 1
2 tbsp	coarse salt 25 mL

1. In a bowl, whisk together Worcestershire sauce, whisky, sugar, pepper, garlic and ginger until sugar is dissolved. Place tenderloin in a long, glass baking dish; pour marinade over top, turning beef to coat. Cover and marinate in the refrigerator for 24 hours, turning and basting occasionally.

2. Remove tenderloin from the marinade, shaking off excess. Place on foil-lined baking sheet. Rub all over with salt. Roast in a 500°F (260°C) oven for 10 minutes. Turn over and roast for 10 to 15 minutes longer or until a meat thermometer registers 140°F (60°C) for rare. The meat should be quite pink inside for the best texture and flavour. (Beef can be cooled, wrapped in foil and refrigerated for up to 2 days.)

Hint

The alcohol from the Scotch burns off during the cooking.

Horseradish Sauce

MAKES 2 CUPS (500 ML).

Slightly sweet but with enough tang to be a perfect accompaniment to the beef, this easy sauce keeps well refrigerated for up to 3 days. For 100 people, multiply the recipe by 5.

1-1/2 cups	mayonnaise	375 mL
2/3 cup	horseradish	150 mL
2 tbsp	icing sugar	25 mL

1. In a bowl, whisk together the mayonnaise, horseradish and icing sugar until well blended. (Sauce can be refrigerated for up to 3 days.)

Fruited Wild Rice Salad

MAKES 20 SERVINGS.

Diced fresh mango and dried cherries contribute wonderful flavour and texture to this colourful salad. Wild rice is elegant, but using a bit of orzo (pasta) adds more colour and texture while reducing the amount of wild rice you need. For 100 people, make the recipe in 5 batches. Garnish serving bowls with mango or peach slices and fresh herbs. This salad makes a great make-ahead dish for any kind of party.

5-3/4 cups	water	1.425 L
1	can (10 oz/284 mL) chicken broth	1
2 cups	wild rice	500 mL
1 tsp	salt	5 mL
1 cup	orzo	250 mL
2 cups	dried cherries	500 mL
1 cup	chopped green onions	250 mL
3/4 cup	chopped toasted pecans	175 mL
1/2 cup	chopped fresh parsley	125 mL
1/2 cup	diced celery	125 mL
1/3 cup	white wine vinegar	75 mL
2	cloves garlic, minced	2
1 tbsp	granulated sugar	15 mL
2 tsp	Dijon mustard	10 mL
1/2 cup	vegetable oil	125 mL
1/3 cup	olive oil	75 mL
	Salt and pepper	
2	mangos or peaches, peeled and diced	2

1. In a large saucepan, bring water and broth to a boil. Add rice and salt; return to boil. Reduce heat to medium and simmer, stirring occasionally, for about 40 minutes or until tender. Stir in orzo during the last 5 minutes, adding up to 1/2 cup (125 mL) more water if orzo sticks to the pan. Stir in cherries, green onions, pecans, parsley and celery. Transfer to a large bowl. (Salad can be prepared to this point, cooled, covered and refrigerated for up to 1 day.)
2. Whisk together vinegar, garlic, sugar and mustard. Gradually whisk in the vegetable oil and olive oil. Drizzle over salad and toss. Season to taste with salt and pepper. (Salad can be covered and refrigerated for up to 1 day; let it come to room temperature before serving.) Stir in the diced mangos.

Hint

Dried cherries are absolutely delicious in this salad, but if they are unavailable, dried cranberries would also be good.

The whole feeling of this meal should be relaxed, easy-going and very Spanish. If you can find banderillas in jars at a store that sells Spanish ingredients, they would make a nice addition to the tapas. Banderillas are little skewers of olives, pickles, artichokes, herring, etc.; tapas are hot and cold Spanish appetizers.

An Outdoor Spanish Party

(TAPAS)

MARINATED MUSSELS

SPANISH POTATO OMELETTE

CHORIZO WITH ORANGE ZEST

SHRIMP IN GARLIC SAUCE

OVEN-FRIED ALMONDS

OLIVES

PAELLA-ON-THE-BARBECUE

HEARTS OF PALM AND AVOCADO SALAD WITH GREENS AND LIME VINAIGRETTE

FRESH PEACHES OR MELON

Marinated Mussels

MAKES 6 SERVINGS.

Wonderfully tangy and fresh tasting, these colourful mussels will become a favourite appetizer at any dinner party, but they are particularly appealing as part of a tapas selection. For the best flavour, be sure to make them a day ahead.

2 lb	mussels (about 40 mussels)	1 kg
1/4 cup	chopped onion	50 mL
1	lemon, cut in wedges	1
1/4 cup	olive oil	50 mL
3	cloves garlic, minced	3
3 tbsp	red wine vinegar	45 mL
2 tbsp	chopped fresh parsley	25 mL
1 tbsp	sweet red pepper, minced 15 mL	
2 tsp	small capers	10 mL
1/2 tsp	EACH paprika and grated lemon zest	2 mL
	Salt and pepper	

1. Scrub mussels well, removing beards. Discard any that do not close tightly when tapped against a hard surface.
2. In a large saucepan, bring 1/2 cup (125 mL) water, onion and 1 lemon wedge to a simmer. Add mussels; cover and steam until mussels open, about 5 minutes. Discard any that do not open. Using a slotted spoon, transfer mussels to a bowl. Boil cooking liquid for about 3 minutes to reduce to 1/2 cup (125 mL). Remove lemon wedge.
3. In a large skillet, heat oil over medium heat; cook garlic for 2 minutes. Add mussel liquid, vinegar, parsley, red pepper, capers, paprika, lemon zest, and salt and pepper to taste. Pour into a medium bowl. Remove mussels from the shells and add to the bowl, reserving one half of each shell in the refrigerator. Cover mussels and refrigerate for at least 2 hours or preferably for 24 hours.
4. To serve, arrange reserved mussel shells on a platter. Place one mussel on each shell. Pour marinade over the mussels. Garnish platter with remaining lemon wedges.

Spanish Potato Omelette *(Tortilla de Patatas)*

MAKES 6 TO 8 SERVINGS.

Having nothing in common with the thin Mexican flatbreads except its name, the Spanish tortilla ("little cake") is an omelette. It has become a tapas classic and is considered by some the national dish of Spain. This egg-bound potato and onion pancake is good hot or made ahead and served at room temperature. I particularly remember how good it was hot when I made it in our rented villa in the south of Spain after having been caught in the rain during a visit to one of the mountain villages.

1/2 cup	olive oil 125 mL
4	large potatoes (about 2 lb/1 kg), peeled and thinly sliced 4
	Salt and pepper
1	large Spanish onion, chopped 1
1	clove garlic, minced 1
6	eggs 6

1. In a large ovenproof skillet (preferably cast iron) over medium-high heat, heat the oil. Sprinkle potato slices with salt and pepper to taste; fry in 2 batches, about 10 to 15 minutes each, until golden brown on both sides, turning occasionally with a spatula. Meanwhile, line a bowl with paper towels. With a slotted spoon, transfer the cooked potatoes to the bowl to drain.

2. Remove all but 2 tbsp (25 mL) oil from the skillet. Add onion and garlic; cook over medium-low heat for 20 minutes without browning, stirring often. Remove from heat, spread evenly in the bottom of the pan and layer the potato slices on top.

3. In a small bowl, beat eggs with 1/2 tsp (2 mL) salt and 1/4 tsp (1 mL) pepper; pour over the potatoes. Return the skillet to medium heat. Cook, shaking the pan to prevent sticking, until the bottom and sides are set, 4 to 5 minutes. Meanwhile, preheat broiler.

4. Run a knife around the edge to release sides of tortilla; broil for 2 minutes or until top is set and golden.

5. Run a metal spatula all around the sides and as far under the tortilla as possible. Invert a large plate over top and flip upside down to turn out the omelette. Cut into wedges or cubes to serve hot or at room temperature.

Chorizo with Orange Zest

MAKES 6 SERVINGS.

Chorizo is Spain's most popular sausage. Although produced in endless regional variations, it always includes pork, peppers and garlic. In tapas bars, it is usually sliced and served cold or grilled and served on pieces of bread, accompanied by a full-bodied red wine such as rioja.

1 lb	hot or mild chorizo sausage 500 g
1 tbsp	olive oil 15 mL
1	clove garlic, minced 1
2 tbsp	dry white wine or orange juice 25 mL
1 tsp	grated orange zest 5 mL
1	baguette, sliced 1

1. Slice chorizo into 1/4-inch (5 mm) thick slices.

2. In a large skillet over medium heat, heat the oil. Add garlic and cook until just golden. Add chorizo slices. Brown on both sides, stirring often. Stir in wine and orange zest; simmer until wine has evaporated, about 3 minutes. Drain off fat, if necessary.

3. Serve hot or cold on slices of baguette.

Shrimp in Garlic Sauce (*Gambas al Ajillo*)

MAKES 4 SERVINGS.

After my first exciting trip to Spain, I wrote an article on tapas (those wonderful little bites offered in tascas or tapas bars) for *President's Choice Magazine* and had many people rave about doing all the dishes I gave. This one is especially good with chilled fino sherry and lots of crusty bread to mop up the garlicky juices.

1 tbsp	salt, preferably sea salt	15 mL
1 cup	cold water	250 mL
3/4 lb	large raw shrimp, peeled* and deveined	375 g
3 tbsp	olive oil	45 mL
3	cloves garlic, chopped	3
Pinch	hot pepper flakes (or more to taste)	Pinch
1 tsp	sherry vinegar or white wine vinegar	5 mL
2 tbsp	chopped fresh parsley	25 mL
1/2 tsp	paprika	2 mL

1. In a medium bowl, stir salt into water until dissolved. Add shrimp and let sit at room temperature for 10 minutes. Drain and pat dry.
2. In a large, heavy skillet over medium heat, heat oil until very hot. Add shrimp in a single layer; sprinkle with garlic and hot pepper flakes.
3. Cook for 1-1/2 minutes on the first side; turn and cook about 1 minute on the other side or until shrimp are pink. Stir in vinegar, parsley and paprika. Serve immediately.

Leaving the tail on makes a pretty presentation.

Paella-on-the-Barbecue

MAKES 8 SERVINGS.

Paella was originally cooked outdoors over an open fire and was eaten by families working in the fields. Some restaurants still carry on the tradition, and it was fun to enjoy paella on the beach at Playa de la Herradura when we were spending some time in Andalucia in the south of Spain. The paella pan at the Restaurante El Chambao de Joaquin was 6 feet (1.8 metres) across! However, an inexpensive, thin shallow pan about 15 inches (38 cm) across the base is ideal for this recipe. Paella is an excellent choice for an outdoor summer party. Browning the meats right on the grill gives them a lovely smoky flavour.

3 lb	mixed chicken thighs and drumsticks 1.5 kg
1 lb	chorizo or other spicy, smoked sausage 500 g
1 lb	lean, boneless pork chops or steaks 500 g
	Salt and black pepper
5 cups	chicken stock 1.25 L
1/4 tsp	saffron, crushed 1 mL
2 tbsp	olive oil 25 mL
1	large onion, finely chopped 1
1	EACH sweet green and red pepper, seeded and cut into strips 1
2	tomatoes, peeled, seeded and chopped 2
2	cloves garlic, minced 2
2 cups	arborio rice 500 mL
16	large mussels (about 1 lb/ 500 g), scrubbed and beards removed* 16
2 cups	fresh or frozen (not thawed) green peas 500 mL
2 tbsp	chopped fresh parsley 25 mL
2	lemons, cut in wedges 2

1. Put the chicken, chorizo and pork on the greased grill of the barbecue over medium-high heat; cook for 10 minutes, turning often, until browned. (The chicken will not be cooked through.) Remove chicken to a bowl. Slice chorizo thinly and cut pork into 1-inch (2.5 cm) cubes. Add chorizo and pork to the bowl with chicken. Sprinkle with salt and pepper, then refrigerate. (Can be done a few hours ahead.) Bring stock to a boil in a medium saucepan, add saffron, then set aside.

2. Place paella pan or very large skillet directly on the grill over medium-high heat. Heat oil, then cook onion, sweet peppers, tomatoes and garlic for 10 to 15 minutes, stirring constantly, until thickened and most of the moisture has evaporated. Add rice and stir to coat with tomato mixture. Stir in chicken stock, chicken, chorizo and pork; then cover pan with foil or a lid and bring to a boil. Reduce heat to low on gas barbecue (if using charcoal, draw pan to the edge of the fire), then simmer for 15 to 20 minutes or until rice is almost tender. Add mussels, then steam, covered, for 5 minutes. Add peas, then cook, covered, for 5 minutes. Discard any mussels that have not opened. Taste and adjust seasoning. Garnish with parsley and serve with lemon wedges.

*Discard any open raw mussels that don't close when tapped sharply on the counter.

Note

Spanish cooks do not cover the pan while the rice is cooking, but I like the texture of the rice when it is covered and not stirred during this process. As well, a nice crusty bottom will form this way—part of the enjoyment of the dish.

Hearts of Palm and Avocado Salad with Greens and Lime Vinaigrette

MAKES 8 SERVINGS.

Hearts of palm have a refreshingly tart flavour, and with the lime dressing, this salad makes a delicious foil for the main course.

1	can (14 oz/398 mL) hearts of palm 1
12 cups	torn mixed salad greens (e.g., Boston lettuce, radicchio, endive, romaine) 3 L
1	small red onion, thinly sliced 1
1	large avocado, peeled and sliced 1

LIME VINAIGRETTE

1/2 tsp	grated lime zest 2 mL
2 tbsp	fresh lime juice 25 mL
2 tsp	Dijon mustard 10 mL
Pinch	hot pepper flakes (or more to taste) Pinch
	Salt and pepper
1/3 cup	olive oil 75 mL

1. Rinse the hearts of palm and dry well; cut into bite-sized pieces to make about 2 cups (500 mL). In a salad bowl, toss together the hearts of palm, greens and onion. (Salad can be covered loosely with a damp towel and refrigerated for up to 4 hours.) Just before serving, add the avocado.

1. In a small bowl, whisk together lime zest, lime juice, mustard, hot pepper flakes, and salt and pepper to taste; gradually whisk in the oil. (Vinaigrette can be covered and refrigerated for up to one day. Bring to room temperature and whisk before using.)
2. Just before serving, toss the salad with the vinaigrette.

FALL

MY FALL KITCHEN

Fall is that orderly time of the year that brings renewed responsibilities of study and committees. It's a return to the city after a carefree time at the cottage. It dictates set meal times and more formal entertaining.

The brisk air may mean donning those jackets again, but it does put nature's finishing touch on some of the produce still to harvest. Northern Spy apples welcome a bit of frost, and the rutabaga just wouldn't be the same without it. The end of summer doesn't mean that wonderful fresh fruit and vegetables are finished. Autumn is a true harvest season, right up until the last of the kale and Brussels sprouts are picked out of the snow.

The markets and roadside stands are still piled high with baskets of ripe pears and grapes giving off their intoxicating fragrance. There are colourful mountains of pumpkins and squash, which I can never resist buying so that our shed usually ends up with its own squash mountain.

The fresh, cool air is perfectly suited to heartier meals so we can enjoy some of that squash with the long-roasting turkey that will be the focus of our Thanksgiving dinner, along with the lovely fruit pies that are so much a part of harvest fare.

FALL STARTERS AND SOUPS

IN THE MENUS ...

Gougère Ring

MAKES 6 SERVINGS.

One sunny Sunday, I remember stopping with a couple of friends in a tiny village in Burgundy, France, to buy the makings for a picnic. We found wonderful parslied ham, fruit and vegetables at the farmers' market and in small shops. At the boulangerie, we found Gougère, a rough cheese bread that was so delicious I can taste it still. Gougère remains one of my favourite company appetizers. I developed this easy version for a series of classes I did in Toronto for the late Helen Gougeon, one of my favourite Canadian food writers.

6 or 7	eggs	6 or 7
3/4 tsp	salt	4 mL
5 oz	Gruyère cheese	150 g
4-1/2 tbsp	unsalted butter	70 mL
1-1/4 cups	water	300 mL
1 tsp	EACH Dijon mustard and granulated sugar	5 mL
1/2 tsp	dry mustard	2 mL
1/4 tsp	pepper	1 mL
Dash	hot pepper sauce	Dash
1-1/4 cups	all-purpose flour	300 mL

1. With a fork, beat together one of the eggs and a pinch of the salt for a glaze; set aside.
2. Using the shredding disc of the processor, or by hand, grate the cheese; set aside.
3. In a medium saucepan, bring butter, water, Dijon mustard, sugar, remaining salt, dry mustard, pepper and hot pepper sauce to a boil, stirring to melt the butter. Remove from the heat and immediately add the flour all at once; beat with a wooden spoon for 1 minute or until mixture is well combined and leaves the side of the pan. Cook over medium heat for 2 minutes, stirring constantly.
4. Transfer mixture to the processor, now fitted with a metal blade. Cool for 1 to 2 minutes. Add 5 eggs and process, stopping once to scrape down the side of the bowl, until the eggs are completely incorporated and the mixture is very thick, smooth and shiny, about 30 seconds. If not shiny, process in another egg for 10 seconds. Add three-quarters of the cheese and process for 5 seconds.
5. Grease a baking sheet and sprinkle it with water, shaking off the excess. Using your finger, draw a 9-inch (23 cm) circle for a guide when forming the ring.

6. Using 2 large spoons, drop the dough by spoonfuls onto the circle so that the rounds touch each other to form a ring. With any remaining dough, form another ring of smaller rounds on top. Brush with the egg glaze. Sprinkle with remaining cheese. (Ring can be prepared up to 30 minutes ahead and covered with an inverted bowl.)

7. Place in a 425°F (220°C) oven and immediately reduce the temperature to 400°F (200°C); bake for 25 minutes. Reduce the temperature to 375°F (190°C) and bake for another 20 minutes or until golden brown. Carefully remove the ring to a rack and cool for 5 minutes before placing on a large plate to cut into wedges and serve warm.

Onion-Sage Focaccia

MAKES 4 SERVINGS.

I think onions are underrated as a vegetable. We use them in flavouring soups, stews, dips and sauces, but we seldom think of them as the star of a dish. This simple flatbread is delicious as an appetizer to a light dinner or as an accompaniment to a main-course soup. Prepare the pizza dough (or use bought dough) just to the point where you punch it down.

1	very small Spanish onion, thinly sliced	1
1/4 cup	white wine vinegar	50 mL
2 tbsp	liquid honey	25 mL
	Pizza Dough (recipe follows)	
3/4 cup	freshly grated Parmesan cheese	175 mL
	Cornmeal	
1 tbsp	finely chopped fresh sage (or 1 tsp/5 mL crumbled dried sage)	15 mL
2 tbsp	vegetable oil	25 mL

1. In a small bowl, combine onion, vinegar and honey; let stand at room temperature for at least 30 minutes and no longer than 1 hour, stirring occasionally.

2. Punch down the dough; blend in 1/4 cup (50 mL) of the cheese and form into a ball. Turn out onto a lightly floured surface and cover with a bowl; let stand for 10 minutes. Roll out into a 10-inch (25 cm) circle. Transfer to a pizza pan or baking sheet lightly sprinkled with cornmeal.

3. Make indentations all over the top with your fingertips. Drain onion and scatter over dough. Sprinkle with remaining cheese, then sage and oil.

4. Sprinkle all over with 1 tsp (5 mL) cold water; bake in a 425°F (220°C) oven for 20 to 25 minutes or until golden. Cut into wedges to serve warm.

Pizza Dough

MAKES ONE 12-INCH (30 CM) CRUST. (RECIPE CAN BE DOUBLED.)

This quick and easy homemade pizza dough is very simple to make by hand. However, if you have an electric bread machine, combine the ingredients in the machine according to the order indicated in its accompanying booklet. Use 1-1/2 tsp (7 mL) bread machine yeast (instead of 2 tsp/10 mL regular, active dry yeast) and set your machine to the dough cycle. By using a bread machine, you can eliminate letting the dough rise in a bowl. Whichever way you make it, you can roll it out, wrap it and refrigerate it on the pan for up to 8 hours, or freeze it. Or, wrap the risen dough in plastic wrap, then in a freezer bag and freeze it. Thaw in the refrigerator before rolling it out.

Pinch	granulated sugar	Pinch
2/3 cup	warm water	150 mL
2 tsp	active dry yeast	10 mL
2 tbsp	vegetable oil	25 mL
1-1/2 cups	all-purpose flour (approx.)	375 mL
1/2 tsp	salt	2 mL

1. In a small bowl, combine the sugar and water; sprinkle with yeast and let stand in a warm place until bubbly and doubled in volume, about 5 minutes. Stir in oil.

2. In a large bowl, mix together flour and salt. Make a well in the centre and pour in the yeast mixture. With a fork, gradually blend together the flour and yeast mixtures to form dough. With floured hands, gather dough into a ball.

3. Turn out onto a lightly floured surface; knead for about 5 minutes, adding just enough extra flour to make a soft, slightly sticky dough. Place in a greased bowl, turning once to grease all over. Cover the bowl with greased waxed paper and a tea towel. Let stand in a warm, draft-free place until tripled in size, 1-1/2 to 3 hours.

4. Punch down the dough and form into a ball. Turn out onto a lightly floured surface and cover with a bowl; let stand for 10 minutes. Roll out the dough into a 12-inch (30 cm) circle.

Hot Gazpacho

MAKES 6 SERVINGS.

One cold day as we were touring a little village in the mountains near where we were staying in Southern Spain, we stopped at a family restaurant where we enjoyed the most delicious hot soups. One was garlic and almond, and the other was a special tomato soup. Of course, I asked for the recipes and received very scanty instructions; I did, however, manage to reproduce the tomato soup one cool day at our villa. It's perfect for a fall day at home when local tomatoes and peppers are still around.

3 tbsp	olive oil	45 mL
2	large ripe tomatoes, peeled, seeded and chopped	2
1	onion, chopped	1
1	green pepper, chopped	1
1	clove garlic, minced	1
1/2 tsp	salt	2 mL
1/4 tsp	saffron threads*	1 mL
1/4 tsp	ground cumin	1 mL
1/4 tsp	black pepper	1 mL
4 cups	chicken stock	1 L
4	slices bread, toasted and cubed	4

1. In a large saucepan over medium heat, heat the oil; add tomatoes, onion, green pepper and garlic. Cover and simmer for 10 minutes.
2. Meanwhile, crush the salt, saffron, cumin and pepper together using a mortar and pestle or a small cup and the handle end of a dinner knife. Add to the vegetables with the stock.
3. Bring to a boil, reduce the heat, cover and simmer for 10 minutes. Serve hot garnished with toast cubes.

*Saffron is orange-yellow flavouring made from the dried, red stigmas of a crocus grown in Spain; look for it in specialty food shops. Use sparingly.

Broccoli-Brie Soup

MAKES 4 TO 6 SERVINGS.

Any cheese complements broccoli, but Brie makes this simple soup interesting enough to serve to company or for a family lunch.

1	large bunch broccoli 1
2 tbsp	butter 25 mL
1	onion, chopped 1
1	celery stalk, chopped 1
1	potato, peeled and chopped 1
1 tsp	dried thyme 5 mL
5 cups	chicken stock* 1.25 L
4 oz	Brie cheese (rind removed), diced 125 g
1/4 tsp	EACH salt and black pepper 1 mL

1. Separate broccoli into florets; reserve 3/4 cup (175 mL) tiny florets for garnish. Peel and coarsely chop stems; chop remaining florets.

2. In a large saucepan, melt butter over medium heat. Add onion, celery, potato and thyme; cook for 5 minutes, stirring occasionally. Add stock; bring to a boil. Reduce heat to medium-low; simmer, covered, for about 5 minutes, until potato is tender. Add broccoli; bring back to a boil. Simmer, uncovered, for 3 minutes or until broccoli is just tender.

3. In a blender (a blender makes a smoother soup than a food processor), blend soup in batches until smooth. Pour soup back into saucepan. (Soup can be prepared ahead, cooled, covered and refrigerated for up to 1 day.) When ready to serve, bring soup to a simmer over medium-high heat. Add cheese, salt and pepper, stirring until cheese melts. Do not let soup boil after adding cheese. Ladle into warm soup bowls; garnish with reserved florets.

*If you don't have homemade stock, use two 10-oz (284 mL) cans of chicken broth and 2 cans of water.

FALL MAIN DISHES

Apple Sauerkraut Pork Chops

MAKES 4 SERVINGS.

Bake potatoes and squash in the oven along with this easy skillet supper. Set out some pickled beets, too, and you have a simple, but perfect fall meal.

4	pork chops	4
2 tsp	vegetable oil	10 mL
1/2 tsp	dried thyme	2 mL
	Salt and pepper	
1	pkg (19 oz/540 mL) sauerkraut (or about 1 lb/ 500 g)	1
1	red apple, unpeeled and chopped	1
1/2 tsp	caraway seeds	2 mL
1	bay leaf	1
	Red apple slices	
	Chopped fresh parsley	

1. Trim off any fat from the pork. In a large ovenproof skillet, heat oil over medium heat; brown pork for 2 minutes on each side. Sprinkle with thyme; season with salt and pepper to taste.

2. Meanwhile, drain sauerkraut; rinse under cold water and drain well. In a bowl, combine sauerkraut, chopped apple, caraway seeds, bay leaf and 1/4 tsp (1 mL) pepper; spoon around and under chops in the skillet.

3. Bake, uncovered, in a 350°F (180°C) oven for about 45 minutes or until chops are tender. Discard the bay leaf. Garnish with apple slices and parsley.

TIP

Sauerkraut varies in quality, and I will never find any in a store to match my mother's. However, the "homemade" version available at markets or delis, often in plastic bags, is both tastier and milder than most canned products. All sauerkraut needs to be lightly rinsed to remove excess salt.

Currant-Glazed Pork Roast

MAKES ABOUT 8 SERVINGS.

A good choice for an elegant company meal, this succulent roast pork is good with either scalloped or mashed potatoes. If you wish, substitute stock or cooking water from any vegetables for the water called for in making the sauce.

1 tsp	dry mustard 5 mL
1 tsp	crumbled dried basil 5 mL
1/4 tsp	pepper 1 mL
2 tbsp	EACH dry sherry and soy sauce 25 mL
2	cloves garlic, crushed 2
1	boneless double pork loin, tied (about 4 lb/2 kg) 1
1/4 cup	red currant jelly 50 mL
1 tbsp	cornstarch 15 mL

1. In a small bowl, stir together the mustard, basil and pepper, crushing the basil finely with the back of a spoon. Stir in half of the sherry and half of the soy sauce to make a runny paste. Add garlic.

2. Place pork on a rack in a shallow roasting pan; spread paste all over the roast. Cover and refrigerate for at least 2 hours and up to 6 hours. Remove from the refrigerator 30 minutes before cooking.

3. Roast pork, uncovered, in a 325°F (160°C) oven for about 2 hours or until a meat thermometer registers 160°F (70°C).

4. Meanwhile, in a small saucepan, stir together the remaining sherry, remaining soy sauce and the red currant jelly; heat over medium heat, stirring, until the jelly melts. Spoon some of the mixture over the meat 2 or 3 times during the last 30 minutes of roasting.

5. Remove pork to a carving board; cover loosely with foil and let stand for 10 minutes before carving.

6. Remove and discard excess fat from the pan; stir in about 1 cup (250 mL) water and bring to a boil, stirring to scrape up any brown bits from the bottom of the pan. Stir cornstarch with 2 tbsp (25 mL) of cold water; add to the pan, stirring constantly, and cook over medium heat until sauce is smooth and thickened. Pass in a heated sauceboat with the pork.

Pork and Apple Stew

MAKES 6 TO 8 SERVINGS.

The combination of apples, pork and rosemary is a memorable one in this hearty stew. Serve it with creamy mashed potatoes or crusty bread and a cabbage salad.

2-1/4 lb	boneless pork shoulder or butt	1 kg
1/4 cup	all-purpose flour	50 mL
1 tsp	salt	5 mL
1/4 tsp	pepper	1 mL
1/4 cup	vegetable oil (approx.)	50 mL
2	onions, sliced	2
4	cloves garlic, minced	4
2 cups	apple cider or juice	500 mL
1 tbsp	EACH Dijon mustard and cider vinegar	15 mL
1-1/2 tsp	crumbled dried rosemary	7 mL
5	large apples, peeled and thickly sliced	5
2 cups	diced (1/2 inch/1 cm) rutabaga	500 mL
1	large tomato	1
1/4 cup	chopped fresh parsley	50 mL

1. Cut pork into 1-inch (2.5 cm) cubes. In a bag, combine flour, half of the salt and the pepper; add pork, in batches, and shake to coat. Set aside.

2. In a large Dutch oven or flameproof casserole, heat 1 tbsp (15 mL) of the oil over low heat; cook onions and garlic for 5 minutes. Remove with a slotted spoon to a large bowl.

3. Add pork to the pan in batches and brown over medium-high heat, adding more oil as needed. Remove with a slotted spoon and add to bowl with onions.

4. Pour cider into the pan; bring to a boil, scraping up any brown bits from the bottom of the pan. Return pork and onion mixture with any juices to the pan. Stir in remaining salt, mustard, vinegar, rosemary, three of the apples and the rutabaga. Cover tightly and bring to a boil. Transfer to a 350°F (180°C) oven; bake, stirring occasionally, for about 1-1/2 hours or until pork is tender. (Stew can be prepared to this point, cooled, covered and refrigerated for up to 1 day; reheat gently before continuing.)

5. Meanwhile, in a small, heavy skillet, heat 2 tsp (10 mL) oil over medium-high heat; sauté remaining two apples until tender-crisp, about 3 minutes. Peel, seed and chop tomato. Stir into cooked stew along with sautéed apple and parsley to serve.

Tex-Mex Potato-Beef Casserole

MAKES 4 SERVINGS.

This easy, one-dish supper is one my son, Allen, and his friend, Cherrie, make regularly. Serve it with sour cream if you wish. It's great with a romaine-lettuce and orange salad as well.

1 lb	lean ground beef	500 g
1	onion, chopped	1
2	cloves garlic, minced	2
1 tbsp	chili powder	15 mL
1/4 tsp	EACH ground cumin, hot pepper flakes, dried oregano and salt	1 mL
1	can (19 oz/540 mL) stewed tomatoes	1
1	sweet green pepper, diced	1
1/3 cup	pitted black olives, coarsely chopped	75 mL
4	potatoes (unpeeled), thinly sliced	4
1 tbsp	all-purpose flour	15 mL
1 tbsp	vegetable oil	15 mL
1 cup	shredded Cheddar cheese	250 mL
2	green onions, sliced	2

1. In a large skillet, cook beef, onion and garlic over medium heat, breaking up meat with a spoon, for about 5 minutes or until meat is no longer pink. Drain off any fat.

2. Stir in chili powder, cumin, hot pepper flakes, oregano and salt; cook, stirring, for 1 minute. Stir in tomatoes; cook, stirring occasionally, for about 15 minutes or until mixture is thickened slightly. Stir in green pepper and olives.

3. Meanwhile, in a shallow 8-cup (2 L) baking dish, toss potatoes with flour and oil; spread evenly in the dish. Spoon meat mixture over top. Bake, covered, in a 350°F (180°C) oven for about 45 minutes or until potatoes are tender when the tip of a sharp knife is inserted down through the meat.

4. Sprinkle with cheese; bake, uncovered, for 5 minutes or until cheese is melted. Sprinkle green onions around the edge and serve.

Three-Cheese Meat Loaf

MAKES 4 GENEROUS SERVINGS.

Many people have told me that this is their favourite meat loaf because it's moist and flavourful. Bake some potatoes and squash alongside and toss a spinach salad. Any leftovers are delicious in sandwiches.

	Dry bread crumbs
2	slices Italian-style bread, cubed 2
1/3 cup	milk 75 mL
1 lb	ground beef 500 g
1	small onion, chopped 1
1	sweet green pepper, chopped 1
1/4 cup	freshly grated Parmesan cheese 50 mL
2 tbsp	tomato paste or ketchup 25 mL
1 tbsp	chopped fresh parsley 15 mL
1	egg, lightly beaten 1
3/4 tsp	salt 4 mL
1/4 tsp	EACH pepper and crumbled dried sage 1 mL
1/2 cup	EACH diced mozzarella and Swiss cheese 125 mL

1. Grease a 9 x 5-inch (2 L) loaf pan and sprinkle lightly with bread crumbs.
2. In a large bowl, soak the bread cubes in milk for 5 minutes; with your hands, squeeze out excess moisture. Break up beef with a spoon and add to the bowl; add onion, green pepper, Parmesan cheese, tomato paste, parsley, egg, salt, pepper and sage; with moistened hands, mix together.
3. Press one-third of the meat mixture evenly into prepared pan; sprinkle mozzarella evenly on top. Press another one-third of the meat mixture on top; sprinkle with Swiss cheese. Cover with remaining meat mixture.
4. Bake in a 350°F (180°C) oven for about 1 hour or until a meat thermometer registers 170°F (75°C). Slice to serve.

Veal Shanks Braised with Garlic and Orange

MAKES 4 SERVINGS.

The traditional braising treatment for veal shanks is Osso Buco, a dish that's topped off with garlic, lemon and parsley to serve. Here, I opted for an orange and parsley topping and included lots of garlic that becomes sweet and soft with long cooking right in the sauce. Enjoy with crusty bread, creamy mashed potatoes or polenta along with a green salad.

1/4 cup	olive oil (approx.)	50 mL
2	onions, chopped	2
2	leeks, thickly sliced	2
4	carrots, cut in 1-inch (2.5 cm) pieces	4
1 tbsp	EACH chopped fresh thyme and rosemary (or 1 tsp/5 mL dried)	15 mL
2	bay leaves	2
1 lb	mushrooms, sliced	500 g
4	centre-cut veal shanks (1 inch/2.5 cm thick)	4
1/4 cup	all-purpose flour	50 mL
	Salt and pepper	
1 cup	dry red wine (preferably Pinot Noir)	250 mL
2 cups	beef stock	500 mL
2 tbsp	fresh orange juice	25 mL
12	cloves garlic, peeled	12
1 cup	frozen peas, thawed	250 mL
1/3 cup	chopped fresh parsley	75 mL
1/4 cup	minced orange zest	50 mL

1. In a large Dutch oven, heat 2 tbsp (25 mL) of the oil over medium heat; cook onions, leeks, carrots, thyme, rosemary and bay leaves for 10 minutes, stirring often. Add mushrooms; cook for 4 minutes, stirring occasionally. With a slotted spoon, remove to a bowl.

2. Coat shanks with flour and salt and pepper to taste, shaking off excess. Heat 1 tbsp (15 mL) of the remaining oil in the pan over medium-high heat; brown shanks well, in batches if necessary, adding more oil as needed. Remove to bowl.

3. Sprinkle any remaining flour into the pan; cook, stirring, for 1 minute. Gradually stir in wine; bring to a boil, scraping up any brown bits from the bottom of the pan. Add stock, orange juice and garlic; bring to a boil.

4. Return veal and vegetables with any juices to the pan. Cover and bake in a 350°F (180°C) oven for about 1-1/4 hours or until veal is tender. Discard bay leaves. (Shanks can be cooled, covered and refrigerated for up to 1 day. Reheat gently, stirring often.)

5. Mash some of the garlic into the sauce. Add peas and heat through on top of the stove. Taste and adjust seasoning. Combine parsley and orange zest.

6. Serve with sauce spooned over each shank, sprinkled with parsley mixture.

TIP

With a vegetable peeler, remove only the dark orange part of the rind from 1 large orange. Finely chop with a sharp knife.

Braised Veal with Caramelized Vegetables

MAKES 12 SERVINGS.

Stews often star in my company meals because they are so homey and delicious and, of course, completely make-ahead. Tender pieces of veal and vegetables (kept crisp by doing them separately) combine in a velvety sauce. Serve with lots of crusty bread and a crisp green salad.

6 lb	boneless veal, cut into 1-inch (2.5 cm) cubes 2.7 kg
3/4 cup	all-purpose flour 175 mL
1/2 cup	olive oil (approx.) 125 mL
1 tsp	paprika 5 mL
1/3 cup	minced shallots 75 mL
2 cups	dry vermouth 500 mL
2-1/2 cups	chicken stock 625 mL
2 tsp	crumbled dried sage 10 mL
1/2 tsp	EACH crumbled dried rosemary and thyme 2 mL
	Salt and pepper
1/4 cup	butter 50 mL
2 tbsp	brown sugar 25 mL
2	pkg (each 10 oz/283 g) pearl onions, peeled 2
1-1/2 lb	mini-carrots 750 g
6	small white turnips, peeled and cut into wedges 6
4	parsnips, peeled and cut into 1-inch (2.5 cm) pieces 4
	Sprigs of fresh rosemary, sage or thyme

1. Dry veal and dredge lightly with flour. In a large, heavy casserole or Dutch oven, heat half the oil over medium-high heat; cook veal, in batches and adding oil only if necessary, until browned on all sides. Remove with a slotted spoon to a plate; sprinkle with paprika.

2. In the same casserole, heat more oil if necessary; cook shallots for 3 minutes over medium heat. Stir in vermouth and 1-1/2 cups (375 mL) of the stock; bring to a boil, scraping up any brown bits in the bottom of the pan.

3. Return veal and any juices to the pan; add sage, rosemary, thyme, and salt and pepper to taste. Cover, reduce heat and simmer over low heat for about 1-1/4 hours or until veal is tender, stirring occasionally.

4. Meanwhile, in a deep skillet or shallow stovetop casserole, melt butter and sugar; add onions, carrots, turnips and parsnips, stirring to coat. Sprinkle with salt and pepper to taste; add remaining stock and bring to a boil.

5. Bake, uncovered, stirring occasionally, in a 350°F (180°C) oven for 45 minutes or until vegetables are tender. Stir into cooked veal. (Stew can be cooled, covered and refrigerated for up to 2 days; reheat slowly on the stovetop, stirring often, or place in a 350°F/180°C oven, covered, for about 30 minutes or until heated through.)

6. Serve in heated, shallow soup or pasta bowls, garnished with sprigs of fresh herb.

Hint

Since dry vermouth keeps right on the shelf for a long time without deteriorating, it is handy to use when a recipe calls for dry white wine. It is also less acidic than most wines.

TIP

The secret of tender meat in stew is to simmer it over very low heat.

Lamb Racks Provençale

MAKES 8 SERVINGS.

Seek out oven-ready lamb racks or have your butcher "French" the ends of the bones for this easy and flavourful treatment of a very elegant cut of meat. However, you can easily French the racks yourself by scraping the rib bones clean to about 1 inch (2.5 cm) down from the tips.

4	lamb racks (7 to 8 ribs each)	4
5	cloves garlic	5
1/2 cup	loosely packed parsley sprigs 125 mL	
2 tbsp	olive oil	25 mL
2 tbsp	anchovy paste	25 mL
1 tbsp	red wine vinegar	15 mL
2 tsp	crushed dried rosemary 10 mL	
1 tsp	coarsely ground pepper	5 mL
1/2 tsp	dried thyme	2 mL

1. Dry lamb racks well and score the outside layer of fat diagonally to make small diamonds. In a blender or food processor, process garlic, parsley, oil, anchovy paste, vinegar, rosemary, pepper and thyme until smooth; rub all over racks. Marinate, covered, in the refrigerator for up to 4 hours. Remove from the refrigerator 30 minutes before roasting.

2. Place racks, bone side down, in a shallow roasting pan. Roast in a 450°F (230°C) oven for 10 minutes. Lower the temperature to 350°F (180°C); roast for 20 to 30 minutes longer or until a thermometer registers 140°F (60°C). Let stand, loosely covered with foil, for 10 minutes before carving between the ribs to serve.

Honey-Curried Chicken and Apricots

MAKES 4 SERVINGS.

Full of flavour and quick to put together, this casserole found itself on more than one list of favourites. Serve with rice or baked potatoes and broccoli.

2	onions, thinly sliced	2
1 cup	dried apricot halves	250 mL
4	chicken breast halves, bone in	4
	Salt and pepper	
1/4 cup	liquid honey	50 mL
2 tbsp	fresh lemon juice	25 mL
1 tbsp	curry powder	15 mL
1 tsp	ground cumin	5 mL

1. Arrange onions and apricots in a greased, shallow baking dish just big enough to hold the breasts in a single layer. Arrange chicken, skin side up, on top. Sprinkle with salt and pepper.
2. Combine honey, lemon juice, curry powder and cumin; drizzle over the chicken. (Recipe can be prepared to this point, covered and refrigerated for up to 8 hours; let stand at room temperature for 30 minutes before baking.)
3. Bake, uncovered, in a 375°F (190°C) oven for about 45 minutes or until the chicken is no longer pink inside, basting once or twice.

Oven-Fried Chicken Legs

MAKES 4 SERVINGS.

This is my favourite everyday way to cook chicken. Sometimes I add a few herbs (like Italian seasoning) to the flour mixture and almost always pop potatoes (and maybe some squash ... while I have the oven on) into the oven to bake alongside. Applesauce is good with the crisp-skinned legs and perhaps some green beans or broccoli. If you don't have cornmeal in the house, use all-purpose flour.

1/4 cup	EACH all-purpose flour and cornmeal	50 mL
2 tsp	paprika	10 mL
1/4 tsp	EACH salt and pepper	1 mL
1/2 cup	milk	125 mL
4	chicken legs	4
2 tbsp	fresh lemon juice	25 mL

1. In a plastic bag, combine flour, cornmeal, paprika, salt and pepper. Pour milk into a shallow dish. Shake chicken in flour mixture, dip into milk and then shake again in flour mixture.
2. Place chicken, skin side down, in a greased 13 x 9-inch (3.5 L) baking dish; drizzle with lemon juice. Bake in a 375°F (190°C) oven for 20 minutes; turn chicken over. Bake for 20 to 25 minutes longer or until juices run clear when chicken is pierced and chicken is no longer pink inside.

Variation

For **Sesame Oven-Fried Chicken Legs,** substitute sesame seeds for the cornmeal.

Glazed Roast Duck with Mango-Pecan Stuffing

MAKES 4 SERVINGS.

This recipe yields enough stuffing for two ducks if there are eight people at your table. Pricking the duck's skin and roasting it at a high temperature before stuffing it will eliminate much of the fat.

1	duck (5 lb/2.2 kg)	1
	Salt and pepper	
1/2 tsp	dried rosemary	2 mL
2 tbsp	butter	25 mL
1/2 cup	EACH diced celery and chopped onion	125 mL
2/3 cup	brown rice	150 mL
1/2 tsp	dried thyme	2 mL
2-1/2 cups	chicken stock	625 mL
1/4 cup	chopped fresh parsley	50 mL
1	mango (about 1 lb/500 g), peeled and diced	1
1/2 cup	coarsely chopped pecans	125 mL
1 cup	boiling water	250 mL
3 tbsp	mango chutney, finely chopped	45 mL
2 tbsp	white rum	25 mL
1/2 cup	dry white wine	125 mL
1 tbsp	cornstarch	15 mL

1. Remove any giblets from the duck, reserving them for another use, such as stock. Pat duck dry inside and out with paper towels. Trim off any excess fat and pierce skin all over with a needle. Rub inside and out with 1/2 tsp (2 mL) salt, 1/4 tsp (1 mL) pepper and the rosemary; set aside.

2. To make stuffing, melt butter in a large skillet over medium heat. Add the celery and onion; cook, stirring, for about 5 minutes or until softened. Stir in rice and thyme, then reduce heat to low and cook, stirring, for 5 to 10 minutes, until rice is coated with butter. Stir in 2 cups (500 mL) stock and the parsley; then bring to a boil over high heat. Reduce the heat to medium-low, cover and simmer for 35 to 40 minutes or until rice is tender. Remove from the heat. Stir in mango and pecans, then season generously with salt and pepper. Let cool completely. (Stuffing can be prepared up to 1 day ahead, covered and refrigerated.)

3. Place duck, breast side up, on a rack in a shallow roasting pan. Pour boiling water over duck, then roast, uncovered, in a 450°F (230°C) oven for 30 to 40 minutes or until the skin is well browned. Remove duck from the oven and reduce temperature to 325°F (160°C).

4. Pour off any fat from the roasting pan and carefully stuff duck loosely with cooled rice mixture. Spoon any leftover stuffing into a shallow, buttered baking dish and set aside. (Thirty minutes before the duck is ready, drizzle the dish of reserved stuffing with some of the drippings from the roasting pan, cover with foil or a lid and place in the oven alongside the duck, until heated through and lightly browned on the top.) Truss duck and tie securely. Return duck to the oven and roast for 30 minutes.

continued

5. Meanwhile, stir together the mango chutney and rum in a small bowl. Brush half of this mixture over the duck and roast for 15 minutes. Brush with the remaining mango chutney mixture and roast 15 minutes more or until juices run clear when a thigh is pierced with a skewer, and a meat thermometer inserted in the thigh registers 185°F (85°C). (The duck takes about 1-1/2 hours total in roasting time.) Transfer duck to a warm platter, tent loosely with foil and let stand in a warm place while you make the gravy.

6. Skim off as much fat as possible from the drippings and place the pan over a burner. Stir in remaining stock and wine, then bring to a boil over high heat, stirring to scrape up any brown bits from the bottom of the pan. Stir together the cornstarch and 2 tbsp (25 mL) cold water in a small bowl. Add the mixture to the roasting pan and cook, stirring, for 2 to 3 minutes, until the gravy is smooth and thickened.

7. Carve the duck; pass the gravy in a heated sauceboat with the duck.

Chili-Crusted Salmon Steaks

MAKES 4 SERVINGS.

This simple, but delicious recipe appears in an article on spicy food that Elizabeth Baird and I wrote together for *Canadian Living*. When Elizabeth reminded me how good it was, I made it again and now I understand why it is on her list of favourites.

These salmon steaks are made with chipotle peppers, which are smoked jalapeño peppers. You will find them preserved in rich, mahogany-red adobo sauce, which is just about as smoky and fiery as the peppers themselves.

4	salmon steaks (1-1/2 lb/750 g total) 4
1 tsp	vegetable oil 5 mL
Pinch	EACH salt and pepper Pinch
3 tbsp	light mayonnaise 45 mL
1 tbsp	fresh lime or lemon juice 15 mL
1	chipotle pepper, minced 1
2 tsp	adobo sauce 10 mL

1. Brush one side of each salmon steak with oil; sprinkle with salt and pepper. Turn over. In a small bowl, stir together the mayonnaise, lime juice, chipotle pepper and adobo sauce; spread evenly over top of the steaks. Let stand at room temperature for 30 minutes. (Steaks can be transferred to a plate, covered and refrigerated for up to 2 hours.)
2. Place steaks, oil side down, on a broiler rack or foil-lined baking sheet; broil about 6 inches (15 cm) from the element for about 10 minutes, or until golden and bubbly and the fish flakes easily with a fork.

Hint

Because canned chipotle peppers come in a standard-size can containing more than you need, you can freeze those left. Pour them and the sauce into a freezer bag, gently pressing out the air. Manipulate the bag to separate the peppers so that it will be easy to break off a section of pepper and sauce without thawing the whole package.

Baked Stuffed Whitefish

MAKES 4 SERVINGS.

When we lived in Owen Sound, Ontario, stuffed whitefish was a regular treat. The fish were plucked out of the cold waters of Georgian Bay and sold at the weekly Saturday farmers' market. Baked whole, whitefish is delicious with an old-fashioned bread stuffing—a regular menu item with my son, Allen, and his friend Cherrie.

1/4 cup	butter 50 mL
1-1/2 cups	chopped mushrooms 375 mL
2	stalks celery, diced 2
1	onion, chopped 1
2 tbsp	chopped fresh parsley 25 mL
1 tbsp	chopped fresh sage (or 1 tsp/5 mL crumbled dried sage) 15 mL
1/2 tsp	EACH salt and pepper (approx.) 2 mL
1/2 tsp	ground ginger 2 mL
2 cups	coarse, fresh bread crumbs 500 mL
1	whitefish, cleaned (about 2-1/2 lb/1.25 kg) 1
1 tbsp	vegetable oil 15 mL

1. In a large skillet, melt butter over medium heat; cook mushrooms, celery and onion, stirring occasionally, for 5 minutes or until softened.

2. Stir in parsley, sage, salt, pepper and ginger; cook for 2 minutes. Remove from the heat; stir in bread crumbs.

3. Pat fish cavity dry; sprinkle cavity with salt and pepper to taste. Fill cavity loosely with stuffing; fasten with skewers. Place fish on a greased, rimmed baking sheet; brush with oil.

4. Bake in a 450°F (230°C) oven for 10 minutes per inch (2.5 cm) of thickness, about 25 minutes, or until flesh is opaque and flakes easily when tested with a fork.

Two-Cheese Baked Penne with Roasted Vegetables

MAKES 8 SERVINGS.

High on everyone's list of favourites, this pretty make-ahead casserole is just the kind I like to serve to company. A crisp green salad goes well with the smooth texture of the two deliciously melted cheeses. Use a homemade sauce or a good commercial one.

2	sweet red or yellow peppers, sliced 2
1/2 lb	mushrooms, quartered 250 g
2	small zucchini, sliced 2
2	small red onions, cubed 2
4	cloves garlic, minced 4
1/4 cup	olive oil 50 mL
	Salt and pepper
1/2 cup	chopped fresh parsley 125 mL
2 tbsp	chopped fresh basil (or 2 tsp/10 mL dried basil) 25 mL
2 tsp	chopped fresh rosemary (or 1/2 tsp/2 mL crumbled dried rosemary) 10 mL
5 cups	penne pasta with ridges (1 lb/500 g) 1.25 L
3-1/2 cups	meatless spaghetti sauce 875 mL
1 lb	provolone cheese, shredded 500 g
1 cup	Asiago or Parmesan cheese, freshly grated 250 mL

1. In a large, shallow pan, toss peppers, mushrooms, zucchini, onions, and garlic with oil; spread out and roast in a 450°F (230°C) oven for about 25 minutes or until softened, stirring once or twice. Season to taste with salt and pepper and stir in 1/3 cup (75 mL) of the parsley and the basil and rosemary.

2. Meanwhile, cook the pasta in a large pot of boiling, salted water just until al dente, about 8 minutes. Pour in 2 cups (500 mL) of cold water, drain well and cool. Gently combine with spaghetti sauce, vegetables, provolone and half the Asiago. Transfer to a greased, shallow 3-quart (3 L) baking dish. Sprinkle with remaining Asiago and parsley. (Pasta can be prepared ahead to this point, covered and refrigerated for up to 1 day, or frozen for up to 2 months. Bring to room temperature before reheating, thawing frozen casserole in the refrigerator.)

3. Bake, covered, in a 375°F (190°C) oven for 30 minutes. Uncover and bake 10 to 15 minutes longer or until bubbly.

Curried Harvest Vegetables with Lentils

MAKES 4 TO 6 SERVINGS.

I included many vegetarian dishes in my *New Casseroles and Other One-Dish Meals* cookbook, and this is one of my favourites. Serve it on hot rice (preferably basmati), accompanied with your favourite chutney (like my Hot and Spicy Rhubarb Chutney on page 29).

1 cup	dried red lentils	250 mL
2 tbsp	vegetable oil	25 mL
2	onions, chopped	2
2	cloves garlic, minced	2
1 tbsp	EACH ground cumin and ground coriander	15 mL
2 tsp	turmeric	10 mL
1/2 tsp	pepper	2 mL
1/4 tsp	hot pepper flakes	1 mL
Pinch	EACH cinnamon and cloves	Pinch
2-1/2 cups	chicken or vegetable stock	625 mL
2 tbsp	fresh lemon juice	25 mL
2	carrots	2
1	small winter squash	1
1	small cauliflower	1
1	sweet red pepper	1
1/2 lb	green beans	250 g
	Salt	
1/2 cup	peanuts	125 mL

1. Sort and rinse lentils; set aside.
2. In a large saucepan, heat oil over medium heat; cook onions and garlic for about 3 minutes or until softened. Stir in cumin, coriander, turmeric, pepper, hot pepper flakes, cinnamon and cloves; cook, stirring, for 30 seconds. Stir in lentils to coat well. Stir in stock and lemon juice; bring to a boil. Reduce heat, cover and simmer for 5 minutes.
3. Meanwhile, cut carrots into 1-inch (2.5 cm) thick slices. Peel squash and cut into 1-inch (2.5 cm) cubes. Cut cauliflower into small florets. Cut red pepper into thin strips. Trim beans and cut in half.
4. Stir carrots, squash and cauliflower into lentil mixture; bring to a boil. Reduce heat, cover and simmer for 5 minutes. Stir in red pepper and beans; simmer for 5 minutes. Stir in salt to taste and peanuts. Cook, uncovered, for 5 minutes or until vegetables are tender and lentils have formed a thick sauce. Taste and adjust seasoning. (Curry can be made up to 1 day ahead if you undercook the vegetables slightly. It will thicken if made ahead; thin with more stock or water, if desired, and reheat gently, stirring often.)

Hint

Choose a squash that's relatively easy to peel such as butternut. Pepper squash, with all its ridges, is more difficult.

Roasted Cherry Tomato Clafoutis

MAKES 4 SERVINGS.

I developed this recipe for my casserole cookbook and subsequently made it for a couple of cooking demonstrations. The audience could not believe how simple and good it was. Traditional clafoutis (a kind of cake-like custard) is made with black cherries or other fruit and is served as a dessert. I've added cheese and chosen cherry tomatoes as a savory version that would be just right for a company breakfast, perhaps with some back bacon and interesting bread.

2 cups	cherry tomatoes (1 lb/500 g) 500 mL
2 tbsp	olive oil 25 mL
1 tbsp	chopped fresh thyme (or 1 tsp/5 mL dried) 15 mL
2	cloves garlic, crushed 2
2 tsp	granulated sugar 10 mL
	Salt and pepper
1 cup	light cream 250 mL
3	eggs 3
2 tbsp	all-purpose flour 25 mL
1/2 lb	mozzarella cheese, shredded (about 2 cups/500 mL) 250 g

1. Remove stems from tomatoes. Arrange in a single layer in a shallow 6-cup (1.5 L) baking dish. Drizzle with oil; sprinkle with thyme, garlic, sugar, 1/2 tsp (2 mL) salt and 1/4 tsp (1 mL) pepper. Roast in a 400°F (200°C) oven for 10 to 15 minutes or until the skin shrivels slightly.

2. In a blender, blend cream, eggs and flour until smooth; pour over tomatoes. Sprinkle with cheese. Reduce temperature to 350°F (180°C); bake for about 25 minutes or until puffed and golden. Serve immediately.

FALL SIDES AND SALADS

IN THE MENUS ...

Roasted Fall Vegetables

MAKES 6 SERVINGS.

Make this easy oven dish when the markets are overflowing with a myriad of colourful vegetables. It's perfect to pop into the oven alongside a chicken or a capon.

8	small potatoes, scrubbed and quartered 8
2	onions, cut into wedges 2
4	cloves garlic, crushed 4
1/4 cup	olive oil 50 mL
1/4 tsp	dried thyme 1 mL
1/4 tsp	crumbled dried rosemary 1 mL
1	medium butternut squash, peeled and cut into 3/4-inch (2 cm) cubes 1
1	sweet red pepper, cut into 3/4-inch (2 cm) chunks 1
	Chopped fresh parsley

1. In a roasting pan, toss potatoes, onions and garlic with 3 tbsp (45 mL) of the oil. Sprinkle with thyme and rosemary. Roast, uncovered, in 375°F (190°C) oven for 35 minutes, gently turning once with a metal spatula. Toss squash and red pepper with remaining oil; add to the pan and continue roasting for 10 to 20 minutes longer, or until all vegetables are tender. Sprinkle with parsley to serve.

Purée of Fall Roots

MAKES 4 TO 6 SERVINGS.

This simple and creamy purée is delicious with roast meat or poultry. I like parsnips that have been left all winter in the ground and then dug up early in the spring, but some of my favourite vendors at the local farmers' market do dig them up in the fall.

4	carrots	4
3	parsnips	3
Half	small rutabaga	Half
2 cups	water	500 mL
1 tbsp	brown sugar	15 mL
	Salt and pepper	
1/4 cup	butter	50 mL
2 tsp	fresh lemon juice	10 mL
	Buttered bread crumbs or chopped nuts (optional)	

1. Peel vegetables and cut into 1-inch (2.5 cm) pieces or lengths. In a large, deep skillet, combine vegetables with water, brown sugar, and salt and pepper to taste. Bring to a boil; reduce heat to medium and cook, uncovered, until the water has evaporated and vegetables are very tender, for 20 to 30 minutes, stirring occasionally.

2. Cool slightly; then purée in a food processor or blender with butter and lemon juice. Taste and adjust seasoning. Purée can be served immediately or made a couple of hours ahead and reheated in the top of a double boiler over simmering water or in a microwave oven. Or, place in a greased baking dish, sprinkle with bread crumbs or chopped nuts and reheat, uncovered, in a 350°F (180°C) oven for 20 to 30 minutes or until bubbly.

Rum Baked Squash

MAKES 4 SERVINGS.

This and the variation below are some of my favourite ways to roast squash. It's great with roast pork, ham or poultry.

2	acorn squash 2
	Salt and pepper
4 tbsp	butter 50 mL
4 tsp	brown sugar 20 mL
4 tsp	dark rum 20 mL
	Freshly grated nutmeg
1 tbsp	slivered candied ginger 15 mL
4 tbsp	coarsely chopped walnuts 50 mL

1. Cut squash in half lengthwise; scoop out the seeds and place squash halves, cut side up, in a shallow baking dish. Sprinkle with salt and pepper. Place 1 tbsp (15 mL) butter in each half. Sprinkle the inside of each half with 1 tsp (5 mL) EACH brown sugar and rum and a pinch of nutmeg. Distribute the candied ginger and walnuts among the halves.

2. Add a film of water to the bottom of the dish; cover lightly with foil and bake in a 350°F (180°C) oven for 45 to 55 minutes or until the squash is tender.

Variation

To prepare **Maple Baked Squash**, omit the brown sugar, rum, nutmeg, ginger and walnuts. Sprinkle squash with salt and pepper, cover and bake 30 minutes. Place the butter, 1 tsp (5 mL) maple syrup and a pinch of ground cloves in each half. Bake, uncovered, for 15 to 20 minutes or until tender.

Creamy Garlic-Thyme Custards

MAKES 4 SERVINGS.

When I developed this recipe for a Christmas 2000 menu I was doing for *Elm Street*, my editor, Julia Aitken, added these words to my lead: "These rich, velvety custards are the best thing to come out of a ramekin in years." High praise indeed. She also said they were the ultimate comfort food and she could sit down to eat all four without missing a spoonful.

Make them in pretty little ramekins (small, round dishes for baking and serving) that you can set on or beside each dinner plate.

2	heads garlic 2
2 tsp	olive oil 10 mL
2 tsp	chopped fresh thyme (or 1/2 tsp/2 mL dried thyme) 10 mL
	Salt and pepper
1 cup	whipping cream (35%) 250 mL
3	eggs 3
1/4 tsp	cayenne pepper 1 mL
4	small, fresh thyme sprigs (if available) 4

1. Cut the top off each garlic head to expose garlic and remove any loose, outer parchment skin. Place on a large piece of foil. Drizzle with olive oil and sprinkle with thyme, salt and pepper. Enclose in foil and roast in a 400°F (200°C) oven for about 45 minutes or until soft when package is squeezed. Unwrap and cool. (Garlic can be roasted up to 1 day ahead, covered and refrigerated.)

2. In a blender, combine whipping cream, eggs, 1/2 tsp (2 mL) salt, 1/4 tsp (1 mL) black pepper and cayenne. Turn garlic upside down and gently squeeze out flesh into blender. Blend mixture until smooth.

3. Pour into four buttered 6-oz (175 mL) ramekins or custard cups. (Unbaked custards can be covered and refrigerated for up to 4 hours. Stir each gently before baking.) Place in a shallow pan just big enough to hold them and pour boiling water into the pan to come halfway up the sides of the ramekins. Bake in a 275°F (140°C) oven for about 1 hour to 1 hour and 10 minutes, or until centres of custards are firm to the touch. (Custards can sit at room temperature for up to 2 hours before serving. To reheat, place ramekins on a rack in a large skillet containing about 1 inch (2.5 cm) of simmering water. Cover skillet, then simmer for about 10 minutes or until custards are hot throughout.)

4. Serve at once, garnished with fresh thyme sprigs if available.

Three-Ingredient Creamy Coleslaw

MAKES 6 SERVINGS.

I make this easy salad often to accompany dishes like baked beans (see Maple Baked Beans, page 203) or simply cooked pork chops. Sometimes I make it with four ingredients by adding a shredded carrot.

6 cups	finely shredded green cabbage 1.5 L	
1/2 cup	diced red onion 125 mL	
1/2 cup	diced (unpeeled) English cucumber 125 mL	

1. In a large bowl, toss together cabbage, red onion and cucumber.

DRESSING

2/3 cup	light mayonnaise 150 mL
2 tbsp	cider vinegar 25 mL
4 tsp	granulated or brown sugar 20 mL
1/2 tsp	salt 2 mL
Pinch	paprika Pinch

1. In a small bowl, whisk together mayonnaise, vinegar, sugar, salt and paprika until smooth. Pour dressing over top and toss to coat. Cover and refrigerate for at least 1 hour or up to 4 hours.

Turnip-Apple Slaw

MAKES 8 SERVINGS.

A change from everyday coleslaw, this colourful salad can be made a few hours ahead, covered and refrigerated. White turnips are small cousins of the rutabaga.

4	small, white summer turnips (about 1 lb/500 g total) 4
2	unpeeled red apples, diced 2
2	stalks celery, sliced 2
2/3 cup	sliced green onions (about 4) 150 mL
1/2 cup	light mayonnaise 125 mL
2 tbsp	cider vinegar 25 mL
1 tsp	EACH packed brown sugar and Dijon mustard 5 mL
Pinch	cayenne pepper (or more to taste) Pinch
	Salt and pepper
	Lettuce and celery leaves

1. Peel turnips and coarsely grate. Drain in a sieve to remove any excess liquid. In a large bowl, combine turnips, apples, celery and green onions.
2. Whisk together mayonnaise, vinegar, brown sugar, mustard, cayenne, and salt and pepper to taste. Pour over vegetables and toss to coat well. Spoon into a lettuce-lined bowl and garnish with celery leaves.

Black Bean and Red Pepper Salad

MAKES ABOUT 6 SERVINGS.

Perfect for a buffet or potluck supper, this easy salad will keep for several days in the refrigerator. If you wish to make it even easier, you could use a can of rinsed and drained black beans.

I discovered that although cooking the dried beans in a microwave oven isn't faster than on top of the stove, the beans do have a better texture.

1 cup	dried black beans	250 mL
1/4 cup	olive oil	50 mL
2 tbsp	red wine vinegar	25 mL
1 tsp	salt	5 mL
1/2 tsp	EACH pepper, granulated sugar and ground cumin	2 mL
1	clove garlic, crushed	1
1	sweet red pepper, diced	1
1 cup	Spanish (or other sweet) onion, diced	250 mL
3	stalks celery, sliced	3
1	jalapeño pepper, diced	1
1/3 cup	coarsely chopped fresh coriander or parsley	75 mL

1. Sort and rinse beans. In a saucepan, cover beans with 3 times their volume of cold water; let soak overnight in the refrigerator.
2. Drain beans and place in a 16-cup (4 L) microwaveable casserole; cover with 3-1/2 cups (875 mL) of cold water. Cover and microwave at High for 45 minutes or until tender. (Or, in a large saucepan, cover beans with 3 times their volume of cold water; bring to a boil on top of the stove. Reduce heat and cook, uncovered, for 45 to 60 minutes or until tender.) Drain well.
3. In a small bowl or measuring cup, whisk together oil, vinegar, salt, pepper, sugar, cumin and garlic; pour over beans and toss to coat.
4. In a large bowl, toss together the red pepper, onion, celery and jalapeño pepper; add beans and toss to mix. Gently stir in the coriander. Cover and refrigerate for at least 2 hours for flavours to mingle (and up to 3 days).

FALL DESSERTS

IN THE MENUS ...

Cranberry-Pear Pie
with Pecan Crumble Topping

MAKES 6 SERVINGS.

Cranberries are so delightful that they shouldn't be confined to the role of sauce alone. I buy a huge supply for the freezer after their fall harvest and feature them in everything from cakes, muffins and drinks to breads and pies. Our early settlers called cranberry pies "mock cherry" pies and often made them for Christmas feasting, but such delicious pies make festive eating any time of the year.

Sufficient pastry for a 9-inch (23 cm) shell (see **Pie Pastry,** page 33)

1. Line a deep 9-inch (23 cm) pie plate with pastry. Flute the edges and refrigerate while you prepare the filling.

FILLING

2 cups	cranberries (fresh or frozen, unthawed)	500 mL
3	pears	3
1 tbsp	fresh lemon juice	15 mL
1 cup	granulated sugar	250 mL
2 tbsp	all-purpose flour	25 mL

1. Place cranberries in a large bowl. Peel and thinly slice pears; add to the cranberries. Gently stir in the lemon juice, granulated sugar and flour to combine well. Mound in the pastry shell.

PECAN CRUMBLE TOPPING

1/2 cup	chopped pecans	125 mL
1/2 cup	all-purpose flour	125 mL
1/2 cup	packed brown sugar	125 mL
1/2 cup	butter	125 mL

1. In a large bowl, stir together the pecans, flour and brown sugar. Cut in the butter until the mixture is well blended. Sprinkle evenly over top of the filling. Bake in a 400°F (200°C) oven for 10 minutes. Reduce the heat to 350°F (180°C) and bake about 35 to 40 minutes longer or until cranberries are tender and the topping is golden brown.

Variation

For **Cranberry-Apple Pie with Pecan Crumble Topping,** substitute 3 small or 2 large apples for the pears and proceed as above.

Mocha Pecan Pie

MAKES 8 TO 10 SERVINGS.

This variation on pecan pie, which is not overly sweet, is perfect for company.

6 oz	bittersweet or semisweet chocolate 175 g
1/4 cup	coffee liqueur (one miniature bottle) 50 mL
1 tbsp	instant coffee granules 15 mL
1/2 cup	packed brown sugar 125 mL
1 cup	corn syrup 250 mL
3	eggs, beaten 3
1/4 cup	melted butter 50 mL
2 tsp	vanilla 10 mL
1/4 tsp	salt 1 mL
1 cup	coarsely chopped pecans 250 mL
1	unbaked 9-inch (23 cm) pie shell (see **Pie Pastry,** page 33) 1
1 cup	pecan halves 250 mL
	Ice cream or whipped cream

1. In a 6-cup (1.5 L) heatproof bowl set over simmering water, melt chocolate with coffee liqueur and instant coffee granules. Stir until smooth. Remove from the heat; stir in sugar until dissolved. Stir in corn syrup, eggs, butter, vanilla, salt and chopped pecans.

2. Pour filling into pie shell; arrange pecan halves decoratively on top. Bake in a 350°F (180°C) oven for 45 to 50 minutes or until edges feel set but the centre still jiggles slightly. Let cool on a wire rack before serving. Serve at room temperature with ice cream or whipped cream.

Warm Soft Gingerbread

MAKES 8 SERVINGS.

My husband, Kent, is usually not a dessert-eater, but he loves this old-fashioned cake. When I wrote the recipe for *Homemaker's Magazine,* my editor added this comment to my lead: "This is the best gingerbread you'll ever taste!" Serve it with softly whipped cream flavoured with chopped candied ginger, or top it with warm applesauce. The gingerbread keeps well for several days and can be reheated.

1 cup	butter, softened 250 mL
1/2 cup	packed brown sugar 125 mL
1	egg 1
1 cup	molasses 250 mL
2 tsp	baking soda 10 mL
1 cup	boiling water 250 mL
3 cups	all-purpose flour 750 mL
1 tbsp	ground ginger 15 mL
1/2 tsp	cinnamon 2 mL
1/4 tsp	EACH salt and ground cloves 1 mL

1. In a large bowl, cream together butter and sugar. Beat in egg until light and fluffy. Stir in molasses.
2. In a small bowl, dissolve baking soda in boiling water; set aside. In a medium bowl, sift or stir together flour, ginger, cinnamon, salt and cloves. Add flour mixture to butter mixture alternately with dissolved baking soda mixture, stirring just until blended (do not overmix). Spoon mixture into a greased 9-inch (2.5 L) square cake pan. Bake in a 350°F (180°C) oven for 45 to 55 minutes or until a tester inserted in the centre comes out clean.
3. Serve warm and cut into squares.

Upside-Down Pear Gingerbread

MAKES 8 SERVINGS.

1. Spread an additional 3 tbsp (45 mL) soft butter on the bottom of the pan; sprinkle with 2 tbsp (25 mL) granulated sugar. Arrange 2 large, peeled, cored and sliced pears on top and set aside. Proceed with batter as above and pour it over the pears. Bake as above for 45 to 60 minutes. Cool in the pan for 15 minutes; then invert onto a serving plate. Serve warm and cut into squares.

Oven-Caramelized Pears

MAKES 4 SERVINGS.

I think pears are underrated, so over the years I have written a number of articles on pears and have included them in various menus. This wonderful fruit dessert takes only a few minutes to prepare and can cook while you enjoy your main course. It's best served warm with crisp cookies (like the Pecan Lace Cookies, see page 40) on the side. Use pears that are ripe but firm.

6	pears	6
1/3 cup	granulated sugar	75 mL
1/4 cup	butter, in bits	50 mL
1/2 cup	whipping cream	125 mL
Pinch	EACH nutmeg and ground ginger	Pinch

1. Peel, core and slice pears; arrange them in a well-greased 9-inch (2.5 L) square baking dish. Sprinkle the pears with sugar; dot with butter.

2. Bake, uncovered, in a 500°F (260°C) oven for 30 minutes or until sugar is golden, gently stirring once.

3. Stir together the cream, nutmeg and ginger; pour over the pears. Bake for about 5 minutes or until a light brown syrup has formed.

Cranberry-Pear Compote

MAKES 8 SERVINGS.

If you've ever flown over a cranberry bog during the October harvest, you'll never forget the crimson carpet below. This bright fruit brings lovely colour and lots of bouncy flavour to anything it is combined with. Here, I've teamed it up with fall pears for an easy compote. Or, you could do exactly the same thing with apples, like the Northern Spy, that hold their shape with cooking. On slices of pound cake, with dollops of sweetened whipped cream, either combination makes a delightful fall shortcake.

2 cups	EACH granulated sugar and water 500 mL
1	cinnamon stick 1
8	pears, peeled, cored and each cut into 8 wedges 8
2 cups	fresh or frozen (not thawed) cranberries 500 mL
1/4 cup	fresh lemon juice 50 mL

1. In a medium saucepan, bring sugar, water and cinnamon stick to a boil, stirring until the sugar dissolves. Add pears. Reduce heat to low. Cook, covered, for 5 to 7 minutes, gently turning pears over halfway through cooking time, until pears are tender but not mushy. With a slotted spoon, remove pears to a large serving bowl.

2. Add cranberries to the syrup in the saucepan; bring back to a boil over high heat. Reduce heat to low; cook, covered, for about 4 minutes, until cranberries start to pop. Discard cinnamon stick; stir in lemon juice. Gently stir cranberry mixture into pears. Let cool; refrigerate, covered, for up to 2 days.

Cider-Baked Applesauce

MAKES ABOUT 2 CUPS (500 ML).

I often make this simple, apple-intense sauce when I have a pork roast or chicken in the oven to serve alongside. It's also good as dessert or with yogurt and granola for breakfast (my husband also loves it with toast). Use Empire or McIntosh apples or, if you're lucky enough to find them in an August farmers' market, Yellow Transparents.

5	apples	5
1 tbsp	fresh lemon juice	15 mL
1/4 cup	packed brown sugar	50 mL
Pinch	EACH cinnamon and nutmeg	Pinch
1/4 cup	apple cider or apple juice	50 mL

1. Peel, core and cut apples into eighths; place in an 8-inch (2 L) square baking dish. Toss with lemon juice; sprinkle with brown sugar, cinnamon and nutmeg. Drizzle with cider; stir gently until the sugar dissolves.

2. Cover and bake in a 350°F (180°C) oven for 35 to 45 minutes or until the apples are soft. Mash with a potato masher.

Apple Crisp

MAKES 4 TO 6 SERVINGS.

Fall always evokes the heady fragrance of the freshly picked apples we stored in our fruit cellar on the farm. One of the desserts I remember my mother making was this delicious apple crisp—still a family choice with Cheddar cheese or vanilla ice cream.

8	tart apples (about 2 lb/1 kg)	8
1/2 cup	water	125 mL
1/4 cup	granulated sugar	50 mL
1 tsp	cinnamon	5 mL
1/2 tsp	vanilla	2 mL
Pinch	salt	Pinch
3/4 cup	packed brown sugar	175 mL
3/4 cup	all-purpose flour	175 mL
1/4 tsp	nutmeg	1 mL
1/3 cup	butter	75 mL

1. Peel, core and thinly slice apples. Place in a greased 8-inch (2 L) square baking dish. Stir in water, granulated sugar, 1/2 tsp (2 mL) of the cinnamon, vanilla and salt.

2. In a small bowl, stir together brown sugar, flour, remaining cinnamon and nutmeg. With a pastry blender or two knives, cut in butter until mixture is crumbly; sprinkle over the apple mixture. Bake, uncovered, in a 375°F (190°C) oven for 30 minutes or until the apples are very tender.

Fallen Chocolate Soufflé Cake

MAKES 10 SERVINGS.

This is a great cake for beginners. It's easy to make, uses ingredients you probably have on hand, and looks—and tastes—wonderful. The cake is best served the day it's made.

1-1/4 cups	icing sugar 300 mL
1/2 cup	unsweetened cocoa powder 125 mL
8	eggs, separated 8
1 tsp	vanilla 5 mL
Pinch	EACH cream of tartar and salt Pinch

1. Sift the icing sugar and cocoa together onto a plate; set aside. In a large bowl and using an electric mixer, beat together the egg yolks and vanilla for 5 minutes, until thick and lemon coloured. Reduce the speed to low; blend in sugar mixture. Increase speed to high; beat for about 2 minutes or until mixture is very thick.

2. In a medium bowl and with clean beaters, beat egg whites until foamy. Add cream of tartar and salt; beat until stiff, but not dry, peaks form. Fold one-quarter of the egg whites into the chocolate mixture; fold in the remaining egg whites until no white streaks remain.

3. Pour mixture into a well-greased and floured 9-inch (2.5 L) springform pan; bake in a 325°F (160°C) oven for about 45 minutes or until cake is just set and no longer jiggles when the pan is shaken gently. The top will look dry. (Cake will rise quite high in the pan; so make sure there is no oven rack directly above the cake in the oven.) Gently run the tip of a knife around the inside edge of the pan; let cool completely in the pan on a wire rack. The centre of the cake will fall as it cools, but don't panic—this is normal.

CHOCOLATE CREAM

1 cup	whipping cream 250 mL
1/4 cup	EACH icing sugar and unsweetened cocoa powder 50 mL
1/2 tsp	vanilla 2 mL
1 oz	good-quality semisweet chocolate 25 g

1. In a medium bowl, whisk together cream, sugar, cocoa and vanilla; refrigerate, covered, for at least 30 minutes. Using an electric mixer, beat the cream mixture until soft peaks form.

2. Just before serving, spread chocolate cream into the fallen centre of the cake. Using a vegetable peeler, shave chocolate over the cream.

Anne's Famous Chocolate Chip Cookies

MAKES ABOUT 4 DOZEN.

When my daughter, Anne's, list of favourites arrived, this recipe was, of course, on it with the message, "I can't leave these out!" I discovered that these cookies were also on my son's list. When I included them in my *Comfortable Kitchen Cookbook,* I explained that they are famous because everyone knows how good they are, and Anne, as a young child, could make them in a flash. I have no idea where she got the recipe. Anne's copy is printed in a child's hand with questionable spelling, big chocolate chips drawn on the border, a message at the top saying "very good (Yum)" and a big note at the bottom—"Check in oven before turning on" (this last note because of my habit of drying my pans in a warm oven).

1/2 cup	butter, softened	125 mL
1/2 cup	packed brown sugar	125 mL
1/4 cup	granulated sugar	50 mL
1	egg	1
1 tsp	vanilla	5 mL
1 cup	all-purpose flour	250 mL
1/2 tsp	EACH baking soda and salt	
		2 mL
1 cup	chocolate chips	250 mL
1/2 cup	coarsely chopped walnuts or pecans	125 mL

1. In a large bowl, cream the butter; add brown and granulated sugars and beat well. Beat in egg, then vanilla. Stir in flour, baking soda and salt. Blend in chocolate chips and nuts.
2. Using 2 teaspoons, drop by spoonfuls, 2 inches (5 cm) apart onto ungreased baking sheets. Bake in a 375°F (190°C) oven for 8 to 10 minutes or until golden brown. Remove to cool on a rack.

Sensational Turtle Brownies

MAKES 32 BROWNIES (OR 16 IF USING AS A SUNDAE BASE).

I can't resist starting with a quotation from Pamela Steel's *Great Canadian Cookies* (Prentice Hall Canada, 2000) in which she included this recipe: "These marvelous brownies have become a Canadian standard and I often see them imitated." They have been a definite hit when I've done them for guest appearances at cooking schools and shows, and they have made everyone's list of favourites. For a really decadent sundae, use the brownies as a base and top with chocolate, coffee or vanilla ice cream and Warm Chocolate Truffle Sauce (page 159).

1 cup	butter, in pieces	250 mL
4 oz	unsweetened chocolate, coarsely chopped	125 g
1-3/4 cups	granulated sugar	425 mL
4	eggs, well beaten	4
1 tsp	vanilla	5 mL
1-1/4 cups	all-purpose flour	300 mL
1/2 tsp	salt	2 mL

1. In the top of a double boiler over simmering water, melt butter with the chocolate. Stir in sugar until well combined. Stir in eggs and vanilla. Gradually add the flour and salt, stirring well after each addition.
2. Pour into a greased 13 x 9-inch (3.5 L) baking pan; bake in a 400°F (200°C) oven for 10 minutes. (Batter will not be totally cooked but will be set enough to add the topping.)

TOPPING

1/2 cup	whipping cream	125 mL
1/2 cup	packed brown sugar	125 mL
1/4 cup	butter	50 mL
1-1/2 cups	pecan halves	375 mL
1 cup	chocolate chips	250 mL

1. Meanwhile, in a saucepan, combine cream, brown sugar and butter; bring to a boil and boil for 2 minutes.
2. Sprinkle partially baked base with pecans; drizzle evenly with the caramel syrup. Bake for 8 to 10 minutes or until golden but not browned.
3. Remove from the oven; sprinkle with chocolate chips. Let melt slightly for 1 to 2 minutes; swirl with a knife so that some caramel and nuts show through. Let cool on a rack. Cut into squares.

Warm Chocolate Truffle Sauce

MAKES 3/4 CUP (175 ML).

This rich sauce becomes even more decadent if you stir in 1 tbsp (15 mL) brandy before serving. Pour it over vanilla or mocha ice cream, especially when the ice cream tops Sensational Turtle Brownies (see page 158).

1/4 cup	whipping (35%) cream	50 mL
5 oz	bittersweet or semisweet chocolate, coarsely chopped	150 g
1 tbsp	butter, softened	15 mL

1. In a small, heavy-based saucepan, bring cream to a boil over high heat. Remove the saucepan from the heat and stir in chocolate, then butter until melted. Let cool slightly before serving. (Sauce can be refrigerated, covered, for up to 1 week. Warm over low heat before serving.)

Triple-Decker Squares

MAKES 5 DOZEN.

These easy squares are from my good friend Mary Lou Ruby Jonas and are on my daughter's list of favourites. Anne makes them for potluck suppers where they are always a hit.

2 cups	all-purpose flour	500 mL
1/4 cup	granulated sugar	50 mL
2 cups	butter	500 mL
1 cup	packed brown sugar	250 mL
1/4 cup	corn syrup	50 mL
1	can (about 10 oz/300 mL) sweetened condensed milk	1
1 tsp	vanilla	5 mL
2 cups	semisweet chocolate chips	500 mL

1. In a large bowl, stir together flour and granulated sugar; cut in 1 cup (250 mL) of the butter until mixture is crumbly. Press evenly into a greased 13 x 9-inch (3.5 L) baking pan. Bake in a 350°F (180°C) oven for about 25 minutes or until lightly coloured.
2. Meanwhile, in a saucepan, combine remaining butter, brown sugar, corn syrup and condensed milk; stir over low heat until sugar is dissolved. Bring to a boil over medium heat, stirring constantly; boil gently for 5 minutes, stirring to prevent sticking.
3. Remove from the heat; add vanilla and beat well. Pour over warm base and spread evenly. Let cool on rack.
4. Melt chocolate chips and spread over cooled squares. Let chocolate set before cutting into squares.

FALL

FALL MENUS

When the markets and your garden have been harvested of all the wonderful fresh produce, having people in to share the bounty is one of the season's best treats.

A Fall Harvest Supper

CORN PANCAKES WITH CRÈME FRAÎCHE AND SMOKED SALMON

GINGER SQUASH SOUP

CRANBERRY CHICKEN
WILD RICE LEMON PILAF

BASIL-PEAR SALAD

CHOCOLATE HAZELNUT TORTE

Corn Pancakes

MAKES ABOUT 16 PANCAKES.

Although corn is not used extensively in Europe, the most exquisite corn pancakes I've ever tasted were at the three-star restaurant L'Espérance in Saint-Père-sous-Vézelay, France. Marc Meneau, chef and owner, topped each pancake with a tiny piece of pan-fried liver.

Serve these pancakes topped with chicken livers or a dollop of crème fraîche, a tiny piece of smoked salmon and a sprig of dill. They're also good for breakfast or brunch with maple syrup or honey.

1 cup	cooked corn kernels (2 to 3 ears) 250 mL
1/2 cup	sour cream 125 mL
2	eggs 2
1/3 cup	all-purpose flour 75 mL
1 tsp	granulated sugar 5 mL
1/2 tsp	baking powder 2 mL
1/4 tsp	salt 1 mL
1/4 tsp	freshly grated nutmeg 1 mL
	Unsalted butter for frying

1. In a blender or food processor, combine corn, sour cream, eggs, flour, sugar, baking powder, salt and nutmeg; process for a few seconds just until mixed. Do not overprocess; batter should be runny but not perfectly smooth. Let stand for about 30 minutes.
2. Lightly butter a heated griddle or skillet and heat over medium-high. Drop batter by the tablespoon (15 mL) onto the hot pan; cook for 1 to 2 minutes on each side or until lightly browned. Serve warm.

Ginger Squash Soup

MAKES 6 TO 8 FIRST-COURSE SERVINGS.

A favourite with many and a hit in cooking classes, this simple soup gets wonderful flavour from roasting the squash and slow cooking the leeks to release their sweetness. Use any winter squash available with the equivalent weight.

1	acorn squash (about 2-1/2 lb/1.25 kg) 1
2 tbsp	butter 25 mL
2	leeks, thinly sliced 2
1	small carrot, thinly sliced 1

1. Cut squash in half, remove seeds and place cut side down in a shallow baking dish. Cover with foil and bake in a 350°F (180°C) oven for 40 minutes or until tender. Scrape squash from skin.
2. Meanwhile, in a large saucepan, melt butter over low heat; cook leeks and carrot uncovered, stirring occasionally, for about 40 minutes or until leeks are softened and lightly browned.

4 cups	chicken stock 1 L
1 tsp	ground ginger (or more to taste) 5 mL
1/2 tsp	salt 2 mL
1/4 tsp	pepper 1 mL
1/2 cup	light cream or milk 125 mL
	Sour cream and snipped chives

3. Stir in stock, cooked squash, ginger, salt and pepper; cover and simmer over medium heat for 20 minutes. Transfer to a blender or food processor (a blender makes a smoother soup) and purée until smooth; return to the saucepan. (Recipe can be prepared to this point, covered and refrigerated for up to 24 hours.)

4. Stir in cream and gently heat through without boiling. Taste and adjust seasoning, if necessary. Garnish each serving with a swirl of sour cream and a sprinkling of chives.

Cranberry Chicken

MAKES 8 SERVINGS.

This easy and pretty company dish is adapted from a recipe in my *Quick Chicken* cookbook. It is wonderful served with a wild rice pilaf and a green salad.

12 oz	cranberries, fresh or frozen (not thawed) (3-1/2 cups/875 mL) 375 g
1/3 cup	granulated sugar 75 mL
2 tbsp	cornstarch 25 mL
1/2 cup	mild liquid honey 125 mL
1 tbsp	fresh lemon juice 15 mL
8	large, skinless, boneless chicken breast halves (3 lb/1.5 kg total) 8
2 tbsp	vegetable oil 25 mL
	Salt and pepper
1/4 cup	orange liqueur or orange juice 50 mL
1 tbsp	grated orange zest 15 mL
	Sprigs of fresh parsley

1. Sprinkle cranberries evenly in a greased 13 x 9-inch (3.5 L) baking dish. Combine sugar and cornstarch and spoon over the cranberries. Drizzle with honey and lemon juice. Place in a 375°F (190°C) oven for 15 minutes, stirring once.

2. Meanwhile, pat chicken dry. In a large skillet over medium-high heat, heat oil. Add chicken in batches and cook until browned on both sides, removing each batch to a plate.

3. Arrange browned chicken on top of cranberry mixture. Sprinkle with salt and pepper, orange liqueur and zest. Return to the oven and bake for about 30 minutes or until chicken is no longer pink inside, covering with foil if chicken or cranberries get too brown. Remove chicken to a warm platter; stir cranberry sauce well and spoon over top. Garnish with parsley sprigs.

Wild Rice Lemon Pilaf

MAKES 8 SERVINGS.

Wild rice is special to serve at dinner parties and celebrations. Here, I've extended this treat by combining it with some white rice as a wonderful, full-flavoured accompaniment to the chicken.

4 cups	chicken stock 1 L
1 cup	wild rice, rinsed (6 oz/175 g) 250 mL
1/4 cup	butter 50 mL
2 tbsp	fresh lemon juice 25 mL
1 tbsp	grated lemon zest 15 mL
2	onions, chopped 2
1-1/2 cups	long-grain white rice 375 mL
1 cup	chopped pecans, lightly toasted 250 mL
1/2 cup	chopped fresh parsley 125 mL

1. In a large saucepan, combine the stock, wild rice, 1 tbsp (15 mL) of the butter, lemon juice and half the zest; bring to a boil. Cover and reduce heat to medium-low; simmer for 35 minutes.

2. Meanwhile, in a large skillet, melt remaining butter over medium heat; cook onions until softened, about 8 minutes. Add white rice and stir to coat; stir into wild rice mixture after it has cooked for 35 minutes. Bring to a boil, reduce heat, cover and simmer over medium-low heat until liquid is absorbed, 15 to 20 minutes. Remove from the heat; let stand, covered, for 5 minutes.

3. Stir in remaining zest, pecans and parsley. (Pilaf may be cooled, covered and refrigerated in a casserole dish for up to 2 days. Microwave, covered, at High for 6 to 8 minutes or bake, covered, in a 350°F/180°C oven, stirring occasionally, for about 20 minutes or until heated through.)

Basil-Pear Salad

MAKES 8 SERVINGS.

This simple, refreshing salad is a favourite with a number of people, including the groups I taught at the Saskatchewan Food & Wine Festival. You can arrange the salad on individual plates or make it in one big bowl.

1/2 cup	olive oil 125 mL
1/4 cup	fresh lemon juice 50 mL
	Salt and pepper
1/2 cup	slivered fresh basil leaves 125 mL
4	ripe Bartlett pears 4

1. In a small bowl, whisk together the oil, three-quarters of the lemon juice, and salt and pepper to taste; stir in the basil. (The dressing can be covered and set aside for up to 4 hours.)

2. Core and thinly slice unpeeled pears; toss with remaining lemon juice.

3. Line salad plates with lettuce and arrange pear slices on top. Drizzle with dressing; sprinkle with pine nuts and Parmesan slivers. Sprinkle with freshly ground pepper and serve immediately.

	Red leaf lettuce
	(about 1 small head)
1/3 cup	toasted pine nuts 75 mL
1/3 cup	slivered Parmesan cheese
	75 mL

TIP

To make Parmesan slivers, run a vegetable parer across a short piece of Parmesan cheese.

To toast pine nuts, spread them out on a baking sheet and toast in a 350°F (180°C) oven for about 5 minutes, watching carefully.

Chocolate Hazelnut Torte

MAKES 12 SMALL SERVINGS.

This has been an all-time favourite among my readers, including my good friend Sharon Boyd who makes it often for clients of her catering business. The simplicity of the dessert is well concealed by its wonderful appearance and taste.

1/4 cup	dried apricots, chopped
	50 mL
1/4 cup	Frangelico liqueur or rum
	50 mL
6 oz	bittersweet chocolate, coarsely
	chopped 175 g
1/2 cup	unsalted butter, cut in pieces
	125 mL
3	eggs, separated 3
2/3 cup	granulated sugar 150 mL
1/4 cup	all-purpose flour 50 mL
2/3 cup	ground hazelnuts (filberts)
	150 mL
Pinch	cream of tartar Pinch

1. Combine apricots and Frangelico; set aside.
2. In the top of a double boiler, melt chocolate and butter over simmering water, stirring until smooth. Remove from the heat and cool slightly.
3. In a large bowl, beat egg yolks with 1/2 cup (125 mL) of the sugar until pale and thickened. Stir in chocolate mixture, flour and ground hazelnuts. Stir in apricot mixture.
4. In another large bowl with clean beaters, beat egg whites until foamy. Add cream of tartar and beat at medium speed until soft peaks form. Gradually add remaining sugar and beat until stiff, but not dry, peaks form; stir about one-quarter into chocolate mixture. Fold in remaining whites until just mixed.
5. Scrape batter into well-greased and floured 9-inch (2.5 L) springform pan, tapping on counter to level top. Bake in a 375°F (190°C) oven until the edge is dry but the centre is still moist, about 30 minutes. Do not overbake. Let cool completely on a rack before removing the pan. (Torte can be made to this point, covered, and set aside for up to 1 day.)

GLAZE

1/3 cup	whipping cream 75 mL
6 oz	semisweet chocolate, chopped
	175 g

1. In a small saucepan, bring cream to a boil over medium-low heat; add chocolate and stir until melted and smooth. Let glaze cool until spreadable.
2. Place strips of waxed paper under the edge of the cake; spread cake with the glaze. (Torte can be glazed several hours ahead and left in a cool place.)

Canadian Thanksgiving is probably my favourite holiday. It usually comes with brisk air, sunny skies and those beautiful autumn leaves.

Our family often goes to the Georgian Bay area of Ontario where I grew up and where the apple harvest is an important part of the agricultural scene. The weekend always includes a long walk through the leaves while we all munch on crisp, juicy McIntosh apples and marvel at the wonderful blue of the bay.

The apples, of course, are just a snack in anticipation of the good things dinner will bring—roast turkey and all the trimmings. The turkey I've included in the menu would be an excellent choice for a Christmas table as well. Also delicious at Thanksgiving is the Glazed Roast Duck with Mango-Pecan Stuffing (see page 133).

Thanksgiving

COGNAC PEAR PÂTÉ WITH CRACKERS AND CORNICHONS

SOUTHWESTERN ROAST TURKEY WITH CORN BREAD-PECAN STUFFING

GIBLET GRAVY (SEE PAGE 227)

BAKED CRANBERRY SAUCE (SEE PAGE 228)

MASHED POTATOES

MAPLE BAKED SQUASH (SEE PAGE 143)

STEAMED BROCCOLI

BEET AND ROQUEFORT SALAD

CARAMEL PUMPKIN PIE

Cognac Pear Pâté with Crackers and Cornichons

MAKES 3 CUPS (750 ML).

This easy chicken-liver pâté is creamy and mellow with the addition of a pear. Serve it with crisp crackers, bread or toast and Cornichons (see page 99). My friend and helper, Sharon Boyd, makes it often for parties and lists it among her favourites.

1 cup	unsalted butter	250 mL
1 lb	chicken livers	500 g
1	onion, sliced	1
2	small pears (or 1 large), peeled and thinly sliced	2
1/4 cup	cognac or brandy	50 mL
1/4 cup	whipping cream	50 mL
1 tsp	EACH dry mustard and salt	5 mL
1/4 tsp	EACH ground nutmeg, ground cloves, dried thyme and black pepper	1 mL
Pinch	cayenne pepper	Pinch

1. In a large skillet, melt 1/4 cup (50 mL) of the butter over medium heat; cook livers, stirring, for about 4 minutes or until browned all over yet still pink in the centre. With a slotted spoon, remove to a food processor bowl.

2. Add onion to the pan and cook over medium heat, stirring often, for 5 minutes or until softened. Stir in pears and cook for 4 minutes. Add to chicken livers.

3. Add cognac to the pan and bring to a boil, stirring to scrape up any brown bits from the pan; add to livers. Add cream, mustard, salt, nutmeg, cloves, thyme, pepper and cayenne; process until smooth. With the motor running, add remaining butter, in pieces; process until very smooth. Pour into a crock or other serving dish; cover and refrigerate at least overnight and for up to 3 days.

Southwestern Roast Turkey with Corn Bread–Pecan Stuffing

MAKES 8 TO 10 SERVINGS.

For a *Homemaker's Magazine* Christmas menu entitled "Christmas Around the World," I borrowed flavours from our neighbours to the south for the turkey ... one of the recipes my food editor at the time, Julia Aitken, included in her list of favourites. To go with the roast turkey, make your favourite gravy or the Giblet Gravy on page 227.

continued

CORN BREAD-PECAN STUFFING

1/4 cup	butter	50 mL
6	green onions, chopped	6
3	jalapeño peppers, seeded and sliced*	3
2	stalks celery, chopped	2
2	cloves garlic, minced	2
1 cup	pecan pieces	250 mL
1 cup	chopped fresh parsley	250 mL
1 tbsp	crumbled dried sage	15 mL
1 tsp	EACH dried marjoram, thyme and pepper	5 mL
	Herbed Corn Bread, cubed (recipe follows)	
1-1/2 cups	chicken or turkey stock	375 mL

1. In a large skillet, melt butter over medium heat. Add onions, jalapeño peppers, celery and garlic; cook, stirring, 10 minutes, or until softened. Stir in pecans, parsley, sage, marjoram, thyme and pepper; remove from heat. Stir in corn bread cubes and stock. (Stuffing can be prepared up to 1 day ahead; refrigerate, covered, until just before cooking turkey.)

TURKEY

12 lb	turkey	5.5 kg
Half	lemon	Half
	Salt and pepper	
	Vegetable oil	

1. Remove giblets and neck from turkey; set aside for stock. Rinse turkey inside and out; dry skin and cavity well with paper towels. Rub lemon half all over turkey, inside and out, squeezing juice as you do so. Sprinkle with salt and pepper.
2. Fill neck cavity with stuffing; sew or skewer skin to the back to enclose. Fill body cavity with stuffing; tuck legs under band of skin or tie together with string.
3. Place turkey, breast side up, on a greased rack in a large, shallow roasting pan. Brush all over with oil. Tent turkey with foil, dull side out, tucking in ends but leaving sides open. Roast in a 325°F (160°C) oven for 3 hours, basting every 30 minutes (use vegetable oil until there are enough pan drippings to baste with).
4. Remove foil; cook for 45 to 60 minutes until juices run clear, and a thermometer inserted into the thigh registers 185°F (85°C) and into the stuffing registers 165°F (75°C). Transfer turkey to a heated platter; let stand loosely tented with foil for 20 minutes before carving.

Don't be alarmed by the number of jalapeño peppers; discarding their seeds will make them mild, but wear rubber gloves when handling them or wash your hands with soapy water immediately after.

Herbed Corn Bread

MAKES ONE 8-INCH (20 CM) CORN BREAD (ENOUGH FOR CORN BREAD-PECAN STUFFING, PAGE 170).

This delicious corn bread adds a crumbly texture and great flavour to the stuffing for my Southwestern Roast Turkey. You can make it ahead of time and freeze it, well wrapped, for up to 2 weeks. And, of course, you could make it, slice it, butter it and just eat it!

1 cup	all-purpose flour	250 mL
3/4 cup	cornmeal	175 mL
1 tbsp	EACH granulated sugar and baking powder	15 mL
1 tsp	EACH dried thyme and crumbled dried sage	5 mL
1/2 tsp	salt	2 mL
2/3 cup	milk	150 mL
1/3 cup	vegetable oil	75 mL
1	egg	1

1. In a large bowl, combine flour, cornmeal, sugar, baking powder, thyme, sage and salt.
2. In a glass measure, combine milk, oil and egg; beat lightly. Add milk mixture all at once to dry ingredients; stir with a fork just until dry ingredients are moistened but mixture is still lumpy. Spread batter evenly in a greased 8-inch (2 L) square cake pan. Bake in a 400°F (200°C) oven for 25 minutes, or until bread has risen and looks golden. Let cool in the pan.

Beet and Roquefort Salad

MAKES 8 TO 10 SERVINGS.

Beets are one of my favourite vegetables. They are especially delicious roasted and marinated as they are in this interesting salad. If you have walnut oil, use half walnut and half olive oil. Try to use beets all of the same size for best-looking results.

6	beets (about 2 inches/5 cm in diameter)	6
3 tbsp	fresh lemon juice	45 mL
1 tbsp	Dijon mustard	15 mL
1/3 cup	olive oil (or half walnut and half olive oil)	75 mL
1/2 tsp	granulated sugar	2 mL
Pinch	EACH salt and pepper	Pinch

1. Scrub beets, leaving roots and 1 inch (2.5 cm) of the stem on. Arrange in a small baking dish. Add about 1/4 cup (50 mL) of water to the dish, cover with foil and roast in a 375°F (190°C) oven for 45 to 60 minutes or until tender. Alternatively, in a large pot of boiling salted water, boil beets for 20 to 45 minutes, until tender; drain well. Let beets cool slightly, then remove peel; slice beets into a medium bowl.
2. In a small bowl, combine lemon juice and mustard; whisk in oil until smooth. Whisk in sugar, salt and pepper. Add half of the dressing to the beets; toss to coat well. Refrigerate, covered, until ready to serve or up to 24 hours. Bring to room temperature before serving.

continued

3	heads Belgian endive, outer leaves discarded 3
1	bunch watercress, tough stems removed 1
6 oz	Roquefort cheese, crumbled 175 g
1/2 cup	toasted walnut pieces 125 mL

3. Just before serving, remove enough leaves from the endive to arrange like petals of a flower around the edge of a large, shallow salad bowl or platter. Slice remaining endive crosswise; toss with the remaining dressing. Arrange watercress in the base of the salad bowl; mound sliced endive in the centre. Surround sliced endive with marinated beets. Sprinkle cheese and walnuts over top.

TIP

Beets vary in cooking time according to their age and their size. They store well into the winter but require longer cooking time. Also, the skins slip right off fresh beets, but you have to peel older ones.

Caramel Pumpkin Pie

MAKES 6 TO 8 SERVINGS.

I can't remember how many versions of pumpkin pie I have developed over the years. This pie, richly flavoured with caramelized sugar and a hint of brandy, is one of my favourites. The filling is not high, but you need only a small wedge topped with a little whipped cream to be satisfied.

1/2 cup	granulated sugar 125 mL
1 tbsp	water 15 mL
3/4 cup	corn syrup 175 mL
2 tbsp	brandy 25 mL
2 tbsp	butter, cut in bits 25 mL
3	eggs 3
1 tsp	vanilla 5 mL
Pinch	salt Pinch
1 cup	pumpkin purée 250 mL
1 tsp	cinnamon 5 mL
1/2 tsp	EACH ground ginger and nutmeg 2 mL
	Unbaked 9-inch (23 cm) pie shell (see **Pie Pastry**, page 33)

1. In a small, heavy saucepan over medium heat, combine sugar and water. Heat, stirring, until sugar melts. Increase heat to medium-high and cook, stirring occasionally, until melted sugar is a deep caramel colour. Remove from the heat. Stir in corn syrup. Don't worry if there is a lump or two. Stir in brandy and butter; return to the heat and cook for 1 minute. Remove from the heat and let cool until the mixture stops bubbling.

2. In a large bowl, whisk together eggs, vanilla and salt. Very gradually, whisk in the caramel mixture. Combine pumpkin purée, cinnamon, ginger and nutmeg; whisk into egg mixture. Pour into pie shell. Bake in a 375°F (190°C) oven for 10 minutes. Reduce heat to 325°F (160°C) and bake for 45 minutes longer or until filling is set and crust is golden brown. Let cool on a rack. Serve warm or at room temperature.

WINTER

MY WINTER KITCHEN

When I'm in a Mediterranean country during our winter and can pick rosemary right by the doorstep of a house we are renting, I think, "Why can't we do this at home?" A winter in the Mediterranean is not much of a winter.

Now, the winters here are a different story. In the part of Canada where I live, no self-respecting rosemary bush would be caught out in all that ice and snow. With the cold, however, there comes a certain challenge in my kitchen ... one that leads to creativity. With no fresh produce growing outside my door, I rely on root vegetables and dried beans to create hearty, comforting food. I fill my kitchen windows with the steam from simmering broth and satisfying whole meal soups. In the air is the heady aroma of freshly baked bread and buns.

In the air, too, is the excitement of the holidays and all the good food they bring. I'm never happier than when I know the whole family will be home for Christmas to enjoy all the cookies my son's friend, Cherrie, and I make on our December Saturday of baking and that wonderful goose I always get from a nearby farmer.

After the holidays, I continue to cook filling and warming suppers, then settle down by the fire to watch the slow passage of the season and anticipate the lighter fare of spring when nature's calendar starts its exciting cycle all over again.

WINTER STARTERS

176   HOT AND CLASSY CRAB DIP

177   HAM AND CHEESE SQUARES

178   BAKED HAZELNUT BRIE

179   CREOLE CHICKEN WINGS WITH PEACH

MUSTARD SAUCE

IN THE MENUS ...

Hot and Classy Crab Dip

MAKES ABOUT 1-1/2 CUPS (375 ML).

My daughter, Anne Loxton, often makes this old favourite for company. One Christmas, she and I decided to make it to take to a party, only to discover that our hostess had made the same dip— from my recipe! Place the dish of hot dip in the middle of a platter and surround it with crackers and/or crunchy raw vegetables.

8 oz	light cream cheese	250 g
1	can (6 oz/170 g) crab meat	1
2 tbsp	finely chopped shallots or onion	25 mL
1 tbsp	fresh lemon juice	15 mL
Dash	hot pepper sauce	Dash
1/4 cup	toasted sliced almonds	50 mL
1 tbsp	butter	15 mL

1. In a medium bowl, beat cheese; mash in crab meat. Stir in shallots, lemon juice and hot pepper sauce.
2. Spoon into a small baking dish. Sprinkle with almonds; dot with butter. (Recipe can be prepared to this point up to 1 hour ahead.)
3. Bake in a 350°F (180°C) oven for about 30 minutes or until hot and bubbly.

Ham and Cheese Squares

MAKES ABOUT 6 DOZEN SQUARES.

My son, Allen, and his girlfriend, Cherrie, always make these easy, but pretty appetizer squares for New Year's Eve. They are good for a party because they can be made a day ahead, and everyone will like them. Be sure the ham and cheese slices are very thin and not too salty.

1	pkg (10 oz/284 g) fresh spinach, trimmed	1
2	eggs	2
1	pkg (about 14 oz/397 or 411 g) frozen puff pastry, thawed	1
2 tbsp	Dijon mustard	25 mL
1-1/4 lb	thinly sliced cooked ham	625 g
12 oz	sliced Swiss cheese	375 g
1 tsp	milk (approx.)	5 mL

1. Rinse spinach and shake off excess water. In a large covered pot over medium heat, cook spinach with just the water that clings to the leaves, until wilted, about 2 minutes.

2. Drain and squeeze dry; chop and set aside.

3. Separate 1 of the eggs; set yolk aside for the glaze. Whisk the white with the whole egg; set aside.

4. On a lightly floured surface, roll out half of the pastry and fit into a 16 x 11-inch (40 x 28 cm) jelly roll pan or rimmed baking sheet. Spread with mustard, leaving a 1-inch (2.5 cm) border uncovered. Still leaving the border, top with half of the ham, then half the cheese. Top with spinach; drizzle with egg mixture. Layer the remaining ham and cheese slices on top. Fold pastry border up over filling. Beat reserved egg yolk with milk to make a glaze; brush some over the edges of the pastry. Cover and refrigerate remaining glaze.

5. Roll out remaining pastry into the same size of rectangle; place on top, pressing edges with the floured tines of a fork to seal. Cover with plastic wrap and refrigerate for at least 1 hour or for up to 24 hours.

6. About 1 hour before serving, brush with half the remaining glaze; let stand in the refrigerator for about 30 minutes. Brush with remaining glaze, adding a bit more milk if necessary. With the tip of a sharp knife, score pastry into bite-sized squares; slash 2 or 3 steam vents in the top.

7. Bake in a 425°F (220°C) oven for about 20 minutes or until puffed and golden brown. Let stand for 10 minutes before cutting into squares.

Baked Hazelnut Brie

MAKES 8 SERVINGS.

This easy, warm appetizer or snack found its way into more than one list of favourites. Provide butter knives so everyone can spread the warm cheese on toast and apple slices.

1/4 cup	olive oil	50 mL
1/3 cup	fresh whole-wheat bread crumbs	75 mL
1/3 cup	finely chopped hazelnuts (filberts)	75 mL
1 lb	Brie cheese	500 g
	Watercress or lettuce leaves	
3	red apples (unpeeled), thinly sliced	3
	Fresh lemon juice	
	Hot toast triangles	

1. Pour the oil into a small shallow bowl. In another bowl, combine the bread crumbs and hazelnuts. Cut Brie into serving-sized wedges; dip into the oil and roll gently in bread-crumb mixture. Place in a shallow baking dish, leaving at least 1 inch (2.5 cm) between wedges; drizzle with any remaining oil. Cover and refrigerate for at least 1 hour or overnight.

2. Uncover and bake cheese in a 325°F (160°C) oven for 10 to 15 minutes or until brown on the outside and soft and hot inside. (Don't worry if cheese starts to ooze.)

3. Meanwhile, arrange watercress on individual plates; fan apple slices over top. Sprinkle apple with lemon juice. Make toast triangles and arrange on each plate, leaving just enough room for cheese wedges.

4. With a metal spatula, transfer cheese wedges to plates; serve immediately.

Creole Chicken Wings with Peach Mustard Sauce

MAKES 8 APPETIZER SERVINGS OR 4 MAIN-COURSE SERVINGS.

Mary Lou Ruby Jonas was my assistant when I developed this recipe for *Canadian Living,* and we discovered (by accident!) that roasting the wings at a high temperature made them crusty on the outside, tender and juicy within. Mary Lou listed these spicy wings in her favourites.

3 lb	chicken wings	1.5 kg
4	cloves garlic, minced	4
2 tsp	EACH dry mustard and paprika	10 mL
1 tsp	EACH dried thyme and granulated sugar	5 mL
1/2 tsp	EACH cayenne pepper, salt and black pepper	2 mL
1/4 cup	lemon juice	50 mL

PEACH MUSTARD SAUCE

1/2 cup	peach jam	125 mL
1 tbsp	Dijon mustard	15 mL
2 tsp	diced pimiento or fresh red pepper	10 mL
1 tsp	cider vinegar	5 mL

1. Cut tips from wings and reserve for stock if desired; separate wings at joints. In a small bowl, stir together garlic, mustard, paprika, thyme, sugar, cayenne, salt and black pepper. Blend in lemon juice to make a paste. Using a pastry brush, brush paste over wings. Arrange wings, meaty side down, in a single layer on lightly greased, foil-lined baking sheets. Let stand for 30 minutes at room temperature.

2. Bake, uncovered, in a 475°F (240°C) oven for 30 to 40 minutes or until brown and crisp, turning after 15 minutes.

1. In a saucepan over low heat, melt jam. Stir in mustard, pimiento and vinegar. Pass the sauce separately for dipping.

WINTER WHOLE MEAL SOUPS

Old-Fashioned Split Pea Soup

MAKES 8 TO 10 SERVINGS.

When I wrote my *Vegetable Cookbook,* I did a lot of research on Canadian vegetables and learned the origin of this popular soup. Since dried peas were easy to carry, they played an important part in the diet of voyageurs who combined them with salt pork and water to make a hearty soup. No matter what other soups I make, this is our family's favourite—updated with the use of a meaty ham bone and some fresh vegetables.

As with most soups, this one improves in flavour if made one day and reheated the next. It will thicken quite a bit upon cooling and freezes well.

1 lb	dried green split peas (2-1/4 cups/550 mL) 500 g
10 cups	water 2.5 L
1	meaty ham bone 1
1 cup	chopped onion 250 mL
1	large clove garlic, minced 1
1-1/2 tsp	finely chopped fresh marjoram (or 1/2 tsp/2 mL dried) 7 mL
1/4 tsp	black pepper 1 mL
1 cup	finely chopped celery with leaves 250 mL
1 cup	shredded carrot 250 mL
2 tbsp	minced fresh parsley 25 mL
	Salt
	Croutons for garnish (see **Dandelion Salad with Croutons,** page 26)

1. In a large kettle, cover peas with the water. Add ham bone, onion, garlic, marjoram and pepper. Bring to a boil. Cover, reduce heat and simmer for 2 hours, stirring occasionally.
2. Remove the bone and cut off any meat. Dice the meat and return it to the soup with celery, carrot and parsley. Simmer, covered, another 45 minutes, stirring occasionally. Add salt to taste and serve hot, garnished with croutons.

Spanish Clam & Shrimp Soup with Picada

MAKES ABOUT 6 SERVINGS.

I have wonderful memories of the vast array of fresh fish and seafood in the markets in Spain where it would be easy to find the ingredients for this delicious soup. Picada, a flavourful paste of garlic, bread, nuts and olive oil, can be swirled on top of each bowl to thicken it and add even more flavour. Prosciutto is the substitute for the Spanish air-cured ham traditionally used for this soup. Look for clam juice in the fish department of the supermarket.

2 lb	small clams 1 kg
4 cups	clam juice or fish stock 1 L
1/4 tsp	saffron threads* 1 mL
2 tbsp	olive oil 25 mL
1/3 cup	diced prosciutto 75 mL
1	small onion, minced 1
2	tomatoes, peeled, seeded and chopped 2
2 cups	water 500 mL
1 lb	large shrimp, shelled, deveined and halved 500 g
1 cup	peas, fresh or frozen, thawed 250 mL
2 tbsp	minced fresh parsley 25 mL
	Salt and pepper
	Picada (recipe follows)

1. Pour 1 cup (250 mL) of water into a skillet and add the clams. Cover and bring to a boil. Reduce heat and simmer for 5 minutes. Remove clams that are open. Cover again and simmer for 5 minutes. Repeat if necessary, but discard any clams that don't open.

2. Remove clams from shells and discard shells; strain cooking liquid and reserve.

3. Reserve 1/4 cup (50 mL) of the clam juice to add to the picada. Warm the remainder and add the saffron to it. Set aside for 20 minutes.

4. In a large saucepan, heat oil over medium heat. Cook prosciutto and onion until onion is soft. Add tomatoes; cover and cook for 5 minutes. Gradually stir in water, clam juice with saffron and reserved clam cooking water. Simmer for 5 minutes. Add shrimp, peas, parsley and cooked clams. Simmer gently for about 3 minutes or until shrimp is pink. Season with salt and pepper.

5. Serve soup in hot bowls; serve picada in a little bowl to pass so that each person can add a swirl if he or she wishes.

PICADA

3/4 cup	blanched whole almonds 175 mL
1/2 cup	olive oil 125 mL
2	slices homemade-style white bread, crusts removed 2
5	cloves garlic, chopped 5
1	jalapeño pepper, seeded and minced 1
	Salt

1. In a dry skillet over medium heat, stir almonds until pale brown; remove almonds and set aside. Add half the oil to the skillet; cook bread, turning, until light brown on both sides. Remove skillet from the heat and let bread sit in the pan to soak up the oil.

2. In food processor, combine remaining oil, garlic, almonds and jalapeño. Process 30 seconds. Add bread and process for 4 minutes, scraping sides. Season with salt to taste. Add reserved clam juice to loosen the picada and transfer to a small bowl.

Saffron is orange-yellow flavouring made from the dried, red stigmas of a crocus grown in Spain; look for it in specialty food shops. Use sparingly.

Oyster Stew

MAKES 4 SERVINGS.

Our family loves oysters ... smoked, cooked or raw on the half shell—our traditional Christmas Eve treat. Over the years, I have written articles on the molluscs and have developed many recipes for them. This Oyster Stew, duplicating the one my mother used to make, was on everyone's list of favourites. It's a thin stew (actually a soup) that has been one of the most popular ways of enjoying oysters since the 19th century. Thick chowders laden with vegetables and pork are appropriate for more strongly flavoured shellfish such as clams, while oysters taste best in this simple preparation. Accompany the stew with soda biscuits.

1/4 cup	butter 50 mL
2 cups	fresh oysters in their liquor 500 mL
3 cups	milk, scalded 750 mL
1/2 cup	whipping cream 125 mL
1/4 tsp	white pepper 1 mL
Pinch	nutmeg Pinch
	Salt and paprika

1. In a large heavy saucepan, melt the butter over low heat; simmer the oysters with their liquor until their edges begin to curl, about 3 minutes. Stir in scalded milk, cream, pepper, nutmeg and salt to taste. Heat through but do not boil.
2. Ladle into heated bowls. Sprinkle with paprika. Serve immediately.

Vietnamese Beef Noodle Soup

MAKES 6 MAIN-COURSE SERVINGS.

For a truly authentic soup, make your own beef broth by simmering 2 pounds (1 kg) beef shank with water, cinnamon and star anise for 3 or 4 hours. Or take a short-cut, as I have done, by steeping the spices in 3 cans of beef broth.

8 oz	sirloin steak	250 g
1 tbsp	peanut or vegetable oil	15 mL
2 tbsp	bottled or canned red curry paste	25 mL
7-1/2 cups	beef broth (three 10 oz/284 mL cans diluted with water)	1.8 L
2	star anise*	2
1	stick (2 inches/5 cm) cinnamon, broken	1
1	pkg (14 oz/400 g) fresh wonton noodles	1
1 cup	bean sprouts	250 mL
1/2 cup	EACH fresh coriander leaves, Asian (Thai) basil leaves and fresh mint leaves	125 mL
2	limes, cut in wedges	2
1/4 cup	sliced green onions	50 mL
	Fish sauce and hot pepper sauce	

1. Slice steak thinly across the grain into 3 x 1/8-inch (7 cm x 3 mm) strips. In a large saucepan, heat oil over medium-high heat. Add steak and cook, stirring, for 2 to 3 minutes, until browned. With a slotted spoon, remove to a bowl. Add red curry paste and cook, stirring, for 1 to 2 minutes, until fragrant. Add broth, star anise and cinnamon; bring to a boil, stirring up any brown bits from the bottom of the pan. Reduce heat to low and simmer, uncovered, for 20 minutes. Discard star anise and cinnamon. Keep soup warm.

2. Meanwhile, prepare noodles in boiling water according to package directions. Prepare garnishes by arranging bean sprouts, coriander, basil, mint, lime wedges and green onions in attractive piles on a large round platter. Set in the middle of the table with small containers of fish sauce and hot pepper sauce.

3. Add cooked noodles and beef to simmering stock to heat through. Ladle soup into large, warm soup bowls and have your guests add their own garnishes, sauces and a squeeze of lime juice.

Star anise is a star-shaped spice with a vibrant aniseed (licorice-like) flavour. Look for star anise and fish sauce in Asian grocery stores.

Hungarian Goulash Soup

MAKES 8 GENEROUS SERVINGS.

This wonderful main-course soup, a long-time favourite in our family, was a recipe I learned from a Hungarian chef. As well, my good friend Elizabeth Baird, food editor at *Canadian Living*, says it has remained her favourite of all my recipes since she first tasted it on one of her visits to our home in Owen Sound, Ontario.

2 tbsp	lard, shortening or vegetable oil 25 mL	
1-1/2 lb	lean beef, cubed (3/4 inch/2 cm) 750 g	
2	onions, sliced 2	
2 tbsp	caraway seeds, crushed* 25 mL	
1 tbsp	sweet paprika 15 mL	
1/2 tsp	salt (approx.) 2 mL	
1	can (19 oz/540 mL) tomatoes, undrained and chopped 1	
1-1/4 tsp	dried basil 6 mL	
2	sweet green peppers, diced 2	
1/4 cup	water 50 mL	
4	potatoes, peeled and diced 4	
7 cups	beef broth 1.75 L	
1-1/4 tsp	dried marjoram 6 mL	
3/4 tsp	pepper 4 mL	
1/4 lb	egg noodles 125 g	

1. In a large, heavy-bottomed saucepan, melt lard over medium-high heat; cook meat until browned all over. Add onions and cook until softened, about 5 minutes.
2. Remove from the heat; stir in caraway seeds, paprika and salt. Return to low heat; cover and cook for 20 minutes, stirring occasionally.
3. Stir in tomatoes, basil, green peppers and water; bring to a boil. Reduce heat, cover and simmer for about 1 hour or until meat is almost tender, adding a little water, if necessary, to prevent sticking.
4. Add potatoes and broth; bring to a boil. Reduce heat, cover and cook until potatoes and meat are tender, about 30 minutes. Taste and add more salt if necessary. Stir in marjoram and pepper; cook for 2 minutes. (Recipe can be prepared to this point, cooled, covered and refrigerated. Reheat slowly, stirring often.)
5. Stir in noodles; cook for about 7 minutes or until tender but firm. Ladle into heated bowls.

Crush caraway seeds with a mortar and pestle or place in a sturdy plastic bag and roll firmly with a rolling pin.

Oxtail and Barley Soup

MAKES 6 TO 8 SERVINGS.

This was one of my editor, Julia Aitken's, favourites among the recipes I included in an article called "Humble Cuts," which I wrote for one of the first issues of *Elm Street*. Oxtail takes a long time to cook—4 to 5 hours in this case—but needs little preparation, and the flavour it gives to this warming soup is worth the wait.

1 tbsp	vegetable oil (approx.)	15 mL
2 lb	oxtail (cut into sections at each vertebra)	1 kg
2	EACH onions, carrots and celery stalks, diced	2
2	cloves garlic, minced	2
2	bay leaves	2
1/2 tsp	EACH dried marjoram, thyme, savory and granulated sugar	2 mL
5 cups	water	1.5 L
2-1/2 cups	beef stock	625 mL
1	can (19 oz/540 mL) tomatoes, undrained and chopped	1
1/2 cup	dry red wine	125 mL
3/4 cup	pearl barley	175 mL
	Salt and black pepper	
Half	pkg (10 oz/284 g) fresh spinach, chopped	Half

1. In a large Dutch oven over medium-high heat, heat oil. Add oxtail and brown well all over. Remove to a plate. Reduce heat to medium and add a little more oil if necessary. Add onions, carrots, celery, garlic and bay leaves; then cook, stirring, for 5 minutes or until vegetables are softened. Stir in marjoram, thyme, savory and sugar. Add back oxtail and any juices. Stir in water, beef stock, tomatoes and wine; then bring to a boil. Cover and cook in a 300°F (150°C) oven for 4-1/2 to 5 hours or until meat is falling from the bones. Remove from the oven and let cool a little.

2. When meat is cool enough, pull it away from the bones, discarding bones and returning meat to the pot. (Soup can be prepared to this point, covered and refrigerated for up to 2 days.)

3. Skim off any fat from the soup. Stir in barley and bring to a boil on top of the stove. Reduce heat to medium-low and simmer, covered, for 25 to 30 minutes or until barley is tender. Season with salt and pepper to taste. Discard bay leaves. Stir in spinach, then cook, covered, for 2 to 4 minutes or just until spinach is wilted but still bright green.

4. Ladle soup into warm bowls. (Any leftover soup will thicken upon standing; so thin it with extra broth or water.)

TIP

If your Dutch oven has wooden or plastic handles, cover them with a double thickness of foil before transferring the pot to the oven. Alternatively, if you don't have a Dutch oven large enough, use a covered roasting pan.

Baked Tuscan Vegetable and Bread Soup

MAKES ABOUT 6 SERVINGS.

Rather like a stew, this really thick vegetable soup is usually made a day or two ahead in Italy's Tuscany region where its name, Ribollita, means "recooked" or "reboiled." It starts with a rich minestrone that's layered in a casserole with crusty bread. When it sits, the flavour develops; then it's baked until steaming and tender inside, crusty and golden on top.

5 cups	chicken stock 1.25 L
1 lb	chicken breasts, skinned (bone in) 500 g
2	bay leaves 2
3 tbsp	olive oil 45 mL
1	onion, chopped 1
2	cloves garlic, minced 2
2	carrots, diced 2
2	stalks celery, diced 2
1	sweet green pepper, diced 1
2 cups	chopped cabbage 500 mL
1 tsp	EACH dried thyme and rosemary 5 mL
1	can (19 oz/540 mL) tomatoes, coarsely chopped (undrained) 1
1/4 tsp	pepper 1 mL
1	pkg (10 oz/284 g) fresh spinach, chopped 1
1/2 cup	chopped fresh parsley 125 mL
1	small zucchini, thinly sliced 1
1	can (19 oz/540 mL) white kidney beans, drained and rinsed 1
8	thick slices of stale Italian or French bread 8
1 cup	freshly grated Parmesan cheese 250 mL

1. In a large saucepan, bring chicken stock, chicken breasts and bay leaves to a boil; reduce heat, cover and simmer for about 20 minutes or until chicken is no longer pink inside. Remove chicken and discard bones; dice meat and set aside. Discard bay leaves. Keep stock warm.

2. Meanwhile, in a large skillet, heat 2 tbsp (25 mL) of the oil over medium heat; cook onion, garlic, carrots and celery for 10 minutes, stirring occasionally. Add remaining oil, green pepper, cabbage, thyme and rosemary; cook over low heat, stirring occasionally, for 10 minutes.

3. Add vegetable mixture to the stock in saucepan along with tomatoes and pepper; bring to a boil. Reduce heat, cover and simmer for 30 minutes. Add spinach, parsley, zucchini, kidney beans and reserved diced chicken; cook for 5 minutes. Remove 1 cup (250 mL) of the soup and set aside.

4. Ladle half of the remaining soup into a 24-cup (6 L) Dutch oven or casserole; cover with 4 of the bread slices and 1/2 cup (125 mL) of the Parmesan cheese. Cover with remaining soup; layer with remaining bread. Drizzle reserved soup over top; sprinkle with remaining Parmesan cheese. (Recipe can be prepared to this point, cooled, covered and refrigerated for up to 24 hours.)

5. Bake, covered, in a 350°F (180°C) oven for 20 minutes (45 minutes if refrigerated). Uncover and bake for 20 minutes longer (45 minutes if refrigerated) or until hot.

6. Serve soup in large, warmed bowls. Garnish with a drizzle of olive oil and a sprinkle of Parmesan cheese, if desired.

WINTER MAIN DISHES

Roast Beef with Pan Gravy

MAKES 6 TO 8 SERVINGS.

Not really a recipe so much as *just cooking* the "king of roasts." For the gravy, use beef broth or a combination of beef broth, dry red wine and/or vegetable water (reserved from cooking potatoes or other vegetables). Using the same method, you can cook as big a roast as you wish.

1	standing rib roast of beef (about 6 lb/2.7 kg)	1
	Salt and pepper	
3 tbsp	all-purpose flour	45 mL
2-1/2 cups	liquid (see above)	625 mL

1. Place beef, rib side down, in a large, shallow roasting pan; sprinkle with salt and pepper. Roast, uncovered, in a 450°F (230°C) oven for 20 minutes. Reduce temperature to 325°F (160°C) and roast for about 15 minutes per pound (500 g) or until a meat thermometer reaches 140°F (60°C) for rare.

2. Transfer beef to a warm serving platter; tent with foil and set aside in a warm place to rest for 20 minutes before carving so that juices can relax back into the meat.

3. To make gravy, skim fat from pan drippings (reserve if making Yorkshire Puddings, see page 190); stir in flour. Set roasting pan over medium heat; cook for 1 minute, stirring constantly. Gradually stir in liquid and any juices that have accumulated on the platter under the beef. Bring to a boil, stirring constantly. Reduce heat to low; simmer for 5 minutes or until thickened. Season to taste with salt and pepper.

4. Carve the beef and pass gravy in a heated sauceboat with the roast.

Yorkshire Puddings

MAKES 12 PUDDINGS.

My family doesn't think a roast of beef is complete without Yorkshire Puddings. This easy recipe is one I have been making for years. The secret to their success is to make the batter ahead to rest and become cold; then grease the muffin cups well and be sure they are very hot when you pour in the batter.

2	eggs	2
1/2 tsp	salt	2 mL
1 cup	all-purpose flour	250 mL
1 cup	milk	250 mL
1/4 cup	beef drippings	50 mL

1. In a blender, combine eggs, salt, flour and milk in that order. Process until a smooth batter forms, scraping down the sides of the bowl once or twice. Refrigerate, covered, for at least 1 hour.
2. Thoroughly grease the cups of a 12-cup muffin pan with some of the drippings; spoon a thin film of beef drippings into each cup. Place in a 400°F (200°C) oven for 5 minutes or until the fat is very hot. Divide the batter evenly among the cups; bake for 15 minutes. (Don't open the door at any time during their baking.) Reduce the temperature to 375°F (190°C); bake for 15 minutes, until puffed and golden. Serve at once.

Daube of Beef with Orange

MAKES 8 TO 10 SERVINGS.

This was a favourite for many of my readers, perhaps because it is such a great dish to serve to company. From southern France, it is a layered stew that is truly no-tend as it simmers away in the oven, sending forth the most enticing of aromas. Serve it with lots of crusty bread or mashed potatoes and a green salad. If you wish, substitute 1 cup (250 mL) beef stock and 1/4 cup (50 mL) EACH orange juice and red wine vinegar for the wine.

1	large orange	1
3 lb	stewing beef, cut into 2-inch (5 cm) cubes	1.5 kg
1-1/2 cups	dry red wine	375 mL
2 tbsp	olive oil	25 mL
1 tsp	EACH salt and dried thyme	5 mL
1/2 tsp	pepper	2 mL
1	bay leaf	1
3	cloves garlic, crushed	3
1/2 lb	side bacon slices, cut into 2-inch (5 cm) pieces	250 g
1/2 lb	small mushrooms	250 g
8	carrots, sliced	8
16	pearl onions, blanched and peeled (or 4 small onions, quartered)	16
1/2 cup	all-purpose flour	125 mL
2-1/2 cups	beef stock	625 mL
2 tbsp	tomato paste	25 mL

1. Cut a long, 1/2-inch (1 cm) wide strip of rind (without white part) from the orange. In a large bowl, combine beef, orange rind strip, wine, oil, salt, thyme, pepper, bay leaf and garlic. Cover and marinate in the refrigerator for at least 6 hours or overnight.

2. Arrange one-third of the bacon over the bottom of a 20- or 24-cup (5 or 6 L) casserole; cover with half of the mushrooms, then half of the carrots, then half of the onions. Reserving marinade, toss beef with flour to coat completely; arrange half over the vegetables. Repeat layers once. Cover with remaining bacon.

3. Stir stock and tomato paste into the marinade; pour over the casserole. Cover and bake in a 325°F (160°C) oven for 3-1/2 to 4 hours or until beef is very tender. Discard bay leaf and orange rind. (Stew can be cooled, covered and refrigerated for up to 2 days. Let stand at room temperature for 30 minutes before reheating in a 325°F/160°C oven for 30 to 45 minutes or more, until bubbly. The reheating time depends on how long it has been refrigerated and the type of casserole dish you are using.)

Spicy Shepherd's Pie with Feta-Potato Topping

MAKES 6 SERVINGS.

This casserole is a far cry from the usual leftover meat-potatoes-and-gravy combination, but it's just as comforting. Try it with ground lamb some time, too.

2	medium eggplants (2 lb/1 kg total)	2
	Salt	
1-1/2 lb	lean ground beef	750 g
1	onion, chopped	1
4	cloves garlic, minced	4
1	can (19 oz/540 mL) tomatoes, drained and chopped	1
1 tsp	EACH dried oregano, ground cumin, cinnamon and allspice	5 mL
	Pepper	
1 tbsp	olive oil	15 mL
1/2 lb	mushrooms, quartered	250 g
2	carrots, finely chopped	2
Pinch	hot pepper flakes	Pinch
1/2 cup	chopped fresh parsley	125 mL
6	potatoes, peeled and quartered	6
2 cups	crumbled feta cheese (1/2 lb/250 g)	500 mL
1/2 cup	freshly grated Parmesan cheese	125 mL
1	egg	1

1. Peel eggplants; cut into 1-inch (2.5 cm) cubes. Place in a colander; sprinkle lightly with salt. Set aside to drain while you prepare the remaining ingredients.
2. In a large nonstick skillet, cook beef, onion and half of the garlic over medium-high heat for 5 minutes, stirring often, until beef is no longer pink and onion is softened. Drain off any fat. Stir in tomatoes, oregano, cumin, cinnamon, allspice, and salt and pepper to taste. Transfer to a 12-cup (3 L) casserole.
3. Rinse eggplant; pat dry on paper towels. In the same skillet, heat oil over medium heat. Add eggplant, mushrooms, carrots, hot pepper flakes and remaining garlic to the skillet. Cook for 10 minutes, stirring often. Stir in the parsley; spoon evenly over meat mixture.
4. Meanwhile, cook potatoes in salted water to cover for about 20 minutes, until tender. Drain well, reserving cooking water. Return potatoes to saucepan; dry out slightly over low heat. Remove from heat and mash; add feta, Parmesan, egg, and salt and pepper to taste. Beat until smooth, adding about 2 tbsp (25 mL) reserved water to make potatoes fluffy. Spread potatoes over top of eggplant mixture. (Cool, cover and refrigerate if making ahead. Remove from refrigerator 30 minutes before baking.) Bake, uncovered, in a 400°F (200°C) oven for 50 to 60 minutes, or until bubbly, covering top with foil if it gets too brown.

Mexican Beef Pie

MAKES 6 SERVINGS.

A crunchy cornmeal mixture provides an easy crust for this spicy beef pie. It's perfect for a family supper, served with a crisp green salad.

FILLING

1 lb	lean ground beef	500 g
3	cloves garlic, minced	3
1	onion, chopped	1
2 tsp	chili powder	10 mL
1 tsp	dry mustard	5 mL
1/4 tsp	EACH cumin, hot pepper flakes, dried oregano and salt	1 mL
1	can (14 oz/398 mL) tomatoes, undrained	1
Half	sweet green pepper, diced	Half
1	can (14 oz/398 mL) kidney beans, undrained	1

CORNMEAL TOPPING

3/4 cup	coarse cornmeal	175 mL
1/2 cup	all-purpose flour	125 mL
1/2 tsp	EACH baking soda, salt and granulated sugar	2 mL
1 cup	shredded Cheddar cheese	250 mL
3/4 cup	buttermilk or sour milk*	175 mL
1	egg	1
2 tbsp	vegetable oil	25 mL

1. In a large skillet, cook beef, garlic, onion, chili powder, mustard, cumin, hot pepper flakes, oregano and salt over medium heat for 5 minutes, breaking up beef with a spoon. Stir in tomatoes, breaking them up with a spoon; cook, uncovered, for 20 minutes, stirring occasionally. Stir in green pepper. Arrange half of the mixture in a shallow 8-cup (2 L) casserole. Top with half of the beans. Repeat layers; set aside.

1. In a large bowl, combine cornmeal, flour, baking soda, salt and sugar. Stir in cheese.
2. In a small bowl, stir together buttermilk, egg and oil. Add buttermilk mixture to dry ingredients, stirring only enough to combine. Spread cornmeal topping evenly over beef/bean mixture. Bake in a 450°F (230°C) oven for about 15 minutes or until topping is set and lightly browned.

To sour milk, place 1 tbsp (15 mL) vinegar in a liquid measuring cup; then pour in milk to the 3/4-cup (175 mL) level. Let stand for 15 minutes before using. If using buttermilk, shake carton well before pouring.

Beef Curry

MAKES 4 TO 6 SERVINGS.

When I lived in London, Ontario, our next-door neighbour taught me to make this delicious curry with spices her father sent to her from Bombay. It's a simple recipe, good for family or entertaining because it's even better made one day and served the next. If you like curries hotter, add more crushed chilies. Serve it with basmati rice and set out little dishes of raisins and peanuts to sprinkle on top.

1-1/2 lb	lean beef (round steak or chuck) 750 g
3	cloves garlic, crushed 3
2 tbsp	minced fresh ginger 25 mL
1-1/2 tsp	EACH ground turmeric (approx.), ground cumin and ground coriander 7 mL
1 tsp	salt 5 mL
Pinch	hot pepper flakes Pinch
2 tbsp	vegetable oil (approx.) 25 mL
4	onions, chopped 4
1 tsp	EACH ground cloves and cinnamon 5 mL
1	can (19 oz/540 mL) tomatoes, undrained 1
	Chopped fresh coriander

1. Cut beef into 1-inch (2.5 cm) cubes. In a small bowl, combine beef, garlic, ginger, turmeric, cumin, coriander, salt and hot pepper flakes, mixing well with hands. Cover with foil and let stand at room temperature for 30 minutes.

2. In a large saucepan, heat oil over medium heat; cook onions for 7 minutes, stirring often. Stir in cloves, cinnamon and a pinch more turmeric; push to one side of the pan.

3. With a slotted spoon, transfer meat to the pan; cook, stirring often and adding more oil if necessary, until meat loses its pinkness. Stir in meat juices that have accumulated in the bowl along with tomatoes; bring to a boil. Reduce heat to low; cover and simmer for about 1-1/2 hours or until meat is very tender, stirring occasionally. (Curry can be cooled, covered and refrigerated for up to 2 days. Reheat slowly, stirring often.) Taste and adjust seasoning if necessary. Sprinkle with coriander to serve.

Note

If you have a pressure cooker, put a little water in it; use a heatproof bowl to hold the beef mixture, cover it with foil and place it on a rack inside. Pressure-cook for 10 minutes to draw out juices before browning the meat.

Texas Red

MAKES 4 TO 6 SERVINGS.

Texas-style chili traditionally contains no beans but is hearty enough to satisfy the biggest appetite. If you like less heat, just reduce the jalapeños in this spicy chili; of course, if you want it spicier, just add more.

2 lb	boneless beef (blade roast or round steak) 1 kg
3 tbsp	vegetable oil 45 mL
1/4 cup	chili powder 50 mL
3	onions, chopped 3
4	cloves garlic, minced 4
1	can (28 oz/796 mL) crushed or diced tomatoes (undrained) 1
1 tbsp	EACH packed brown sugar and red wine vinegar 15 mL
2 tsp	ground cumin 10 mL
1 tsp	EACH dried oregano, paprika and salt 5 mL
2	jalapeño peppers, seeded and minced 2

1. Trim beef well and cut into 3/4-inch (2 cm) cubes. In a skillet, heat oil over medium-high heat; brown beef, in batches. With a slotted spoon, transfer to a large saucepan. Add the chili powder to beef and set aside.
2. Add onions and garlic to the skillet; cook over medium heat for 5 minutes. Stir into meat along with the tomatoes. Bring to a boil; reduce heat, cover and cook for 20 minutes.
3. Stir in brown sugar, vinegar, cumin, oregano, paprika and salt; cook for 2 hours, covered, over low heat.
4. Stir in jalapeño peppers; cook, uncovered, for 10 minutes. Taste and adjust seasoning.

TIP

Wear rubber gloves when cutting the jalapeño peppers.

Chicken Stew with Parsley Dumplings

MAKES ABOUT 4 SERVINGS.

This is one of my husband, Kent's, all-time favourite suppers, and I must admit there is nothing more comforting than a steaming pan of chicken stew topped with fluffy dumplings. Be sure to use a pot large enough to allow 3 inches (8 cm) of space for the dumplings to rise.

1	chicken (3 lb/1.5 kg) or 4 bone-in breast halves	1
2 tbsp	all-purpose flour	25 mL
1/4 tsp	EACH salt, pepper and paprika	1 mL
1 tbsp	EACH butter and vegetable oil (approx.)	15 mL
4	small red potatoes, quartered	4
2	EACH parsnips, carrots and onions, quartered	2
2	stalks celery, diagonally sliced	2
4 cups	water or chicken stock	1 L
1/2 tsp	dried thyme	2 mL
1/4 tsp	crumbled dried sage	1 mL
2	bay leaves	2
1 cup	frozen peas	250 mL

1. If using a whole chicken, cut into pieces, cutting the breast into 4, the back into 2 and separating the drumsticks from the thighs. Wipe with paper towels.
2. In a sturdy plastic bag, combine the flour, salt, pepper and paprika. Shake chicken in the bag in batches to coat with flour mixture.
3. In a large saucepan, melt butter with the oil over medium heat. Add chicken in batches and brown on all sides, adding more oil if needed; remove browned pieces to a warm bowl or plate.
4. Pour off all but 2 tbsp (25 mL) of the pan drippings. Add potatoes, parsnips, carrots, onions and celery to the pan; cook for 5 minutes, stirring often. Stir in water; bring to a boil, scraping up any brown bits from the bottom of the pan.
5. Return chicken and any juices; stir in thyme, sage and bay leaves. Return to a boil; reduce heat to very low, cover and simmer until chicken is tender and no longer pink inside, about 25 minutes if using breasts and 45 minutes if using the whole chicken. Remove and discard bay leaves. Stir in peas. Taste and adjust seasoning if necessary.

PARSLEY DUMPLINGS

2 cups	sifted cake and pastry flour	500 mL
4 tsp	baking powder	20 mL
1/2 tsp	salt	2 mL
2 tbsp	chopped fresh parsley	25 mL
2 tbsp	shortening	25 mL
2/3 cup	milk (approx.)	150 mL

1. Meanwhile, stir or sift together flour, baking powder and salt in a large bowl; stir in parsley. Cut in shortening until mixture is the consistency of oatmeal. Stir in milk, adding a few more drops if necessary to make a sticky dough.
2. Evenly dust a large plate with flour. With a tablespoon, cut out dumplings and drop onto floured plate. Quickly drop dumplings onto gently simmering stew, spacing them evenly; cover pan tightly and simmer, without lifting the lid, for 15 minutes. Serve immediately.

Fiesta Chicken and Sausage Stew

MAKES 8 SERVINGS.

A perfect main course to take away to the chalet or to the potluck supper next door, this satisfying stew is even better made a day ahead and reheated. Serve with crusty white or corn bread and a green salad.

8	chicken legs (about 4 lb/2 kg) 8
1 tsp	EACH oregano, marjoram and dry mustard 5 mL
1/2 tsp	EACH salt, pepper and ground cumin 2 mL
1/4 tsp	cayenne pepper 1 mL
2 tbsp	olive oil 25 mL
1-1/2 lb	chorizo, Italian or other spicy fresh sausage, thinly sliced 750 g
12	cloves garlic, halved 12
4	carrots, cut into large chunks 4
2	onions, sliced 2
2	sweet red or yellow peppers (or a combination), cut into thin strips 2
1	jalapeño pepper, seeded and diced 1
1	can (28 oz/796 mL) plum tomatoes, drained and quartered 1
1/4 cup	chopped fresh parsley or coriander 50 mL

1. Wipe chicken with a damp cloth. In a small bowl, stir together oregano, marjoram, mustard, salt, pepper, cumin and cayenne. Rub over chicken pieces and refrigerate, covered, in a large bowl for 1 hour.

2. In a large skillet, heat half the oil over medium-high heat and brown sausages well, about 10 minutes. With a slotted spoon, remove to drain on paper towels. Add remaining oil to the same skillet; brown chicken, in batches, for about 5 minutes a side. Transfer to a large, shallow casserole.

3. Discard all but 2 tbsp (25 mL) of the drippings from the skillet; cook garlic, carrots and onions, covered, over medium heat for about 7 minutes, stirring occasionally, until carrots are slightly tender. Add sweet and jalapeño peppers; cook for 2 minutes. Arrange vegetables with sausages around chicken pieces. Add tomatoes to the skillet and bring to a boil, scraping up any brown bits from the bottom. Pour over the chicken.

4. Bake, covered, basting often, in a 400°F (200°C) oven for 45 to 50 minutes or until juices run clear when the thickest part of the chicken thigh is pierced and the chicken is no longer pink near the bone. (Stew can be cooled, covered and refrigerated for up to 2 days; reheat in a 350°F/180°C oven for about 30 to 40 minutes or until bubbly.) Sprinkle with parsley to serve.

Honey-Garlic Chicken Wings

MAKES 4 SERVINGS.

I've been doing chicken wings like this for many years, and no matter how else I prepare wings, my family likes these best. Now Allen and Anne are making them in their own homes. Serve the quick and easy braised wings with rice and green peas for a fast supper treat.

3 lb	chicken wings	1.5 kg
2 tbsp	peanut or vegetable oil	25 mL
1/3 cup	soy sauce, preferably low-salt	75 mL
2 tbsp	liquid honey	25 mL
2 tbsp	dry sherry	25 mL
2	cloves garlic, crushed	2
1 tbsp	minced fresh ginger	15 mL

1. Remove tips from wings and reserve for stock if desired. Separate wings at the joint.
2. In a wok or large skillet, heat oil over high heat; stir-fry wings for 3 to 4 minutes or until browned.
3. Stir together soy sauce, honey, sherry, garlic and ginger; pour over wings and stir to coat well.
4. Reduce heat to low; cover and simmer for about 30 minutes or until the wings are tender and the sauce is thickened, stirring often near the end of the cooking time to make sure sauce doesn't burn.

Maple-Orange Crown Roast of Pork

MAKES 8 SERVINGS.

This was a recipe in the first article I wrote for *Canadian Living* and a dish my friends Gary and Diane Slimmon made long before they met me. It was on their list of favourites.

A crown roast is usually easy to find around holiday time. If not, ask your butcher to make a crown of two rib loin sections (backbone removed) tied together so that the ribs are on the outside, the meat on the inside. Have the bones Frenched—meat and fat trimmed off the tips.

A note about the stuffing: the celery-mushroom stuffing in this recipe could also be used in a pork loin roast.

12 rib	crown roast of pork (about 6 to 7 lb/about 3 kg) 12 rib
	Salt and pepper
1/4 cup	butter 50 mL
1 cup	chopped celery 250 mL
1 cup	finely chopped mushrooms 250 mL
1/2 cup	chopped onion 125 mL
1/4 cup	finely chopped fresh parsley 50 mL
1/2 tsp	grated orange rind 2 mL
1/2 tsp	dried basil 2 mL
1/4 tsp	dried thyme 1 mL
1/4 tsp	crumbled dried sage 1 mL
1 cup	dry bread crumbs 250 mL
1/2 cup	maple syrup 125 mL
1/2 cup	orange juice 125 mL
	Parsley sprigs and orange slices

1. Place the roast, bone tips up, on a rack in a shallow roasting pan. Season with salt and pepper. Make a ball of aluminum foil and press into the middle to keep roast open. Wrap bone tips with bits of foil. Roast in a 325°F (160°C) oven for 30 minutes.

2. Meanwhile, to make the stuffing, melt the butter in a large skillet over medium heat. Add celery, mushrooms and onion; cook until onion is translucent, 5 to 8 minutes. Remove from the heat. Stir in parsley, orange rind, 1/2 tsp (2 mL) salt, 1/4 tsp (1 mL) pepper, and the basil, thyme and sage. Stir in bread crumbs to mix well. Combine maple syrup and orange juice; set aside.

3. Remove foil from the centre of the roast and pack centre with stuffing, mounding it high. Roast for another 1-1/2 to 2 hours or until a meat thermometer registers 160°F (70°C), basting the pork with the maple-orange mixture every 15 minutes during the last hour and covering the stuffing with foil if the top becomes too brown.

4. Remove roast to a warm platter and tent with foil for 15 minutes.

5. Remove foil from bone tips and decorate with paper frills, if desired, to serve. Garnish platter with parsley and orange slices, cut halfway through and twisted. Slice between ribs to serve.

TIP

For easier handling, place roast on an oiled 9- to 10-inch-diameter (23 to 25 cm) tart pan bottom before setting on the rack.

Bistro-Style Lamb with Garlic Crust

MAKES 10 SERVINGS.

This is the type of casserole I love serving to company with a salad and a fruit dessert. Although the list of ingredients is lengthy, the recipe is easy to prepare and uses items you probably already have in your kitchen. I developed the recipe for *Homemaker's Magazine,* and Carolyn Gall Casey (the tester at the time) said, "It was the best recipe to come through the kitchen, and years after I could still taste it."

1 lb	dried white beans (2 cups/500 mL) 500 g
6	carrots, sliced 6
4	onions, chopped 4
1	bouquet garni* 1
1/4 lb	salt pork or bacon, diced 125 g
2-3/4 lb	lean, boneless lamb shoulder 1.375 kg
1/3 cup	all-purpose flour 75 mL
	Salt and pepper
2 tbsp	olive oil (approx.) 25 mL
2-1/2 cups	beef stock 625 mL
1/4 cup	tomato paste 50 mL
1 tbsp	Dijon mustard 15 mL
1	large head garlic, cloves peeled and halved 1
1 tsp	EACH dried thyme, marjoram and crumbled rosemary 5 mL

1. Sort and rinse beans. In a medium saucepan, cover beans with 6 cups (1.5 L) water; let soak overnight in the refrigerator. (Or, cover with water and bring to a boil; boil for 2 minutes. Remove from heat; cover and let stand for 1 hour.)

2. Drain beans; cover again with cold water and bring to a boil. Add half of the carrots, half of the onions and the bouquet garni. Bring to a boil. Reduce heat and simmer, covered, for about 40 minutes or until beans are tender but not mushy. Drain and discard bouquet garni.

3. Meanwhile, in a large saucepan, cook salt pork over medium-high heat until browned and crisp, about 4 minutes. With a slotted spoon, remove to drain on paper towels. Add remaining carrots and onions to the pan; cook for 5 minutes over medium heat; with a slotted spoon, remove to a bowl.

4. Meanwhile, trim lamb and cut into 2-inch (5 cm) pieces. In a sturdy bag or bowl, combine flour, 1/2 tsp (2 mL) salt and 1/4 tsp (1 mL) pepper; add lamb and shake to coat well. If the drippings in the pan are not at least 1 tbsp (15 mL), add half the oil to the pan. Cook lamb in batches over medium-high heat for 3 to 4 minutes until it is browned on all sides, removing each batch as it browns to the bowl with the vegetables. Add more oil to the pan as needed.

5. Add stock, tomato paste, mustard, garlic, thyme, marjoram and rosemary to the saucepan. Bring to a boil, scraping up any brown bits from the bottom of the pan. Return lamb, vegetables and salt pork to the saucepan; bring to a boil. Reduce heat to medium-low; simmer, covered, for about 1 hour or until lamb is tender.

GARLIC CRUST

1/4 cup	butter	50 mL
3	large cloves garlic, minced	3
12	1/2-inch (1 cm) slices French baguette (approx.)	12
1 tbsp	Dijon mustard	15 mL

6. Stir in cooked bean mixture; transfer to a 16-cup (4 L) casserole. (Recipe can be prepared to this point, covered and refrigerated for up to 2 days. Remove from the refrigerator 30 minutes before baking; then reheat, covered, in a 350°F/180°C oven for 20 minutes before adding crust.)

1. In a large skillet, melt butter over low heat; stir in garlic. Spread bread with mustard; arrange slices, mustard side down, in skillet. Heat for 3 to 5 minutes, turning slices once, until butter is absorbed. Arrange bread slices, mustard side down, over lamb mixture. Bake in a 350°F (180°C) oven for 30 to 40 minutes, or until casserole is bubbly and crust is golden brown.

Bouquet garni: Tie 1 tbsp (15 mL) thyme sprigs or 1 tsp (5 mL) dried thyme, 3 parsley sprigs and 2 bay leaves inside the ribs of 2 short stalks of celery.

Quick Cassoulet

MAKES 10 TO 12 SERVINGS.

The mere title is an oxymoron. A true cassoulet (a stew of beans and meat, which I have made on occasion after inspiring visits to southwestern France) is made from "confit," or preserved goose, dried beans and a selection of meats like lamb and pork. It takes about 4 days to prepare. There's no doubt that it is wonderful, but as we all age, both time and health dictate a lighter, faster version. I hope I've retained much of the wonderful flavour of the dish. It's great for feeding a crowd and perfect for carrying to the chalet on the weekend.

4 lb	duck 2 kg
1 lb	garlic farmer's sausage 500 g
1 tsp	vegetable oil 5 mL
4	cloves garlic, minced 4
2	onions, coarsely chopped 2
1/2 cup	dry white wine 125 mL
1	can (28 oz/796 mL) crushed tomatoes, undrained 1
1/2 tsp	EACH dried thyme and savory 2 mL
2	bay leaves 2
Pinch	granulated sugar Pinch
	Salt and pepper
4	cans (19 oz/540 mL each) white pea or navy beans 4
2 cups	fresh bread crumbs 500 mL
1/3 cup	chopped fresh parsley 75 mL

1. Remove any loose fat from the duck; cut duck into small serving pieces and set aside.

2. Place backbone, wing tips, neck and giblets in a medium saucepan. Cover with 3 times as much cold water. Bring to a boil, then reduce the heat to medium-low. Simmer, partially covered, for 1 hour; set aside.

3. Meanwhile, cut sausage into 1/2-inch (1 cm) slices. In a large flame-proof casserole, heat oil over medium-high heat; brown sausage for 5 minutes. Remove with a slotted spoon to drain on paper towels.

4. In the same casserole, in 2 batches, brown duck pieces well on all sides so that they render as much fat as possible; set aside. Pour out and reserve all but 2 tbsp (25 mL) drippings. Add garlic and onions to the casserole; cook, stirring, over medium heat for 5 minutes. Stir in wine; bring to a boil, scraping up any bits in the bottom of the pan. Stir in tomatoes, thyme, savory, bay leaves, sugar, and salt and pepper to taste. Add sausage and duck pieces. Bring to a boil; cover and reduce heat to medium-low. Simmer for 1-1/2 hours or until the meat is very tender, stirring often.

5. Drain and rinse beans. Add to casserole with enough duck stock (about 1 cup/250 mL) from simmering bones to make a very moist, but not soupy, mixture. Discard bay leaves. (Recipe can be prepared ahead to this point and frozen for up to 3 months. Thaw in the refrigerator to proceed.)

6. In a medium bowl, combine bread crumbs, parsley and 1/4 cup (50 mL) reserved drippings. Sprinkle evenly over casserole. (Recipe can be prepared up to this point and refrigerated, covered, for up to 1 day. Add 10 minutes or so to heating time.)

7. Bake, uncovered, in a 350°F (180°C) oven for about 45 minutes or until a golden-brown crust has formed and the casserole is bubbly.

Maple Baked Beans

MAKES 6 SERVINGS.

In my cookbook, *New Casseroles and Other One-Dish Meals,* you will find Sharon Boyd's recipe for Baked Beans, which are absolutely delicious. When she makes them for a potluck supper, they always disappear quickly. My baked beans are simpler, but good, and they make an easy, satisfying supper. I stick some slices of side pork in a pan to bake alongside them for an hour, and I add a creamy cabbage salad and chili sauce to the meal.

2 cups	dried white navy (pea) beans (1 lb/500 g) 500 mL
1-1/2 tsp	dry mustard 7 mL
1-1/2 tsp	pepper 7 mL
1 tsp	salt 5 mL
1	onion, minced 1
1/4 lb	salt pork 125 g
3/4 cup	maple syrup (preferably dark cooking) 175 mL
2 tbsp	molasses 25 mL

1. Sort and rinse beans. In a medium saucepan, cover beans with 6 cups (1.5 L) cold water and let soak overnight in the refrigerator. (Or, cover with water and bring to a boil; boil for 2 minutes. Remove from the heat; cover and let stand for 1 hour.)

2. Drain beans; cover again with cold water and bring to a boil; reduce heat and simmer, covered, for 40 minutes.

3. Reserving cooking liquid, drain and transfer beans to a bean pot or heavy 12-cup (3 L) casserole. Stir in mustard, pepper, salt and onion. Rinse salt pork; dice and stir into beans. Stir in enough reserved liquid to reach the top of the beans.

4. Cover and bake in a 325°F (160°C) oven for about 5 hours or until beans are very tender, stirring occasionally and adding more cooking liquid or water, if necessary, to ensure that the beans do not become too dry.

5. Stir in maple syrup and molasses and bake, uncovered, for 30 minutes.

Vegetable Lasagna

MAKES 10 TO 12 SERVINGS.

I've had many people tell me that this moist and hearty vegetarian version has been their favourite lasagna recipe since it first appeared in *Homemaker's Magazine* several years ago. Served with garlic bread and a crisp green salad, it's perfect for a party.

2 tbsp	vegetable oil 25 mL
2	onions, chopped 2
2	cloves garlic, minced 2
1/2 lb	mushrooms, sliced 250 g
1	sweet green pepper, chopped 1
1	can (28 oz/796 mL) plum tomatoes 1
1	can (14 oz/398 mL) tomato sauce 1
2	carrots, shredded 2
1/4 cup	chopped fresh parsley 50 mL
1 tsp	EACH dried basil and oregano 5 mL
	Granulated sugar and salt to taste
1/4 tsp	pepper 1 mL
Pinch	hot pepper flakes Pinch
1	pkg (10 oz/284 mL) spinach 1
9 to 15	lasagna noodles, depending on size 9 to 15
2	eggs 2
1 lb	low-fat ricotta cheese, drained if necessary 500 g
Pinch	nutmeg Pinch
1 lb	part-skim mozzarella cheese, shredded 500 g
1 cup	freshly grated Parmesan cheese 250 mL

1. In a medium saucepan, heat oil over medium heat. Add onions, garlic, mushrooms and pepper. Cook, stirring often, for 5 minutes. Add tomatoes and their juice, cutting up tomatoes as finely as possible. Stir in tomato sauce, carrots, parsley, basil, oregano, sugar, salt, pepper and hot pepper flakes. Bring to a boil, cover, reduce heat and simmer for 30 minutes, stirring occasionally.

2. Meanwhile, in a heavy saucepan, cook spinach, covered, with only the water that clings to its leaves after washing, for 2 to 5 minutes, or until just wilted. Drain well in a sieve and when cool enough to handle, squeeze any moisture out with your hands. Chop finely and set aside.

3. In a large pot of boiling salted water, cook noodles according to package directions. Drain, rinse with cold water, drain again and spread out on clean tea towels on a flat surface.

4. In a food processor, whirl eggs, ricotta cheese, nutmeg and cooked spinach until fairly smooth.

5. Spread one-quarter of the tomato sauce in the bottom of a greased 13 x 9-inch (3.5 L) baking dish. Arrange a single layer of noodles on top. Spread with half of the ricotta mixture, then one-quarter of the tomato sauce, one-third of the mozzarella and one-third of the Parmesan. Repeat these layers once. Arrange remaining noodles on top; spread with remaining tomato sauce and sprinkle with remaining cheese. The dish will be quite full but will accommodate everything. (The recipe can be made ahead, covered and refrigerated for up to 24 hours.)

6. Bake, uncovered, in a 350°F (180°C) oven for 30 minutes. Cover with foil and bake another 10 to 15 minutes or until hot and bubbly. Allow an additional 10 to 15 minutes if previously refrigerated. Let stand for 10 minutes before cutting into squares to serve.

Note

The baked lasagna can be frozen, in its entirety, in part or in individual portions. Just cool and place in a foil-lined baking dish just the size of the lasagna, in individual servings or in servings for 3 or 4. Seal the foil tightly all around the lasagna and place in the freezer until solid. You can then return the dish to your cupboard.

Thawing the lasagna isn't necessary; slip it out of the foil and back into its baking dish. It will take about 1-1/2 hours in a 350°F (180°C) oven, covered. If you thaw the lasagna before reheating, defrost it in the refrigerator and allow 20 to 25 minutes in a 350°F (180°C) oven.

Parmesan Baked Fillets

MAKES 2 SERVINGS, EASILY DOUBLED FOR 4.

This quick and easy treatment is good on any kind of fish fillets. Team them up with steamed broccoli and oven-fried potato slices for a simple but delicious supper.

1/2 cup	light mayonnaise	125 mL
1/4 cup	finely chopped fresh parsley	50 mL
1/2 tsp	finely chopped fresh thyme (or a pinch dried thyme)	2 mL
1/4 cup	EACH dry bread crumbs and freshly grated Parmesan cheese	50 mL
1/2 lb	fish fillets	250 g

1. In a small bowl, stir together mayonnaise, parsley and thyme. On waxed paper or in a shallow dish, mix bread crumbs with cheese. Pat fillets dry with paper towels.

2. Spread mayonnaise mixture on both sides of fillets. Dip each into crumb mixture, turning to coat; place on greased baking sheet (or one lined with greased foil).

3. Bake in a 450°F (230°C) oven for 8 to 10 minutes or until fish is opaque and flakes easily when tested with a fork.

WINTER SIDES AND SALADS

IN THE MENUS ...

Old-Fashioned Scalloped Potatoes

MAKES 4 SERVINGS.

When I was writing my *Comfortable Kitchen Cookbook,* I decided to include a recipe for the simple potato dish that so many people love. When I make scalloped potatoes, I arrange a thin layer of potatoes and onions, then sprinkle them with a bit of flour, salt and pepper, repeating until the dish is full. Then I pour in milk until I can see it from the top, dot everything with butter and bake. In my recipe, I wanted to provide quantities so that even a novice cook could make scalloped potatoes without going to the trouble of making a cream sauce.

My son, Allen, makes this dish all the time but complained that my recipe in the book didn't call for enough milk. I retested it for this book and found that the quantity of milk was just right for a deep casserole. But Allen was making it in a shallow gratin dish, the only 8-cup one he had. So, if you make scalloped potatoes in a shallow dish, you might need more milk. The shape does make a difference.

2 lb	potatoes (7 to 8), peeled	1 kg
2 tbsp	all-purpose flour	25 mL
1 tsp	salt	5 mL
1/4 tsp	pepper	1 mL
1	small onion, thinly sliced	1
2 tbsp	butter	25 mL
2 cups	milk	500 mL

1. Dry potatoes well; thinly slice. In a large bowl, toss together potatoes, flour, salt and pepper; layer half in a greased 8-cup (2 L) casserole. Sprinkle with half the onion; dot with half the butter. Repeat layers. Pour in the milk.

2. Cover and bake in a 350°F (180°C) oven for 30 minutes. Uncover and bake 30 to 35 minutes longer until golden and bubbly.

Baked German Potato Salad

MAKES 4 TO 6 SERVINGS.

My good friends Gary and Diane Slimmon list this hearty, warm salad among their favourites and serve it with sausage and pickled beets. When I developed the recipe, I called for 16 small potatoes, but it works just as well with bigger, older potatoes.

5	red potatoes, scrubbed and halved 5
5	slices side bacon, diced (about 1/4 lb/125 g) 5
2	stalks celery, sliced 2
1	onion, chopped 1
2 tbsp	all-purpose flour 25 mL
1/2 tsp	EACH dry mustard and salt 2 mL
1/4 tsp	pepper 1 mL
1/2 cup	cider vinegar 125 mL
1/3 cup	granulated sugar 75 mL
1 cup	water 250 mL
1/4 cup	chopped fresh parsley 50 mL

1. In a saucepan of boiling salted water, cook potatoes until barely tender when pierced with the tip of a knife, about 15 minutes. Do not over-cook. Drain and cut into 1/4-inch (5 mm) thick slices. Arrange in a greased, shallow 8-cup (2 L) baking dish.

2. In a large skillet over medium heat, fry bacon until crisp. Remove with a slotted spoon and set aside to drain on paper towels.

3. Add celery and onion to the drippings in the pan. Cook over medium heat for 3 minutes. Stir in flour, mustard, salt and pepper; cook for 2 minutes, stirring.

4. Stir in vinegar, sugar, then water all at once, stirring constantly; bring to a boil and cook for 1 minute. Stir in parsley and cooked bacon; pour over potatoes and toss gently to coat. (Recipe can be prepared to this point, covered and refrigerated for up to 6 hours. Remove from refrigerator 30 minutes before baking.)

5. Bake, uncovered, in a 375°F (190°C) oven for 45 minutes or until bubbly. Serve hot or warm.

Tarragon Mushroom Salad

MAKES 8 SERVINGS.

This marinated mushroom salad from my vegetable cookbook has been one of my daughter, Anne's, favourites for many years. For this recipe, use ordinary, white button mushrooms.

1 lb	fresh mushrooms	500 g
1	medium Spanish onion, thinly sliced	1
2/3 cup	tarragon vinegar	150 mL
1/2 cup	vegetable oil	125 mL
2 tbsp	water	25 mL
1	large clove garlic, crushed	1
1 tbsp	granulated sugar	15 mL
1-1/2 tsp	salt, or to taste	7 mL
1/4 tsp	pepper	1 mL
1 tbsp	chopped fresh parsley	15 mL

1. Clean mushrooms and place in a large container. Separate the onion rings and add to mushrooms.
2. In a small bowl, stir together vinegar, oil, water, garlic, sugar, salt and pepper, until sugar is dissolved. Pour over the mushrooms and onion. Gently mix together. Cover and refrigerate for at least 8 hours, stirring occasionally.
3. To serve, drain mushrooms and onion; place in a small serving bowl and sprinkle with parsley.

WINTER DESSERTS

IN THE MENUS ...

Lemon Mousse

MAKES 12 TO 16 SERVINGS.

This easy, delicious dessert has been part of our New Year's Eve dinner for as long as I can remember. I serve it with a selection of Christmas cookies. Mousse is one of those desserts you don't make every day, but for a special dinner you can splurge on the calories.

7	eggs	7
1-1/3 cups	granulated sugar	325 mL
1/3 cup	butter, melted	75 mL
1-1/2 cups	fresh lemon juice (6 to 7 lemons)	375 mL
3 cups	whipping cream	750 mL
1-1/2 tbsp	grated lemon zest (outer rind)	20 mL

1. In a large bowl, combine the eggs and sugar. With an electric mixer, beat at medium speed until mixture is pale, about 5 minutes. Gradually beat in butter in a thin stream. Stir in lemon juice.
2. Pour into the top of a double boiler and cook over simmering water, stirring constantly, for about 15 minutes or until the mixture thickens into a custard. Transfer to a clean, large bowl and refrigerate for at least 1 hour, stirring twice. (Recipe can be prepared to this point, covered and refrigerated for up to 1 day.)
3. In a large bowl, beat cream until soft peaks form. Fold into the cold custard. Fold in the lemon zest. Transfer to a chilled serving bowl or individual dishes. Serve immediately or cover and refrigerate for up to 2 hours.

Hint

Be sure to remove zest from lemons before you juice them. Wrap the zest well and refrigerate until you are ready to use it.

Rich Light Fruit Cake

MAKES 10 LB (4.5 KG) OF CAKE (4 SMALL CAKES).

I included a good selection of fruit cake recipes in my Christmas cookbook (now called *Canadian Christmas Cooking*). This recipe was reprinted in *The Toronto Star* and then requested by readers for a number of years. The cake is dense, fruit filled and very distinctive with its taste of ginger and pecans ... one of my favourites, too. Although moist and delicious even after a few days, let it ripen for 3 to 4 weeks for best results.

1/2 cup	granulated sugar	125 mL
1 cup	water	250 mL
1 tbsp	corn syrup	15 mL
3 cups	white seedless raisins	750 mL
3 cups	red candied cherries, chopped	750 mL
3 cups	green candied cherries, chopped	750 mL
2-2/3 cups	candied pineapple, chopped	650 mL
2-1/3 cups	candied citron peel, diced	575 mL
1 cup	candied orange peel, diced	250 mL
3/4 cup	candied ginger (6 oz/175 g jar, drained), chopped	175 mL
1/2 cup	candied lemon peel, diced	125 mL
4 cups	pecan halves	1 L
2-1/4 cups	blanched almond halves or whole almonds	550 mL
1 cup	brandy	250 mL
2 cups	butter, at room temperature	500 mL
4 cups	all-purpose flour	1 L
8	eggs	8
2-1/2 cups	granulated sugar	625 mL

1. Make a syrup by boiling the 1/2 cup (125 mL) sugar and water together in a small saucepan for 5 minutes. Stir in the corn syrup and set aside.

2. In a large glass bowl, combine all the fruit and nuts. Stir in 1/2 cup (125 mL) of the syrup and all of the brandy. Mix thoroughly, cover and let sit for 24 hours, occasionally stirring gently.

3. When you are ready to bake the cake, prepare four 9 x 5-inch (2 L) loaf tins or other pans. Grease the pans with butter and line them with a buttered, double thickness of parchment paper.

4. To prepare the batter, cream the butter well in a large bowl. Gradually add the flour, creaming to blend smoothly. In another bowl, beat the eggs lightly, and gradually beat in the sugar. Stir both mixtures together until smooth, but do not overmix. Add the fruit and nuts gradually with any liquid, folding and mixing together gently with your hands.

5. Turn into prepared pans and bake in a 250°F (120°C) oven for about 4 hours, or until a skewer inserted in the centre of each cake comes out clean of batter.

6. Cool for 30 minutes in the pans on racks; then turn cakes out onto the racks. Carefully remove the paper and cool completely.

TIP

After the cake is cool, wrap in brandy-moistened cheesecloth, then plastic wrap and foil; keep in an airtight tin in the refrigerator. If you keep the cheesecloth moist (not wet), the cake will keep for years. There is no need to freeze it.

Shortbread

No matter what other fancy cookies we come up with, everyone still loves good old-fashioned buttery shortbread. Here are three different treatments I developed for the traditional cookie for *Canadian Living*, all using the original recipe from my book, *Canadian Christmas Cooking*. Although the cookies can be frozen for up to 6 months, shortbread is at its melt-in-your-mouth best if baked and enjoyed within 2 weeks. For the most tender results, be sure to refrigerate the dough for the amount of time given.

2 cups	unsalted butter, softened 500 mL
1 cup	icing sugar 250 mL
4 cups	all-purpose flour 1 L
1/2 tsp	salt 2 mL

1. In a large bowl, cream the butter thoroughly; beat in the sugar until light and fluffy. Gradually add the flour and salt and gently mix well. Knead dough very gently until smooth and soft but not oily. Shape and bake as directed below. Remove to wire racks and let cool. Store in an airtight container.

Pan Shortbread Bars

MAKES 5 DOZEN.

1. Pat dough into ungreased 15 x 10-inch (38 x 25 cm) jelly-roll pan; smooth surface with the back of a spoon. Score into 2-1/2 x 1-inch (6 x 2.5 cm) rectangles; prick each 3 times. Cover lightly and refrigerate until firm, at least 2 hours.
2. Cut out rectangles and place 1/2 inch (1 cm) apart on ungreased baking sheets. Place in a 325°F (160°C) oven and immediately reduce temperature to 275°F (140°C). Bake for 30 minutes; turn baking sheets and bake for 5 to 10 minutes longer, or until bars are firm and golden on the bottom and sand-coloured on top.

Rolled Shortbread Cookies

MAKES 5 TO 6 DOZEN.

1. Form dough into a ball; wrap in waxed paper and refrigerate overnight.
2. Remove from refrigerator a few minutes before using. Working with a small portion of the dough and keeping the rest wrapped, roll out dough between 2 sheets of waxed paper to 1/4-inch (5 mm) thickness.

With floured cookie cutter, cut into desired shapes and place on ungreased baking sheets. Decorate with candied fruit or candies and place in a 325°F (160°C) oven. Immediately reduce temperature to 275°F (140°C) and bake for 20 to 25 minutes, or until cookies are firm and golden on the bottom and sand-coloured on top.

Moulded Shortbread

MAKES 3 CIRCLES.

1. Lightly butter the pattern on a 6-1/2-inch (16 cm) shortbread mould; dust with flour. Divide dough into 3 parts. Pat each portion one by one into the mould; invert onto ungreased baking sheet and remove mould with the aid of a knife tip. (Alternatively, on baking sheet, mound each portion about the same size as the mould. Press with mould and then remove and trim dough.) Refrigerate for at least 2 hours to set design.

2. Place in a 325°F (160°C) oven; immediately reduce temperature to 275°F (140°C). Bake for 20 minutes; turn baking sheets and bake for 10 to 15 minutes longer, or until shortbread is firm and golden on the bottom and sand-coloured on top.

Hint

Use unsalted butter when it's listed because it is a fresher butter and will make a difference in the taste of the baked cookies.

Sour Cherry Almond Bars

MAKES 20 BARS.

I couldn't resist combining sour cherries with the flavour that goes so well with them. These bars are particularly good with homemade cherry jam.

1 cup	all-purpose flour	250 mL
1/2 cup	ground almonds	125 mL
1/3 cup	packed brown sugar	75 mL
1/3 cup	butter, cubed	75 mL
3/4 tsp	almond extract	4 mL
3/4 cup	sour cherry jam	175 mL
1 tbsp	fresh lemon juice	15 mL
3/4 cup	sliced almonds	175 mL

1. Grease an 8-inch (2 L) square cake pan; line sides with waxed or parchment paper. Set aside.

2. In a food processor or bowl, mix together the flour, ground almonds and sugar. Add butter; sprinkle with 1/4 tsp (1 mL) of the almond extract. Pulse or cut in with a pastry blender or two knives until dough is in coarse crumbs.

3. Gently press handfuls of dough together; press evenly into prepared pan. Bake in a 350°F (180°C) oven for about 15 minutes or until light golden; let cool on a rack.

4. In a food processor or bowl, combine jam, remaining almond extract and lemon juice until smooth; spread evenly over base. Sprinkle with sliced almonds. Bake in a 350°F (180°C) oven for 25 to 30 minutes or until bubbling and almonds are light golden. Let cool on a rack; cut into bars.

Mocha Hazelnut Nanaimo Bars

MAKES 32 BARS.

There is no mistake—everyone loves the classic three-layered cookie. But once you've added the wonderful flavour of coffee to a Nanaimo Bar, you'll have one more reason to thank the folks in Nanaimo, British Columbia.

1-1/2 cups	graham cracker crumbs	375 mL
1 cup	flaked, sweetened coconut	250 mL
1/2 cup	finely chopped toasted hazelnuts	125 mL
2/3 cup	butter	150 mL
1/3 cup	unsweetened cocoa powder	75 mL
1/4 cup	granulated sugar	50 mL
1 tbsp	instant coffee granules	15 mL
1	egg, lightly beaten	1

FILLING

2 cups	icing sugar	500 mL
1/4 cup	butter, softened	50 mL
1 tbsp	instant coffee granules	15 mL

MOCHA TOPPING

2 tbsp	butter	25 mL
1 tbsp	instant coffee granules	15 mL
4 oz	semisweet chocolate, coarsely chopped	125 g

1. In a large bowl, stir together the crumbs, coconut and hazelnuts; set aside.
2. In a saucepan, heat together the butter, cocoa, sugar and coffee granules over low heat, stirring, until butter is melted. Remove from the heat; whisk in the egg. Stir into crumbs until well mixed. Press into a greased 8-inch (2 L) square cake pan; bake in a 350°F (180°C) oven for 10 minutes. Let cool on a rack.

1. In a bowl, beat half of the icing sugar with butter. Mix coffee granules with 2 tbsp (25 mL) water; beat into butter mixture along with remaining icing sugar. Spread over cooled base.

1. In a bowl over a saucepan of hot (not boiling) water, melt butter with coffee granules; add chocolate and stir until melted and smooth. Spread over filling.
2. Refrigerate for about 2 hours or until chocolate is firm. Let stand at room temperature for 5 minutes to soften slightly before cutting into bars.

TIP

Always taste nuts before you use them to make sure they are fresh, and store them in the freezer to ensure they keep fresh.

To toast hazelnuts, spread them out on a baking sheet and place in a 350°F (180°C) oven for 5 to 8 minutes or until darkened slightly and fragrant. Immediately enclose in a clean tea towel and rub the hot hazelnuts until most of the skins are removed.

Chocolate Ginger Tassies

MAKES 36 TARTLETS.

For these sophisticated, but easy tassies (small cups), start with melt-in-your-mouth, pat-in pastry and fill with preserved ginger (the kind that comes in the jar with syrup) and a dollop of chocolate ganache.* These tartlets are a great addition to a tray of dainties—at Christmas or for any party.

1/3 cup	butter, softened	75 mL
1/4 cup	icing sugar, sifted	50 mL
1	egg yolk	1
1/2 tsp	vanilla	2 mL
1 cup	all-purpose flour	250 mL
1 tbsp	cornstarch	15 mL
Pinch	salt	Pinch

1. In a bowl, beat butter with sugar until fluffy. Beat in the egg yolk and vanilla. Stir together the flour, cornstarch and salt; gradually stir into the butter mixture to form a smooth dough.
2. Place a rounded teaspoonful (5 mL) of dough into each of thirty-six 1-1/4-inch (3 cm) mini-tart tins; evenly press over the bottom and up the sides, and make an indentation in the centre. Bake in the centre of a 325°F (160°C) oven for about 18 minutes or until shells are golden. Let cool in the pan for 5 minutes; transfer to racks to let cool completely.

FILLING

1/4 cup	drained preserved ginger, finely chopped	50 mL
1/2 cup	granulated sugar	125 mL
1/4 cup	whipping cream	50 mL
2 tbsp	butter	25 mL
4 oz	semisweet chocolate, chopped	125 g

1. Divide the ginger evenly among the shells. In a small saucepan, bring sugar, cream and butter to a boil, stirring. Remove from the heat. Add chocolate, stirring until melted. Let cool just to room temperature. Spoon about 1 tsp (5 mL) into each shell. Let cool until set.

Ganache is a chocolate and cream filling used in cakes, truffles and tartlets.

Chocolate Rum Balls

MAKES 2-1/2 DOZEN.

These are my son-in-law, Rob Loxton's, favourite Christmas cookies, and he's not alone. I have people I hardly know coming up to me in the supermarket to say they have made them and they are the best rum balls they have ever tasted. They're pretty served in petit-four cases.*

1 cup	blanched ground almonds 250 mL
1 cup	sifted icing sugar 250 mL
1-1/4 tsp	powdered instant coffee 6 mL
3 oz	unsweetened chocolate 75 g
5 tbsp	dark rum 75 mL
1 tbsp	milk 15 mL
1/2 cup	dark chocolate vermicelli or unsweetened cocoa powder 125 mL

1. Place almonds in a large bowl and sift in the icing sugar and instant coffee. Grate the chocolate and stir into the mixture. Sprinkle 3 tbsp (45 mL) of the rum and all of the milk over the dry ingredients. Stir until the mixture is evenly moistened and is a uniform dark brown. Refrigerate for 10 minutes.

2. Shape mixture into a ball and knead several times. Using your hands, roll into 3/4-inch (2 cm) balls. Dip each ball into remaining rum, shake off excess moisture and roll in vermicelli to coat thickly. Place on wax paper to dry at room temperature for 1 hour. Place in an airtight container and refrigerate. Let ripen for a few days before serving.

Petit-four cases are miniature paper cups designed to hold tiny cakes.

Dark Chocolate-Ginger Truffle Squares

MAKES ABOUT 80 SQUARES.

These decadent truffles are a tribute to my husband, who loves the chocolate-covered ginger we can buy at our great local candy shop, Reid's, in Cambridge. Much easier and faster than round truffles, they are made in a baking pan, then cut into tiny squares. They are lovely presented in little petit-four cases* with coffee after dinner.

1/2 cup	whipping cream 125 mL
12 oz	bittersweet chocolate, chopped 375 g
2 tbsp	brandy or liqueur 25 mL
3 tbsp	candied ginger, finely chopped 45 mL
	Cocoa powder

1. Line an 8-inch (2 L) square baking pan with plastic wrap; set aside.

2. In a small, heavy saucepan, bring cream to a boil. Remove from heat; whisk in chocolate until melted. Whisk in brandy until smooth; stir in ginger. Spoon mixture into prepared pan, spreading evenly. Refrigerate, covered, at least 3 hours or overnight.

3. Holding plastic wrap, carefully remove truffle mixture from pan and invert onto a cutting board; remove plastic wrap. With a long, sharp knife, cut into 3/4-inch (2 cm) squares. Sift cocoa lightly over truffle squares. Refrigerate in an airtight container for up to 2 weeks or freeze for up to 2 months.

*Petit-four cases are miniature paper cups designed to hold tiny cakes.

WINTER

WINTER MENUS

Regardless of whether we celebrate Christmas, this is the time of year that brings lots of parties and special dinners. Throughout the book, you'll find many special recipes just right for such events, but I'm going the more traditional route for a Christmas Dinner. This menu is very much like the Christmas Dinner that might have been celebrated here by the early settlers in the 19th century, evidence, indeed, that good things last.

A Traditional Christmas Dinner

FRESH SEAFOOD SALAD

ROAST GOOSE WITH ONION-SAGE STUFFING

GIBLET GRAVY

BAKED CRANBERRY SAUCE

WHIPPED POTATO CASSEROLE

RUTABAGA AND CARROT PUFF

BUTTERED BRUSSELS SPROUTS

STEAMED FIG PUDDING

CARAMEL BRANDY SAUCE

Fresh Seafood Salad

MAKES 6 TO 8 SERVINGS.

This colourful salad is a refreshing first course for a celebration dinner.

24	mussels in their shells (3/4 lb/375 g) 24
3/4 cup	dry white wine 175 mL
1/4 cup	finely chopped onion 50 mL
1 tsp	grated lemon zest (outer rind) 5 mL
3/4 lb	raw medium shrimp, peeled and deveined 375 g
3/4 lb	skinned salmon fillet, cut into 1-inch (2.5 cm) pieces 375 g
1/2 cup	mayonnaise 125 mL
2 tsp	EACH capers, Dijon mustard and chopped fresh parsley 10 mL
	Black pepper
1/2 cup	EACH thinly sliced red onion and fennel or celery 125 mL
	Boston or leaf lettuce
	Lemon wedges

1. Scrub mussels and cut off beards; discard any that remain open after you've tapped them on the counter. In a large saucepan, combine wine, 1/4 cup (50 mL) onion and lemon zest; bring to a simmer. Add mussels; cook, covered, for about 5 minutes or until mussels open (discard any that don't open). With a slotted spoon, remove mussels to a plate.

2. Add shrimp and salmon to the saucepan. Cover; bring to a simmer. Cook for about 4 minutes or just until shrimp turn pink and are firm to touch, turning shrimp and salmon after 2 minutes to ensure even cooking since liquid will not cover fish. With a slotted spoon, remove shrimp and salmon to a bowl.

3. Remove mussels from their shells; add to the shrimp and salmon. Refrigerate, uncovered, until cold.

4. Bring liquid remaining in the saucepan to a boil; boil until it is reduced to about 1/3 cup (75 mL). Strain into a large bowl; let cool.

5. Add mayonnaise, capers, mustard and parsley to the cooled liquid, along with pepper to taste. Stir in chilled seafood, red onion and fennel; toss gently to coat well. Refrigerate, covered, for at least 3 hours or up to 8 hours.

6. To serve, line salad plates with lettuce leaves. Spoon seafood mixture on top of lettuce; garnish with lemon wedges.

Note

In most supermarkets, the vegetable fennel is mistakenly labelled anise. Fennel is a white bulb that looks like a swollen bunch of celery; anise is a feathery herb whose seeds are used for flavouring.

Roast Goose with Onion-Sage Stuffing

MAKES 8 SERVINGS.

I developed this method of cooking goose for my *Canadian Christmas Cooking* book, first published in 1979 as *The Christmas Cookbook,* and then I contributed a similar recipe to the *Canadian Living Christmas Book.* I still use the recipe every Christmas because it produces a crisp-skinned, grease-free bird that is a treat indeed. When I was doing research for my book, I learned that geese were useful additions to pioneer farms because their down provided warm quilts for cold winter nights; their feathers and wings made excellent dusters; their eggs were worth four hens' eggs; and they made good watch "dogs." Best of all, they provided a beautiful Christmas dinner long before people raised and ate turkey, a holiday dinner that's still very special.

10 lb	goose	4.5 kg
1/4 cup	raisins	50 mL
1/2 cup	dry red wine	125 mL
1/4 cup	butter	50 mL
2 cups	minced onion	500 mL
1	large tart apple, peeled and minced	1
1 cup	minced celery with leaves	250 mL
1/2 cup	coarsely chopped pecans	125 mL
6 cups	coarse, fresh bread crumbs	1.5 L
1 tsp	granulated sugar	5 mL
1 tsp	crumbled dried sage	5 mL
1/2 tsp	EACH salt, pepper and dried savory	2 mL
Half	lemon	Half
4 cups	boiling water or stock	1 L

1. Remove any loose fat from the goose. Wipe off and dry thoroughly inside and out. Reserve the neck, wing tips, gizzard and heart for stock. Chop the liver for the stuffing.
2. To prepare the stuffing, combine the raisins with the red wine in a small saucepan and bring to a boil; boil for 3 minutes. Remove from the heat and cool. Reserving wine, drain raisins.
3. In a large skillet, melt the butter; add the onion, apple and goose liver; sauté until the onion is translucent and the liver loses its pinkness. Add the celery and mix well. Remove from the heat and stir in pecans and raisins.
4. In a large bowl, combine the bread crumbs, sugar, sage, salt, pepper and savory.
5. Add the onion-liver mixture and combine thoroughly. Cool. (Stuffing can be covered and refrigerated for up to 1 day. Stuff goose just before roasting.)
6. Rub the goose inside and out with the lemon half, squeezing out the juice as you go; sprinkle inside with salt and pepper.
7. Stuff the neck cavity loosely with some of the stuffing and fasten the neck skin to the body with a skewer. Stuff the body cavity loosely with the rest of the stuffing. Tie or sew shut. Tie the legs close to the body. Using a needle, prick the skin and fatty layer all over (without penetrating the lean meat) to allow the fat to escape.

continued

8. Put the goose, breast side down, on a greased rack in a shallow roasting pan. Pour 2 cups (500 mL) boiling water over the goose. (Pouring boiling water over the goose and roasting it will help remove the excess fat.) Roast in a 400°F (200°C) oven for 20 minutes, uncovered.

9. Reduce the heat to 325°F (160°C) and roast for 1 hour. With foil-protected oven mitts, lift out the goose onto a platter and pour off all the liquid from the roasting pan. Baste the goose with some of the reserved wine. (Keep the wine warm for basting as the goose cooks.)

10. Turn the goose on one side on the rack, prick all over again and pour over it 2 cups (500 mL) boiling water. Roast for 30 minutes. As before, lift out the goose and pour off all the liquid and baste with some of the wine. Turn the goose on its other side and roast for 30 minutes. Prick the goose all over again; lift out and pour off the drippings; baste again with wine. Place on its back and roast for about 1 to 1-1/2 hours longer or until juices run clear when a thigh is pierced and a meat thermometer registers 190°F (90°C). The total roasting time will be about 3-1/2 to 4 hours in all. Transfer the goose to a cutting board; cover loosely with foil and let stand for 15 minutes before carving.

TIP

Carving a goose demands a different technique from carving a turkey. Use a more rigid knife because of the narrow body and close-set legs and wings. Remove the wing with a chef's knife by cutting down through the shoulder joint. Cut through the skin in an arc around the leg. Press the knife down between the thigh and body. Cut through the joint to free the leg. Cut the leg in two. Using a long, slender carving knife, carve the breast into lengthwise slices slightly diagonal to the breastbone.

Giblet Gravy

MAKES 8 SERVINGS.

When I roast a turkey or a goose and make gravy, I just do it, but I decided to measure everything out and give specific instructions to create a recipe for my Christmas cookbook.

STOCK

	Giblets (neck, wing tips, gizzard and heart from goose or turkey)
	Cold water
1	small onion, coarsely chopped 1
1	stalk celery with leaves 1
1	large sprig parsley 1
1	carrot, coarsely chopped 1
4	peppercorns 4
1/2 tsp	EACH salt and dried thyme 2 mL

1. Place giblets in a saucepan and pour in cold water to cover them. Bring to a boil and skim off any foam. Add onion, celery, parsley, carrot, peppercorns, salt and thyme. Bring to a boil again. Reduce heat, cover and simmer for about 2 hours. Remove the giblets and reserve. Strain the liquid, discarding the vegetables and peppercorns. Chop the giblets and reserve in the refrigerator if using in the gravy.

GRAVY

3 cups	giblet stock 750 mL
2 tbsp	cornstarch 25 mL
1/4 cup	cold water 50 mL
	Salt and pepper

1. Remove any excess fat from the drippings left in the roasting pan after the bird is done. Pour the giblet stock into the pan and heat, stirring up the brown bits from the bottom of the pan.
2. Dissolve the cornstarch in cold water and add, stirring constantly. Simmer the gravy for about 5 minutes or until smooth and thick. If you prefer it thinner, gradually stir in more hot stock or hot water.
3. Taste for seasoning and add salt and pepper to taste. Stir in cooked giblets if using and heat through. Serve in a warm gravy boat.

Baked Cranberry Sauce

MAKES 1-1/3 CUPS (325 ML) SAUCE.

I love cranberries. Over the years I've gone to see the harvest here in Ontario and in British Columbia. I've written articles about the bouncy berry and have included them in countless recipes. Cranberry sauce is the most popular way to use the fruit, complementing roast turkey, goose, pork or duck. The instructions on the supermarket package of berries are easy and good, but I also like to bake the berries.

2 cups	fresh cranberries 500 mL	
1 cup	lightly packed brown sugar 250 mL	
1/4 tsp	ground cloves 1 mL	

1. Wash the cranberries and place them in a 4-cup (1 L) baking dish. Sprinkle the brown sugar and cloves over them. Cover and bake for 30 minutes in a 350°F (180°C) oven, stirring occasionally.

Whipped Potato Casserole

MAKES 10 SERVINGS.

This make-ahead mashed potato casserole is on almost everyone's list of favourites. My family, in particular, would be very disappointed if it did not appear on our Christmas table. The recipe was initially published in 1979 in the first edition of my Christmas cookbook, now called *Canadian Christmas Cooking*.

If you wish, you can use light cream cheese and light sour cream.

10 to 12	medium potatoes, peeled 10 to 12
1/4 cup	butter 50 mL
8 oz	cream cheese, cubed 250 g
1 cup	sour cream 250 mL
	Salt and pepper
2 tbsp	butter, melted 25 mL
1/4 cup	EACH fine, fresh bread crumbs and chopped fresh parsley 50 mL

1. Cook the potatoes in boiling, salted water in a covered saucepan for 20 to 30 minutes, or until tender. Drain well and return to heat briefly to dry.
2. Mash potatoes with the butter. Add the cream cheese, sour cream, and salt and pepper to taste. Beat until creamy.
3. Spoon into greased 2-quart (2 L) casserole. Combine the melted butter with the crumbs and parsley; sprinkle evenly on top. Cool, cover tightly and refrigerate overnight.
4. Remove from the refrigerator 30 minutes before reheating. Bake, covered, in a 350°F (180°C) oven for 20 minutes. Uncover and bake about 10 minutes longer or until hot throughout.

Rutabaga and Carrot Puff

MAKES 8 SERVINGS.

During the winter months, we have a good quantity of locally grown root vegetables that are stored so well that they have more nutrients than imported fresh vegetables, which have to travel many miles to get here. Rutabaga—yellow turnip—has long been a Canadian favourite as a side dish with roast turkey or chicken. Here, carrots add their own special sweetness in this lovely dish that can be made ahead of time and reheated. You can, of course, omit the carrots and use an extra-large rutabaga if you wish to have a straight Rutabaga Puff.

1	rutabaga	1
4	carrots	4
Half	onion, chopped	Half
1-1/2 cups	chicken stock	375 mL
1/4 cup	butter	50 mL
1 tbsp	brown sugar	15 mL
Pinch	nutmeg	Pinch
2	eggs, lightly beaten	2
2 tbsp	flour	25 mL
1 tsp	baking powder	5 mL
	Salt and pepper	
1/4 cup	finely chopped pecans or hazelnuts	50 mL

1. Trim and peel rutabaga and carrots; cut into 1/2-inch (1 cm) chunks. Combine rutabaga, carrots, onion, stock, 3 tbsp (45 mL) of the butter, sugar and nutmeg in a large saucepan. Bring to a boil, reduce heat and cook, partially covered, for about 45 minutes or until vegetables are very tender, stirring occasionally.

2. With a slotted spoon, transfer vegetables to a food processor or blender. Set cooking pan over high heat and boil remaining liquid, stirring constantly, for 2 to 3 minutes or until reduced to about 1 tablespoon (15 mL). Add liquid to processor and purée until very smooth. Transfer to mixing bowl and cool to room temperature.

3. Stir in eggs, flour, baking powder, and salt and pepper to taste. Transfer to a buttered 6-cup (1.5 L) casserole or soufflé dish. Melt remaining butter and stir together with nuts. Sprinkle evenly around edge of the dish to make a border. (Casserole can be covered and refrigerated for up to 1 day. Bring to room temperature for 30 minutes before reheating.) Bake, uncovered, in a 350°F (180°C) oven for about 30 minutes or until puffed, firm and golden brown.

Steamed Fig Pudding

MAKES 12 SERVINGS.

There are many people who still love a good steamed pudding on the Christmas table. This pudding, which I usually make for my family, is from my *Canadian Christmas Cooking*. It is lighter than most and a favourite of many. Serve it hot with your favourite sauce or the easy Caramel Brandy Sauce that follows.

	Granulated sugar
8 oz	dried figs 250 g
3/4 cup	butter 175 mL
1 cup	granulated sugar 250 mL
2	eggs 2
1 tsp	grated orange zest (outer rind) 5 mL
2 cups	all-purpose flour 500 mL
1 tsp	baking powder 5 mL
1 tsp	ground mace* 5 mL
1 tsp	cinnamon 5 mL
1/2 tsp	salt 2 mL
3/4 cup	orange juice 175 mL
1 tsp	vanilla 5 mL
1/2 cup	slivered blanched almonds 125 mL

1. Grease two 4-cup (1 L) pudding moulds or bowls, line each bottom with a circle of greased waxed paper and sprinkle the insides with granulated sugar.
2. Using scissors, clip the stems from the figs; then grind the figs in a food processor or meat grinder. You should have 1 cup (250 mL) ground figs.
3. In a large bowl, cream the butter; add the sugar and cream thoroughly together. Beat the eggs; add to the creamed mixture and beat well. Stir in the figs and orange zest.
4. Sift together the flour, baking powder, mace, cinnamon and salt; stir into the creamed mixture alternately with the orange juice. Stir in vanilla and almonds.
5. Turn batter into prepared moulds and cover each with a circle of greased waxed paper; cover with lid if using a mould. To cover a bowl, make a 1-inch (2.5 cm) pleat across the middle of a piece of foil and place over the bowl. Press sides down and tie with string around the top.
6. Place on a rack in a large pot. Pour boiling water around the moulds to two-thirds of the way up the moulds. Steam for 2-1/2 to 3 hours, or until a cake tester inserted in the middle comes out clean. (If using a ring mould, steam for 1-1/2 to 2 hours.)
7. Remove the moulds from the water. Let the puddings set for about 5 minutes; then turn out onto a warm plate and serve hot. (Puddings can be made up to 2 months ahead. Cool, wrap well and freeze or refrigerate. To heat, resteam puddings in the moulds for 1 to 1-1/2 hours, or turn out onto a serving plate, cover with a large microwaveable bowl and reheat at High for 5 to 10 minutes or until hot.)

*Mace is an aromatic spice made from the dried, outer covering of the kernel of a nutmeg.

Caramel Brandy Sauce

MAKES ABOUT 2 CUPS (500 ML).

This easy sauce is delicious with any steamed pudding.

1 cup	packed brown sugar	250 mL
1-1/2 tsp	cornstarch	7 mL
1 cup	light cream	250 mL
1/4 cup	butter	50 mL
2 tbsp	brandy	25 mL
1 tsp	vanilla	5 mL

1. Combine the brown sugar and cornstarch in the top of a double boiler. Gradually add the cream and stir until the sugar is dissolved. Place over simmering water. Add the butter and cook, stirring constantly, until the mixture is smooth and thickens slightly. Cook for 10 minutes longer, stirring often.
2. Remove from the heat and stir in brandy and vanilla. Serve hot.

The good, unpretentious fare found in neighbourhood bistros in France is tailor-made for a casual supper for close friends, whether or not they are celebrating someone's birthday. Set out tumblers (not your best stemmed wine glasses) for a French red wine like a Bordeaux or Burgundy and relax over good, simple food that's perfect for a winter evening.

Bistro Birthday Party

TOMATO AND CHEESE TART

PAN-FRIED STEAK WITH SHALLOT SAUCE

POMMES FRITES

MIXED GREENS WITH MUSTARD VINAIGRETTE

CARAMELIZED BAKED APPLES

SILKY CINNAMON ICE CREAM

Tomato and Cheese Tart

MAKES 4 TO 6 SERVINGS.

Several times we have rented a house or an apartment in southwestern France and have been invited to wonderful parties. This simple but delicious tart is typical of the food we enjoyed. Serve it as an appetizer, or to make the tart a lovely main course for lunch, add a little chopped smoked ham after you spread the crust with mustard. Garnish with a fresh sprig of one of the herbs if available.

	Pastry for a 9-inch (23 cm) single-crust pie (see **Pie Pastry** page 33)
2 cups	cherry tomatoes 500 mL
1 tbsp	Dijon mustard 15 mL
1/2 lb	Gruyère cheese, shredded (2 cups/500 mL) 250 g
1 tsp	dried basil 5 mL
1/4 tsp	dried thyme 1 mL
Pinch	pepper Pinch
1 tbsp	olive oil 15 mL

1. On a lightly floured surface, roll out the pastry thinly; ease into a 9- or 10-inch (23 or 25 cm) tart tin with a removable base, making sure to push pastry down into corners. Trim the edges; prick pastry base all over with a fork. Line with parchment paper; arrange pie weights or dried beans in the pie crust. Bake in a 400°F (200°C) oven for 15 minutes. Reduce temperature to 375°F (190°C). Remove weights and paper from pie crust; prick pastry with a fork. Bake 15 minutes until pastry is pale golden. Cool on a rack.

2. Cut tomatoes in half; arrange cut side down on paper towels. Set aside while you prepare remaining ingredients.

3. Spread pie crust with mustard; sprinkle with half the cheese. Arrange tomatoes, cut side up, on top of cheese; sprinkle with basil, thyme and pepper. Sprinkle remaining cheese evenly over tomatoes; drizzle with oil. Bake in a 375°F (190°C) oven for about 30 minutes or until cheese melts. Let cool slightly in the pan on a rack; remove tart from the pan. Serve warm, cut in wedges.

Pan-Fried Steak with Shallot Sauce

MAKES 4 SERVINGS.

This simple steak and its easy sauce are just right for casual winter entertaining.

4	6-oz (175 g) boneless strip-loin steaks (3/4-inch/2 cm thick) 4
1 tbsp	whole black peppercorns 15 mL

1. Pat steaks dry on paper towels. Using a mortar and pestle or base of a heavy skillet, crush peppercorns coarsely. Rub peppercorns into both sides of steaks; let stand, covered, at room temperature for 30 minutes.

2. In a very large, heavy (preferably cast-iron) skillet, heat oil over high heat. Add steaks to skillet; cook over high heat for 3 minutes on each

continued

2 tbsp	sunflower or vegetable oil 25 mL
1/4 cup	chopped shallots 50 mL
1 cup	dry red wine or beef stock 250 mL
1/2 cup	whipping cream 125 mL
1 tbsp	Dijon mustard 15 mL
	Salt and pepper

side for medium-rare (stand back; oil may splatter). Transfer to a warm platter and cover with foil; keep warm.

3. Pour off all but 1 tbsp (15 mL) of the fat from the skillet. Add shallots to the skillet; cook, stirring, over medium heat for 1 minute. Add wine; bring to a boil, scraping up any browned bits from the bottom of the skillet. Boil for 3 to 5 minutes, until liquid is syrupy. Stir in the cream; boil for 3 to 5 minutes until the sauce thickens slightly. Stir in the mustard and salt and pepper to taste.

4. Divide steaks among four warm dinner plates; add any juices that have accumulated on the platter to the sauce in the skillet. Stir well. Spoon sauce evenly over steaks; serve at once.

Pommes Frites

MAKES 4 SERVINGS.

The secret of making crisp, non-greasy French fries is having the oil at the right temperature and frying the potatoes twice. If you have an electric deep-fryer, follow the manufacturer's instructions. These fries are perfect with Pan-Fried Steak.

4	baking potatoes (about 2-1/2 lb/1.1 kg) 4 Vegetable oil for deep-frying Salt

1. Peel potatoes and cut into 1/2-inch (1 cm) thick strips, dropping them into a large bowl of ice water as you work.

2. Just before frying, drain potatoes well; spread them out on crumpled paper towels. Dry potatoes thoroughly.

3. Pour enough oil into a deep-fryer or large saucepan to come 3-1/2 inches (9 cm) up the sides of the saucepan. Heat the oil over high heat until a candy thermometer registers 270°F (132°C). Fry the potatoes in 4 batches for 3 to 5 minutes, until potatoes are tender and pale golden. Remove from the oil; drain on crumpled paper towels. Repeat with remaining potatoes. (Frites can be prepared up to 1 hour ahead at this point.)

4. Heat oil remaining in saucepan over high heat until a candy thermometer registers 385°F (196°C). Fry frites in 2 batches for 2 to 4 minutes, shaking deep-fryer basket occasionally, or stirring once or twice, until frites are crisp and golden. Drain on crumpled paper towels. Sprinkle with salt and serve immediately.

Caramelized Baked Apples

MAKES 4 TO 6 SERVINGS.

Bistro desserts are homey classics that never go out of style. Here's an update of an old favourite that's easy to make and needs no last-minute attention—a winning dessert for any type of menu.

1/2 cup	sultana raisins or currants 125 mL
2 tbsp	Calvados, brandy or apple juice 25 mL
4	large baking apples (Northern Spy, Idared or Spartan) 4
1/4 cup	butter, melted 50 mL
1/4 cup	granulated sugar 50 mL
1/4 cup	packed brown sugar 50 mL
1/2 tsp	cinnamon 2 mL

1. In a small bowl, combine the raisins and Calvados; set aside while you prepare the apples.
2. Cut unpeeled apples in half crosswise (around their "waists"); scoop out the cores with a melon baller or small teaspoon. In a 13 x 9-inch (3 L) baking dish, arrange apples cut side up. Spoon raisin mixture evenly into the hollow in each apple. Drizzle apples evenly with butter; sprinkle with granulated sugar. Bake, uncovered, in a 375°F (190°C) oven for 30 minutes or until apples are tender.
3. Sprinkle apples evenly with brown sugar and cinnamon. Broil 5 inches (12 cm) from a hot broiling element for 3 to 5 minutes or until tops caramelize. Spoon over apples any cooking juices in the dish.
4. Serve warm with Silky Cinnamon Ice Cream (recipe follows), vanilla ice cream or softly whipped cream.

Silky Cinnamon Ice Cream

MAKES ABOUT 4 CUPS (1 L).

A chopped cinnamon stick and ground cinnamon lend a wonderfully spicy flavour to this luscious ice cream, making it a perfect match for Caramelized Baked Apples.

1-1/2 cups	whipping cream 375 mL
1 cup	table cream 250 mL
1	2-inch (5 cm) cinnamon stick 1
1/2 cup	granulated sugar 125 mL
Pinch	ground cinnamon Pinch
3	egg yolks 3

1. In a medium saucepan, heat whipping and table cream over medium-high heat for 7 to 10 minutes until bubbles form around the edge (do not boil).
2. In a blender, coarsely chop the cinnamon stick. Stir the chopped stick into the cream, along with the sugar and ground cinnamon; stir until sugar dissolves. Reduce heat to very low; let stand, covered, for 10 minutes (do not boil), tasting occasionally to make sure the flavour isn't too strong.

continued

3. In a small bowl, whisk egg yolks lightly; whisk in a little of the hot cream mixture. Pour egg yolk mixture back into saucepan; cook over medium-low heat, stirring constantly, for 5 minutes or until mixture is thick enough to coat the back of a spoon (do not boil).

4. Strain mixture through a sieve into a clean bowl; let cool, stirring often. Refrigerate, covered, for at least 2 hours or until thoroughly chilled. Freeze in an ice cream maker according to manufacturer's instructions. (Ice cream can be packed into a container and stored in the freezer for up to 2 days; remove to the refrigerator for 30 minutes before serving.)

YEAR ROUND

MY
YEAR-ROUND
KITCHEN

Each section of the book celebrates the good food of a season, but there are some recipes in each that could be appropriate any time of the year. The Lemon Mousse Cheesecake, nice and light for spring, would be as welcome in the fall. Cheddar Chutney Tarts, which just happen to be part of a summer menu, are sure to become standard fare whenever you entertain a crowd. Family favourites like Old-Fashioned Baked Macaroni and Cheese or Honey-Curried Chicken and Apricots will probably find their way onto your supper table right through the year. In this last chapter, I've added more all-season family favourites: a One-Pot Spaghetti Supper, Easy Rice Pudding and Salmon Loaf. And there's elegant Crisp Coconut Chicken with Mango Salsa—just right for impressing a special person any time the mood strikes because mangos come to us year-round from different corners of the world.

There are a few recipes, however, like Easy Basic Meat Broth and salad dressings that defy any seasonal category since they use basic techniques that will make your everyday cooking easier and more delicious.

When you have mastered Tea Biscuits, you will find joy in baking. Even the Blueberry Streusel Muffins, wonderful in blueberry season, are so good you will probably want to make them with frozen berries, too, as your "in-house" muffins. The Chelsea Buns are my favourite for treating the Christmas morning crowd, but they are also perfect to take to the summer cottage where they will be a delight both to serve and eat...as I hope you find everything from my kitchen at any time of the year.

YEAR-ROUND RECIPES

Salmon Loaf

MAKES 4 SERVINGS.

When you think there's nothing in the house for supper, remember that a couple of cans of salmon from the cupboard make a quick nutritious loaf the whole family will like. It's equally good as a hot entrée or cold as part of a salad plate.

1-1/2 cups	cracker crumbs (about 36 soda crackers) 375 mL
1/2 cup	milk 125 mL
2	cans (7.5 oz/213 g each) salmon 2
1/4 cup	finely diced celery 50 mL
2	eggs, slightly beaten 2
2 tbsp	fresh lemon juice 25 mL
1/4 tsp	EACH salt, pepper and paprika 1 mL
Pinch	cayenne Pinch

1. In a large bowl, soak crumbs in milk for 5 minutes.
2. Stir in salmon with its juice, mashing to crush bones and flake salmon. Stir in celery, eggs, lemon juice, salt, pepper, paprika and cayenne. Pack firmly into a greased 9 x 5-inch (2 L) loaf pan. Set in a bigger pan of hot water. Bake in a 350°F (180°C) oven for 40 minutes or until golden on top. If serving hot, let sit, covered loosely with foil, for 5 minutes before cutting in slices.

Blueberry Streusel Muffins

MAKES 24 MUFFINS.

These moist, blueberry-rich muffins are the best you will ever taste. I must give full credit to my friend Mary Lou Ruby Jonas who shared the recipe with me. If using frozen berries, do not thaw first.

STREUSEL TOPPING

1/4 cup	granulated sugar	50 mL
1/4 cup	all-purpose flour	50 mL
1/2 tsp	cinnamon	2 mL
1/4 cup	butter	50 mL

1. In a small bowl, combine sugar, flour and cinnamon; cut in butter until crumbly. Set aside.

MUFFINS

1/2 cup	butter, softened	125 mL
1-1/4 cups	granulated sugar	300 mL
2	eggs	2
1 tsp	grated lemon zest (outer rind)	5 mL
4 cups	all-purpose flour	1 L
4 tsp	baking powder	20 mL
1/2 tsp	salt	2 mL
1-1/4 cups	milk	300 mL
4 cups	blueberries, preferably wild	1 L

1. In a large bowl, cream butter with sugar until fluffy; beat in eggs, one at a time. Stir in lemon zest.
2. Sift or stir together flour, baking powder and salt. Add flour mixture alternately with milk to creamed mixture, stirring just enough to combine, but do not overmix. Gently stir in blueberries.
3. Spoon into 24 greased muffin cups. Sprinkle each with some of the Streusel Topping. Bake in a 375°F (190°C) oven for 25 to 30 minutes or until tops are firm to the touch.

Hint

An ice cream scoop is an excellent tool to use to spoon the batter into the muffin cups.

Classic Tea Biscuits

MAKES ABOUT 20 BISCUITS.

When my mother disappeared with a cup and came back with cream from the basement, we knew there would be flaky, hot tea biscuits for lunch. These aren't made with cream, but they are nice and tender—old-fashioned and easy to make! I love to serve them hot with fruit preserves for a company breakfast.

2 cups	all-purpose flour	500 mL
4 tsp	baking powder	20 mL
1 tbsp	granulated sugar	15 mL
1/2 tsp	salt	2 mL
1/2 cup	shortening	125 mL
1	egg, beaten	1
2/3 cup	milk (approx)	150 mL

1. In a large bowl, sift or stir together the flour, baking powder, sugar and salt; cut in shortening until mixture is like fine meal.
2. Stir together egg and milk; add to flour mixture all at once, stirring with a fork until dough follows the fork around the bowl. (If too dry, add a bit more milk for a soft, sticky dough.)
3. Turn out onto a lightly floured surface; knead gently 20 times. Pat or roll to an even 1/2-inch (1 cm) thickness. Using a cookie cutter or top of a glass, cut into 2-inch (5 cm) circles.
4. Bake on ungreased baking sheet in 450°F (230°C) oven for about 10 minutes or until golden brown.

Chelsea Buns

MAKES 36 BUNS.

My friend Mary Lou Ruby Jonas worked as my assistant for years. During that time, I did a story for *Canadian Living* by visiting a family home in Waterloo, Ontario, to investigate their traditional holiday fare. There I met Mary Karen Gosselink who made a wonderful refrigerator yeast dough for a Christmas Coffee Cake. Mary Lou now uses that dough with my syrup and method from *Canadian Christmas Cooking*. She divides the buns into foil pans, covers them well and freezes them as soon as they're formed. On Christmas Eve morning, the buns are thawed and popped into the oven.

3/4 cup	granulated sugar	175 mL
2-1/2 cups	warm water	625 mL
2	pkg active dry yeast (2 tbsp/25 mL)	2
3/4 cup	vegetable oil	175 mL
2	eggs	2

1. Dissolve 1-1/2 tsp (7 mL) of the sugar in 1/2 cup (125 mL) of the water. Sprinkle yeast into water; let stand for 10 minutes or until frothy.
2. In a large warm bowl (preferably of a large electric mixer), stir together remaining sugar and water, oil, eggs and salt. Briskly stir yeast mixture with a fork; add to egg mixture. Beat in 3 cups (750 mL) of the flour; beat for 5 minutes. Beat in enough of the remaining flour, 1/2 cup

2 tsp	salt 10 mL
8 cups	all-purpose flour (approx) 2 L
1-3/4 cup	lightly packed brown sugar 425 mL
3/4 cup	butter, at room temperature 175 mL
1/4 cup	hot water 50 mL
3/4 cup	red and green maraschino or candied cherries (mixed) 175 mL
1 cup	seedless raisins 250 mL
1/2 cup	pecan halves 125 mL
1 tbsp	cinnamon 15 mL

(125 mL) at a time, to make soft dough that comes away from the bowl. Turn out onto a floured surface; knead for 8 minutes or until dough is smooth and elastic.

3. Shape dough into a ball; place in a greased bowl, turning to grease all over. (Dough can be covered and refrigerated overnight or for up to 3 days; it will rise in the refrigerator. Before rolling it out, bring to room temperature for 1 to 2 hours.) Cover and let rise in a warm place for about 1-1/2 hours or until doubled in bulk.

4. Punch down the dough, knead 2 or 3 times; divide into 3 pieces and let rest, lightly covered, for 10 minutes on a board.

5. Meanwhile, prepare the syrup for the buns. In a small saucepan, combine 1 cup (250 mL) of the brown sugar, 1/4 cup (50 mL) of the butter and the hot water. Stir over medium heat until the butter melts; then boil for 2 minutes. Immediately pour into three greased 10-inch (1.5 L) round pans and tilt pans to spread evenly.

6. Drain the cherries thoroughly and cut them into halves. Divide the cherries, raisins and pecans among the pans, sprinkling them evenly over the bottoms.

7. Roll out each piece of dough into a 14 x 9-inch (35 x 23 cm) rectangle; spread each with one third of the remaining butter, softened. Sprinkle each with one third of the remaining brown sugar and one third of the cinnamon. Roll up each from the long side into a tight roll to enclose the brown sugar mixture, pinching seam firmly to seal.

8. Cut each roll into 12 pieces. Arrange, cut side down, in the prepared pans. Grease the tops, cover with greased waxed paper and a damp towel and let rise in a warm place for about 45 minutes, or until double in bulk. (Alternatively, cover and let rise in the refrigerator overnight. Bring to room temperature before baking. Or, cover with greased waxed paper, foil and enclose in a freezer bag and freeze for up to 2 weeks. Replace the freezer bag and foil with a tea towel. Set out at room temperature overnight before baking. Then set on a heating pad turned to low or other warm place for an hour.)

9. Bake in a 375°F (190°C) oven for about 25 minutes or until golden brown. Place waxed paper under racks. As soon as the buns come out of the oven, turn the pans upside down on racks. Allow the syrup to run over the buns and remove the pans.

Easy Rice Pudding

MAKES 4 TO 6 SERVINGS.

I used to make this old-fashioned dessert often when my children were at home. I prepared it in a flash right in the baking dish. It's actually cooked rice left from supper the night before, baked in a custard. Once, I forgot to include the rice, and my family never let me forget my "riceless" rice pudding.

1 cup	cooked rice	250 mL
1/2 cup	packed brown sugar	125 mL
2	eggs, beaten	2
2 cups	milk	500 mL
1/2 cup	raisins	125 mL
1 tsp	grated lemon zest (outer rind)	5 mL
1/2 tsp	vanilla	2 mL
1/4 tsp	salt	1 mL
	Grated nutmeg	
	Milk (optional)	

1. In a 6-cup (1.5 L) casserole, combine the rice, sugar and eggs; stir well to blend. Stir in the milk, raisins, lemon zest, vanilla and salt; sprinkle with nutmeg to taste.
2. Place casserole in a pan of hot water; bake in a 325°F (160°C) oven for about 1 hour or until almost set. Serve warm or cold; pour milk over the pudding, if desired.

Easy Basic Meat Broth

MAKES ABOUT 11 CUPS (2.75 L).

A good broth or stock makes a great difference in enhancing the taste of a soup or sauce. Homemade broth is not difficult to make and freezes very well. If you wish, use all beef or all chicken. If using all chicken, you can dispense with the browning; you will probably get a nice broth in 3 to 4 hours of simmering.

2-1/4 lb	meaty beef soup bones	1 kg
3/4 lb	meaty chicken bones (necks, wings, backs)	375 g
1	unpeeled onion, in chunks	1
1	unpeeled carrot, in chunks	1
1 tbsp	vegetable oil	15 mL
2	stalks celery, in chunks	2
1	large fresh tomato, coarsely chopped (or 2 canned tomatoes, chopped)	1
4	sprigs parsley	4
1	bay leaf	1
Pinch	thyme	Pinch
1-1/2 tsp	salt, preferably coarse pickling	7 mL

1. Place bones, onion and carrot in a shallow roasting pan and drizzle with oil. Roast in a 450°F (230°C) oven for 45 minutes, stirring occasionally.

2. Reserving pan, transfer contents to a large stock pot or kettle with celery, tomato, parsley, bay leaf, thyme and salt. Pour in 14 cups (3.5 L) cold water and slowly bring to a boil, skimming any scum from the surface.

3. Meanwhile, add 2 cups (500 mL) water to the browning pan and bring to a boil, scraping up any brown bits from the bottom of the pan. Add to the kettle, reduce heat and simmer gently, uncovered, for 5 to 6 hours or until a rich broth develops.

4. Strain through a fine sieve into a large bowl, pushing hard on solids. Discard solids and let broth cool. Refrigerate, covered, for up to 2 days or freeze for up to 6 months. Remove fat from the top before you use or freeze broth.

Mustard Vinaigrette

MAKES 1/2 CUP (125 ML).

This simple dressing is wonderful on soft and crisp lettuces, with radicchio and Belgian endive. Always be sure the greens are perfectly dry so that the dressing will adhere to them and use only enough dressing to lightly coat the greens, about 1/4 cup (50 mL) for 8 cups (2 L) of lightly packed leaves.

1	clove garlic, minced	1
Pinch	salt	Pinch
1 tsp	extra strong Dijon mustard	5 mL
1 tbsp	white wine vinegar or red wine vinegar	15 mL
1/3 cup	extra virgin olive oil	75 mL
	Black pepper	

1. In a small bowl, mash garlic with salt. Stir in the mustard until smooth, then add vinegar. Whisking constantly, add the oil in a stream and pepper to taste.

Roquefort or Stilton Dressing

MAKES 1/3 CUP (75 ML).

The strong flavours of blue cheeses are an excellent match for juicy slices of ripe pear. Imagine this wonderful combination on a salad of arugula, Belgian endive, celery and toasted walnuts. It is also good on any salad with escarole or radicchio. Be sure the greens are dry and use the dressing sparingly—about 1/4 cup (50 mL) for 8 cups (2 L) of lightly packed leaves.

1/4 cup	crumbled Roquefort or Stilton	50 mL
2 tsp	sherry vinegar or red wine vinegar	10 mL
1 tsp	red wine vinegar	5 mL
3 tbsp	extra virgin olive oil	45 mL
	White pepper	

1. In a small bowl, stir together Roquefort or Stilton, sherry vinegar and red wine vinegar until blended. Whisking constantly, add olive oil in a stream. Season with white pepper to taste.

One-Pot Spaghetti Supper

MAKES ABOUT 4 SERVINGS.

This easy pasta dish was certainly on my daughter's list, but she calls it "Glop" the name my friend Jean Medley gave it when she made it regularly for her growing boys. It's a great recipe for people with limited time or limited pots and pans. Enjoy it with a green salad and some crusty bread.

1 lb	lean ground beef	500 g
1	clove garlic, minced	1
1 tsp	EACH dried basil, dried oregano, paprika and granulated sugar	5 mL
1/2 tsp	salt	2 mL
1/4 tsp	EACH black pepper and hot pepper flakes	1 mL
2 cups	water	500 mL
1	can (14 oz/398 mL) tomato sauce	1
1	can (14 oz/398 mL) tomatoes, undrained	1
1/4 cup	chopped fresh parsley	50 mL
3/4 cup	freshly grated Parmesan cheese (approx)	175 mL
1/2 lb	spaghetti, broken	250 g

1. In a large deep skillet or shallow Dutch oven, cook beef over medium-high heat until it loses its pink colour; keep breaking it up with a wooden spoon. Drain off fat. Reduce heat to medium and stir in garlic, basil, oregano, paprika, sugar, salt, pepper and hot pepper flakes. Cook, stirring, for 2 minutes.

2. Stir in water, tomato sauce, tomatoes, parsley and 1/4 cup (50 mL) of the cheese; bring to a boil, stirring up any brown bits from the bottom of the pan. Reduce heat, cover and simmer for 45 minutes. (Recipe can be prepared to this point, cooled, covered and refrigerated or frozen. Bring to a simmer before continuing.)

3. Stir in spaghetti, making sure all the pasta is covered with sauce. Cover and simmer, stirring occasionally, for 10 to 15 minutes or until pasta is tender but firm. Serve in bowls, passing around remaining Parmesan cheese separately.

TIP

It is not always possible to find a variety of sizes in canned tomatoes. If you have to use half a 28 oz (796 mL) can of tomatoes, remember that you can freeze the other half to use next time.

Crisp Coconut Chicken with Mango Salsa

MAKES 2 SERVINGS.

This delicious chicken stays moist under its crisp coating, which happily teams up with a tropical-tasting sauce. A favourite with students when I've done guest cooking classes, it is easy to make but festive enough for a company meal. Serve with rice and a simple vegetable stir-fry.

1	clove garlic, crushed 1
1 tbsp	Dijon mustard 15 mL
Pinch	ground ginger Pinch
2	skinless boneless chicken breast halves 2
	All-purpose flour
1/4 tsp	EACH salt and pepper 1 mL
1	egg 1
3/4 cup	sweetened flaked coconut 175 mL
1 tbsp	vegetable oil 15 mL
2 tbsp	fresh lime juice 25 mL

MANGO SALSA

1	mango, diced 1
1/4 cup	diced red onion 50 mL
1 tbsp	fresh lime juice or white wine vinegar 15 mL
1 tbsp	chopped fresh coriander or parsley 15 mL
	Salt and pepper
Pinch	hot pepper flakes Pinch

1. In a small bowl, combine garlic, mustard and ginger; spread lightly on both sides of the chicken breasts. Place chicken on waxed paper and sprinkle both sides lightly with flour, salt and pepper.
2. In a shallow bowl, stir egg together with 1 tsp (5 mL) cold water. Place coconut on waxed paper. Dip chicken breasts in egg wash, then in coconut, pressing to make the coconut adhere.
3. In a medium ovenproof skillet, heat oil over medium-high heat; cook chicken 2 minutes a side. Add lime juice to skillet and place in 375°F (190°C) oven for 12 to 15 minutes or until chicken is no longer pink inside.

1. Meanwhile, to prepare the salsa, stir together the mango, red onion, lime juice, coriander, salt and pepper to taste and hot pepper flakes.
2. Arrange salsa on 2 dinner plates and place cooked chicken on top.

Variation

If you make this chicken in the summer when local peaches are available, substitute 2 unpeeled, diced peaches for the mango. Now you have **Crisp Coconut Chicken with Peach Salsa**.

INDEX